THOMA

RELIQUES

OF

ANCIENT ENGLISH POETRY

CONSISTING OF

Old Heroic Ballads, Songs,

AND OTHER PIECES OF OUR EARLIER POETS;

TOGETHER

WITH SOME FEW OF LATER DATE

Volume 3

Elibron Classics
www.elibron.com

Elibron Classics series.

© 2005 Adamant Media Corporation.

ISBN 1-4021-7379-2 (paperback)
ISBN 1-4021-2762-6 (hardcover)

This Elibron Classics Replica Edition is an unabridged facsimile
of the edition published in 1866 by Bernhard Tauchnitz,
Leipzig.

COLLECTION

OF

BRITISH AUTHORS.

VOL. 849.

RELIQUES OF ANCIENT ENGLISH POETRY
BY
THOMAS PERCY.

IN THREE VOLUMES.
VOL. III.

RELIQUES

OF

ANCIENT ENGLISH POETRY:

CONSISTING OF

Old Heroic Ballads, Songs,

AND OTHER PIECES OF OUR EARLIER POETS;

TOGETHER

WITH SOME FEW OF LATER DATE.

BY

THOMAS PERCY,

LORD BISHOP OF DROMORE.

IN THREE VOLUMES

VOL. III.

LEIPZIG

BERNHARD TAUCHNITZ

1866.

CONTENTS

OF VOLUME THE THIRD.

BOOK THE FIRST.

BOOK THE SECOND.

BOOK THE THIRD.

CONTENTS OF VOLUME THE THIRD.

An ordinary Song or Ballad, that is the delight of the common people, cannot fail to please all such readers as are not unqualified for the entertainment by their affectation or their ignorance; and the reason is plain, because the same paintings of Nature which recommend it to the most ordinary reader, will appear beautiful to the most refined.

ADDISON, in SPECTATOR, No. 70.

RELIQUES

OF

ANCIENT POETRY.

&c.

SERIES THE THIRD.

BOOK I.

I.

Poems on King Arthur, etc.

THE third volume being chiefly devoted to romantic sub-
jects, may not be improperly introduced with a few slight
strictures on the old Metrical Romances: a subject the more
worthy attention, as it seems not to have been known to such
as have written on the nature and origin of books of chivalry,
that the first compositions of this kind were in verse, and
usually sung to the harp.

ON THE ANCIENT METRICAL ROMANCES, ETC.

I. The first attempts at composition among all barbarous
nations, are ever found to be poetry and song. The praises
of their gods, and the achievements of their heroes, are
usually chanted at their festival meetings. These are the
first rudiments of history. It is in this manner that the
savages of North America preserve the memory of past
events [1]: and the same method is known to have prevailed

---

[1] Vide Lasiteau, Mœurs de Sauvages, t. 2. Dr. Browne's Hist. of the Rise
and Progress of Poetry.

among our Saxon ancestors, before they quitted their German forests[2]. The ancient Britons had their Bards, and the Gothic nations their Scalds or popular poets[3], whose business it was to record the victories of their warriors, and the genealogies of their princes, in a kind of narrative songs, which were committed to memory, and delivered down from one reciter to another. So long as poetry continued a distinct profession, and while the Bard, or Scald, was a regular and stated officer in the prince's court, these men are thought to have performed the functions of the historian pretty faithfully; for though their narrations would be apt to receive a good deal of embellishment, they are supposed to have had at the bottom so much of truth, as to serve for the basis of more regular annals. At least, succeeding historians have taken up with the relations of these rude men, and, for want of more authentic records, have agreed to allow them the credit of true history[4].

After letters began to prevail, and history assumed a more stable form, by being committed to plain simple prose, these songs of the Scalds or Bards began to be more amusing than useful. And in proportion as it became their business chiefly to entertain and delight, they gave more and more in to embellishment, and set off their recitals with such marvellous fictions as were calculated to captivate gross and ignorant minds. Thus began stories of adventures with giants and dragons, and witches and enchanters, and all the monstrous extravagances of wild imagination, unguided by judgment, and uncorrected by art[5].

This seems to be the true origin of that species of romance which so long celebrated feats of chivalry, and

[2] Germani celebrant carminibus antiquis (quod unum apud illos memoriæ et annalium genus est) Tuistonem, &c. Tacit. Germ. c. 2.

[3] Barth. Antiq. Dan. lib. i. cap. 10.—Wormii Literatura Runica, ad finem.

[4] See "Northern Antiquities, or a Description of the Manners, Customs, &c. of the ancient Danes and other Northern Nations, translated from the French of M. Mallet," 1770, 2 vols. 8vo. (vol. i. p. 49, &c.)

[5] Vide infra, pp. 4, 5, &c.

which at first in metre, and afterwards in prose, was the entertainment of our ancestors, in common with their contemporaries on the Continent; till the satire of Cervantes, or rather the increase of knowledge and classical literature, drove them off the stage, to make room for a more refined species of fiction, under the name of French Romances, copied from the Greek[6].

That our old romances of chivalry may be derived in a lineal descent from the ancient historical songs of the Gothic Bards and Scalds, will be shown below; and indeed appears the more evident, as many of those songs are still preserved in the North, which exhibit all the seeds of chivalry before it became a solemn institution[7]. "Chivalry, as a distinct military order, conferred in the way of investiture, and accompanied with the solemnity of an oath, and other ceremonies," was of later date, and sprung out of the feudal constitution, as an elegant writer has clearly shown[8]. But the ideas of chivalry prevailed long before in all the Gothic nations, and may be discovered as in embryo in the customs, manners, and opinions of every branch of that people[9]. That fondness of going in quest of adventures, that spirit of challenging to single combat, and that respectful complaisance shown to the fair sex (so different from the manners of the Greeks and Romans), all are of Gothic origin, and may be traced up to the earliest times among all the Northern nations[10]. These existed long before the feudal ages, though they were called forth and strengthened in a peculiar manner under that constitution, and at length arrived to their full maturity in the times of the Crusades, so replete with romantic adventures[1].

[6] Viz. Astræa, Cassandra, Clelia, &c.
[7] Mallet, vide Northern Antiquities, vol. i. p. 318, &c.; vol. ii. p. 234, &c.
[8] Letters concerning Chivalry, 8vo. 1763.
[9] Mallet.
[10] Mallet.
[1] The seeds of chivalry sprung up so naturally out of the original manners and opinions of the Northern nations, that it is not credible they arose so late as after the establishment of the feudal system, much less the Cru-

Even the common arbitrary fictions of romance were (as is hinted above) most of them familiar to the ancient Scalds of the North, long before the time of the Crusades. They believed the existence of giants and dwarfs[2]; they entertained opinions not unlike the more modern notion of fairies[3]; they were strongly possessed with the belief of spells and enchantment[4]; and were fond of inventing combats with dragons and monsters[5].

The opinion therefore seems very untenable, which some learned and ingenious men have entertained, that the turn for chivalry, and the taste for that species of romantic fiction, were caught by the Spaniards from the Arabians or Moors after their invasion of Spain, and from the Spaniards transmitted to the Bards of Armorica[6], and thus diffused through

sades. Nor, again, that the Romances of Chivalry were transmitted to other nations, through the Spaniards, from the Moors and Arabians. Had this been the case, the first French Romances of Chivalry would have been on Moorish, or at least Spanish subjects: whereas the most ancient stories of this kind, whether in prose or verse, whether in Italian, French, English, &c., are chiefly on the subjects of Charlemagne and the Paladins, or of our British Arthur and his Knights of the Round Table, &c., being evidently borrowed from the fabulous Chronicles of the supposed Archbishop Turpin, and of Jeffery of Monmouth. Not but some of the oldest and most popular French Romances are also on Norman subjects, as *Richard Sans-peur*, *Robert le Diable*, &c.; whereas I do not recollect so much as one in which the scene is laid in Spain, much less among the Moors, or descriptive of Mahometan manners. Even in *Amadis de Gaul*, said to have been the first Romance printed in Spain, the scene is laid in Gaul and Britain; and the manners are French: which plainly shows from what school this species of fabling was learnt and transmitted to the southern nations of Europe.

[2] Mallet, North. Antiquities, vol. i. p. 36; vol. ii. passim.

[3] Olaus Verel. ad Hervarer Saga, pp. 44, 45. Hickes's Thesaur. vol. ii. p. 311. Northern Antiquities, vol. ii. passim.

[4] North. Antiquities, vol. i. pp. 69, 374, &c.; vol. ii. p. 216, &c.

[5] Rollof's Saga. Cap. xxxv. &c.

[6] It is peculiarly unfortunate that such as maintain this opinion are obliged to take their first step from the Moorish provinces in Spain, without one intermediate resting-place, to Armorica or Bretagne, the province in France from them most remote, not more in situation than in the manners, habits, and language of its Welsh inhabitants, which are allowed to have been derived from this island, as must have been their traditions, songs, and fables,—being doubtless all of Celtic original. See p. 3 of the "Dissertation on the Origin of Romantic Fiction in Europe," prefixed to

Britain, France, Italy, Germany, and the North. For it seems utterly incredible, that one rude people should adopt a peculiar taste and manner of writing or thinking from another, without borrowing at the same time any of their par-

Mr. Tho. Warton's History of English Poetry, vol. i. 1774, 4to. If any pen could have supported this darling hypothesis of Dr. Warburton, that of this ingenious critic would have effected it. But under the general term *Oriental,* he seems to consider the ancient inhabitants of the north and south of Asia as having all the same manners, traditions, and fables; and because the secluded people of Arabia took the lead under the religion and empire of Mahomet, therefore every thing must be derived from them to the northern Asiatics in the remotest ages, &c. With as much reason, under the word *Occidental,* we might represent the early traditions and fables of the north and south of Europe to have been the same; and that the Gothic mythology of Scandinavia, the Druidic or Celtic of Gaul and Britain, differed not from the classic of Greece and Rome.

There is not room here for a full examination of the minuter arguments, or rather slight coincidences, by which our agreeable dissertator endeavours to maintain and defend this favourite opinion of Dr. W., who has been himself so completely confuted by Mr. Tyrwhitt. (See his notes on *Love's Labour's Lost,* &c.) But some of his positions it will be sufficient to mention: such as the referring the Gog and Magog, which our old Christian Bards might have had from Scripture, to the *Jaguiouge* and *Magiouge* of the Arabians and Persians, &c. [p. 13.] — That "we may venture to affirm, that this [Geoffrey of Monmouth's] Chronicle, supposed to contain the ideas of the Welsh Bards, entirely consists of Arabian inventions." [p. 13.] — And that, "as Geoffrey's History is the grand repository of the acts of Arthur, so a fabulous history, ascribed to Turpin, is the groundwork of all the chimerical legends which have been related concerning the conquests of Charlemagne and his twelve peers. Its subject is the expulsion of the Saracens from Spain; and it is filled with fictions evidently congenial to those which characterize Geoffrey's History." [p. 17.] — That is, as he afterwards expresses it, "lavishly decorated by the Arabian Fablers." [p. 58.] — We should hardly have expected that the Arabian Fablers would have been lavish in decorating a history of their enemy; but what is singular, as an instance and proof of this Arabian origin of the fictions of Turpin, a passage is quoted from his fourth chapter, which I shall beg leave to offer, as affording decisive evidence that they could not possibly be derived from a Mahometan source. Sc. "The Christians under Charlemagne are said to have found in Spain a golden idol, or image of Mahomet, as high as a bird can fly. It was framed by Mahomet himself of the purest metal, who, by his knowledge in necromancy, had sealed up within it a legion of diabolical spirits. It held in its hand a prodigious club; and the Saracens had a prophetic tradition, that this club should fall from the hand of the image in that year when a certain king should be born in France," &c. [Vide p. 18, note.]

ticular stories and fables, without appearing to know any thing of their heroes, history, laws, and religion. When the Romans began to adopt and imitate the Grecian literature, they immediately naturalized all the Grecian fables, histories, and religious stories, which became as familiar to the poets of Rome as of Greece itself. Whereas all the old writers of chivalry, and of that species of romance, whether in prose or verse, whether of the Northern nations, or of Britain, France, and Italy, not excepting Spain itself[7], appear utterly unacquainted with whatever relates to the Mahometan nations. Thus with regard to their religion, they constantly represent them as worshipping idols, as paying adoration to a golden image of Mahomet, or else they confound them with the ancient pagans, &c. And indeed in all other respects they are so grossly ignorant of the customs, manners, and opinions of every branch of that people, especially of their heroes, champions, and local stories, as almost amounts to a demonstration that they did not imitate them in their songs or romances: for as to dragons, serpents, necromancies, &c., why should these be thought only derived from the Moors in Spain so late as after the eighth century? since notions of this kind appear too familiar to the Northern Scalds, and enter too deeply into all the northern mythology, to have been transmitted to the unlettered Scandinavians, from so distant a country, at so late a period. If they may not be allowed to have brought these opinions with them in their original migrations from the north of Asia, they will be far more likely to have borrowed them from the Latin poets

[7] The little narrative songs on Morisco subjects, which the Spaniards have at present in great abundance, and which they call peculiarly *Romances*, (see vol. i. book iii. no. xvi., &c.) have nothing in common with their proper Romances (or Histories) of Chivalry, which they call *Historias de Cavallerias:* these are evidently imitations of the French, and show a great ignorance of Moorish manners: (and with regard to the Morisco, or Sorg-*romances*, they do not seem of very great antiquity; few of them appear, from their subjects, much earlier than the reduction of Granada, in the fifteenth century: from which period, I believe, may be plainly traced, among the Spanish writers, a more perfect knowledge of Moorish customs, &c.

appeared both in England and France[1] were composed in
metre, as a rude kind of epic songs. In both kingdoms tales
in verse were usually sung by minstrels to the harp on fes-
tival occasions: and doubtless both nations derived their
relish for this sort of entertainment from their Teutonic an-
cestors, without either of them borrowing it from the other.
Among both people narrative songs on true or fictitious sub-
jects had evidently obtained from the earliest times. But
the professed romances of chivalry seem to have been first
composed in France, where also they had their name.

The Latin tongue, as is observed by an ingenious writer[2],
ceased to be spoken in France about the ninth century, and
was succeeded by what was called the *Romance* tongue, a
mixture of the language of the Franks and bad Latin. As
the songs of chivalry became the most popular compositions
in that language, they were emphatically called Romans, or
Romants; though this name was at first given to any piece
of poetry. The romances of chivalry can be traced as early
as the eleventh century[3]. I know not if the *Roman de Brut*,
written in 1155, was such: but if it was, it was by no means
the first poem of the kind; others more ancient are still ex-
tant[4]. And we have already seen, that, in the preceding
century, when the Normans marched down to the battle of
Hastings, they animated themselves by singing (in some po-

---

[1] The romances on the subject of *Perceval, San Graal, Lancelot du Lac,
Tristan, &c.*, were among the first that appeared in the French language in
Prose, yet these were originally composed in Metre: the Editor has in his
possession a very old French MS. in verse, containing *L'ancien Roman de
Perceval;* and metrical copies of the others may be found in the libraries of
the curious. See a note of Wanley's in Harl. Catalog. no. 2252, p. 49, &c.
Nicolson's Eng. Hist. Library, 3d ed. p. 91, &c. — See also a curious Collec-
tion of old French Romances, with Mr. Wanley's account of this sort of
pieces, in Harl. MSS. Catal. 978, 106.

[2] The author of the Essay on the Genius of Pope, p. 282.

[3] Ibid. p. 283. Hist. Lit. tom. vi. vii.

[4] Voi Préface aux "Fabliaux et Contes des Poëtes François des xii. xiii.
xiv. & xv. siècles, &c." Paris, 1756, 3 tom. 12mo. (A very curious work.)

pular romance or ballad) the exploits of Roland and the other heroes of chivalry[5].

So early as this I cannot trace the songs of chivalry in English. The most ancient I have seen is that of *Horne-child*, described below, which seems not older than the twelfth century. However, as this rather resembles the Saxon poetry than the French, it is not certain that the first English romances were translated from that language[6]. We have seen above, that a propensity to this kind of fiction prevailed among all the Gothic nations[7]: and though, after the Norman conquest, this country abounded with French romances, or with translations from the French, there is good reason to believe that the English had original pieces of their own.

The stories of King Arthur and his Round Table may be reasonably supposed of the growth of this island; both the French and the Armoricans probably had them from Britain[8]. The stories of Guy and Bevis, with some others, were pro-

---

[5] See the account of *Taillefer* in vol. i. Essay, and note. And see Rapin, Carte, &c.—This song of ROLAND (whatever it was) continued for some centuries to be usually sung by the French in their marches, if we may believe a modern French writer, "Un jour qu'on chantoit la *Chanson de Roland*, comme c'étoit l'usage dans les marches. Il y a long temps, dit-il [John King of France, who died in 1364], qu'on ne voit plus de Rolands parmi les Franqois. On y verroit encore des Rolands, lui répondit un vieux Capitaine, s'ils avoient un Charlemagne à leur tête." Vide tom. iii. p. 202, des Essaies Hist. sur Paris de M. de Saintefoix, who gives, as his authority, Boethius in Hist. Scotorum. This author, however, speaks of the complaint and repartee as made in an assembly of the States, *(vocato senatu,)* and not upon any march, &c. Vide Boeth. lib. xv. fol. 327. Ed. Paris. 1574.

[6] See, on this subject, vol. i. Notes on the Essay on the Ancient Minstrels, (s 2) and (G G).

[7] The first romances of chivalry among the Germans were in metre; they have some very ancient narrative songs (which they call *Lieder*), not only on the fabulous heroes of their own country, but also on those of France and Britain, as Tristrain, Arthur, Gawain, and the Knights *von der Tafel-ronde.* (Vid. Goldasti Not. in Eginhart. Vit. Car. Mag. 4to, 1711, p. 207.)

[8] The Welsh have still some very old romances about King Arthur; but as these are in prose, they are not probably their first pieces that were composed on that subject.

bably the invention of English Minstrels [9]. On the other hand, the English procured translations of such romances as were most current in France; and in the list given at the conclusion of these remarks, many are doubtless of French original.

The first *prose* books of chivalry that appeared in our language, were those printed by Caxton [10]; at least, these are the first I have been able to discover, and these are all translations from the French. Whereas romances of this kind had been long current in metre, and were so generally admired in the time of Chaucer, that his rhyme of *Sir Thopas* was evidently written to ridicule and burlesque them [1].

He expressly mentions several of them by name in a stanza, which I shall have occasion to quote more than once in this volume:

"Men speken of Romaunces of pris
    Of Horn-Child, and of Ipotis
        Of Bevis, and Sire Guy,
    Of Sire Libeux, and Pleindamour,
    But Sire Thopas, he bereth the flour
        Of real chevalrie [2]."

Most, if not all of these, are still extant in MS. in some or other of our libraries, as I shall show in the conclusion of

[9] It is most credible that these stories were originally of English invention, even if the only pieces now extant should be found to be translations from the French. What now pass for the French originals were probably only amplifications, or enlargements of the old English story. That the French Romancers borrowed some things from the English, appears from the word Termagant, which they took up from our minstrels, and corrupted into Tervagaunte. See vol. i. p. 62, and Gloss. "Termagant."

[10] Recuyel of the Hystoryes of Troy, 1471. Godfroye of Boloyne, 1481. Le morte de Arthur, 1485. The life of Charlemagne, 1485, &c. As the old minstrelsy wore out, prose books of chivalry became more admired, especially after the Spanish romances began to be translated into English, towards the end of Queen Elizabeth's reign: then the most popular metrical romances began to be reduced into prose, as Sir Guy, Bevis, &c.

[1] See extract from a letter, written by the Editor of these volumes, in Mr. Warton's Observations, vol. ii. p. 139.

[2] Canterbury Tales (Tyrwhitt's Edit.), vol. ii. p. 238.—In all the former editions which I have seen, the name at the end of the fourth line is *Blandamoure*.

this slight Essay, where I shall give a list of such metrical histories and romances as have fallen under my observation.

As many of these contain a considerable portion of poetic merit, and throw great light on the manners and opinions of former times, it were to be wished that some of the best of them were rescued from oblivion. A judicious collection of them, accurately published, with proper illustrations, would be an important accession to our stock of ancient English literature. Many of them exhibit no mean attempts at epic poetry: and though full of the exploded fictions of chivalry, frequently display great descriptive and inventive powers in the bards who composed them. They are at least generally equal to any other poetry of the same age. They cannot indeed be put in competition with the nervous productions of so universal and commanding a genius as Chaucer; but they have a simplicity that makes them be read with less interruption, and be more easily understood: and they are far more spirited and entertaining than the tedious allegories of Gower, or the dull and prolix legends of Lydgate. Yet, while so much stress was laid upon the writings of these last, by such as treat of English poetry, the old metrical romances, though far more popular in their time, were hardly known to exist. But it has happened, unluckily, that the antiquaries, who have revived the works of our ancient writers, have been, for the most part, men void of taste and genius, and therefore have always fastidiously rejected the old poetical romances, because founded on fictitious or popular subjects, while they have been careful to grub up every petty fragment of the most dull and insipid rhymist, whose merit it was to deform morality or obscure true history. Should the public encourage the revival of some of those ancient epic songs of chivalry, they would frequently see the rich ore of an Ariosto or a Tasso, though buried, it may be, among the rubbish and dross of barbarous times.

Such a publication would answer many important uses; it would throw new light on the rise and progress of English poetry, the history of which can be but imperfectly understood if these are neglected: it would also serve to illustrate innumerable passages in our ancient classic poets, which, without their help, must be for ever obscure. For, not to mention Chaucer and Spenser, who abound with perpetual allusions to them, I shall give an instance or two from Shakspeare, by way of specimen of their use.

In his play of *King John*, our great dramatic poet alludes to an exploit of Richard I., which the reader will in vain look for in any true history. Faulconbridge says to his mother, act i. sc. 1,

> "Needs must you lay your heart at his dispose . . .
> Against whose furie and unmatched force,
> The awlesse lion could not wage the fight,
> Nor keepe his princely heart from Richard's hand.
> He that perforce robs lions of their hearts
> May easily winne a woman's:" —

The fact here referred to, is to be traced to its source only in the old romance of *Richard Cœur de Lyon*[3], in which his encounter with the lion makes a very shining figure. I shall give a large extract from this poem, as a specimen of the manner of these old rhapsodists, and to show that they did not in their fictions neglect the proper means to produce the ends, as was afterwards so childishly done in the prose books of chivalry.

The poet tells us, that Richard, in his return from the Holy Land, having been discovered in the habit of "a palmer in Almayne," and apprehended as a spy, was by the king thrown into prison. Wardrewe, the king's son, hearing of Richard's great strength, desires the jailor to let him have a sight of his prisoners. Richard being the foremost, Wardrewe asks him, "if he dare stand a buffet from his hand?" and that on the morrow he shall return him another. Richard consents, and receives a blow that staggers him. On the morrow, having previously waxed his hands, he waits his

---

[3] Dr. Grey has shown that the same story is alluded to in Rastell's Chronicle: as it was doubtless originally had from the romance, this is proof that the old metrical romances throw light on our first writers in prose: many of our ancient historians have recorded the fictions of romance.

antagonist's arrival. Wardrewe accordingly, proceeds the story, "held forth as a trewe man," and Richard gave him such a blow on the cheek, as broke his jaw-bone, and killed him on the spot. The king, to revenge the death of his son, orders, by the advice of one Eldrede, that a lion, kept purposely from food, shall be turned loose upon Richard. But the king's daughter, having fallen in love with him, tells him of her father's resolution, and at his request procures him forty ells of white silk "kerchers;" and here the description of the combat begins:

"The kever-chefes [4] he toke on honde,
And aboute his arme he wonde;
And thought in that ylke while,
To slee the lyon with some gyle.
And syngle in a kyrtyll he stode,
And abode the lyon fyers and wode,
With that came the jaylere,
And other men that wyth him were,
And the lyon them amonge;
His pawes were stiffe and stronge.
The chambre dore they undone,
And the lyon to them is gone.
Rycharde sayd, Helpe, lorde Jesu,
The lyon made to hym venu,
And wolde hym have all to rente:
Kynge Rycharde besyde him glente [5];
The lyon on the breste hym spurned,
That aboute he tourned.
The lyon was hongry and megre,
And bette his tayle to be egre;
He loked aboute as he were madde;
Abrode he all his pawes spradde.
He cryed lowde, and yaned [6] wyde.
Kynge Rycharde bethought hym that tyde
What hym was beste, and to hym sterte,
In at the throte his honde he gerte,
And hente out the herte with his honde,
Lounge and all that he there fonde.
The lyon fell deed to the grounde:
Rycharde felte no wem [7], ne wounde.

---

[4] *i. e.* handkerchiefs. Here we have the etymology of the word, viz. "Couvre le Chef."

[5] *i. e.* slipt aside.   [6] *i. e.* yawned.   [7] *i. e.* hurt.

He fell on his knees on that place,
And thanked Jesu of his grace."

*   *   *   *   *

What follows is not so well, and therefore I shall extract no more of this poem. — For the above feat, the author tells us, the king was deservedly called

Stronge Rycharde Cure de Lyowne.

That distich which Shakspeare puts in the mouth of his madman in *King Lear*, act iii. sc. 4,

Mice and rats and such small deere
Have been Tom's food for seven long yeare,

has excited the attention of the critics. Instead of *deere*, one of them would substitute *geer*, and another *cheer*[8]. But the ancient reading is established by the old romance of *Sir Bevis*, which Shakspeare had doubtless often heard sung to the harp. This distich is part of a description there given of the hardships suffered by Bevis, when confined for seven years in a dungeon:

Rattes and myse and such small dere
Was his meate that seven yere.   Sign. F. iii.

III. In different parts of this work, the reader will find various extracts from these old poetical legends; to which I refer him for further examples of their style and metre. To complete this subject, it will be proper at least to give one specimen of their skill in distributing and conducting their fable, by which it will be seen, that nature and common sense had supplied to these old simple bards the want of critical art, and taught them some of the most essential rules of epic poetry. — I shall select the romance of *Libius Disconius*[9], as being one of those mentioned by Chaucer, and either shorter or more intelligible than the others he has quoted.

If an epic poem may be defined[10] "A fable related by a

---

[8] Dr. Warburton. — Dr. Grey.

[9] So it is entitled in the Editor's MS. But the true title is, *Le beaux Disconus*, or the Fair Unknown. See a note on the Canterbury Tales, vol. iv. p. 333.

[10] Vid. "Discours sur la Poésie Epique," prefixed to TELEMAQUE.

poet, to excite admiration, and inspire virtue, by representing the action of some one hero, favoured by Heaven, who executes a great design, in spite of all the obstacles that oppose him," I know not why we should withhold the name of *epic poem* from the piece which I am about to analyze.

My copy is divided into ix Parts or Cantos, the several arguments of which are as follows.

PART I.

Opens with a short exordium to bespeak attention: the hero is described; a natural son of Sir Gawain, a celebrated knight of King Arthur's court, who, being brought up in a forest by his mother, is kept ignorant of his name and descent. He early exhibits marks of his courage, by killing a knight in single combat, who encountered him as he was hunting. This inspires him with a desire of seeking adventures: therefore clothing himself in his enemy's armour, he goes to King Arthur's court, to request the order of knighthood. His request granted, he obtains a promise of having the first adventure assigned him that shall offer. — A damsel named Ellen, attended by a dwarf, comes to implore King Arthur's assistance to rescue a young princess, "the lady of Sinadone," their mistress, who is detained from her rights, and confined in prison. The adventure is claimed by the young knight Sir Lybius: the king assents; the messengers are dissatisfied, and object to his youth; but are forced to acquiesce. And here the first book closes with a description of the ceremony of equipping him forth.

PART II.

Sir Lybius sets out on the adventure: he is derided by the dwarf and the damsel on account of his youth: they come to the bridge of Perill, which none can pass without encountering a knight called William de la Braunch. Sir Lybius is challenged; they just with their spears: De la Braunch is dismounted: the battle is renewed on foot: Sir William's sword breaks: he yields. Sir Lybius makes him swear to go and present himself to King Arthur, as the first fruits of his valour. The conquered knight sets out for King Arthur's court: is met by three knights, his kinsmen; who, informed of his disgrace, vow revenge, and pursue the conqueror. The next day they overtake him: the eldest of the three attacks Sir Lybius; but is overthrown to the ground. The two other brothers assault him: Sir Lybius is wounded; yet cuts off the second brother's arm; the third yields: Sir Lybius sends them all to King Arthur. In the third evening he is awakened by the dwarf, who has discovered a fire in the wood.

PART III.

Sir Lybius arms himself, and leaps on horseback: he finds two giants roasting a wild boar, who have a fair lady their captive. Sir Lybius, by favour of the night, runs one of them through with his spear: is assaulted by the other: a fierce battle ensues: he cuts off the giant's arm, and at length his head. The rescued lady (an earl's daughter) tells him her story, and leads him to her father's castle; who entertains him with a great feast; and presents him at parting with a suit of armour and a steed. He sends the giant's head to King Arthur.

PART IV.

Sir Lybius, maid Ellen, and the dwarf, renew their journey: they see a castle stuck round with human heads, and are informed it belongs to a knight called Sir Gefferon, who, in honour of his lemman or mistress, challenges all comers: he that can produce a fairer lady, is to be rewarded with a milk-white faulcon, but if overcome, to lose his head. Sir Lybius spends the night in the adjoining town: in the morning goes to challenge the faulcon. The knights exchange their gloves: they agree to just in the market-place: the lady and maid Ellen are placed aloft in chairs: their dresses: the superior beauty of Sir Gefferon's mistress described: the ceremonies previous to the combat. They engage: the combat described at large: Sir Gefferon is in-

2*

curably hurt, and carried home on his shield. Sir Lybius
sends the faulcon to King Arthur, and receives back a large
present in florins. He stays forty days to be cured of his
wounds, which he spends in feasting with the neighbouring
lords.

PART V.

Sir Lybius proceeds for Sinadone: in a forest he meets
a knight hunting, called Sir Otes de Lisle: maid Ellen,
charmed with a very beautiful dog, begs Sir Lybius to bestow
him upon her: Sir Otes meets them, and claims his dog: is
refused: being unarmed he rides to his castle and summons
his followers: they go in quest of Sir Lybius: a battle en-
sues: he is still victorious, and forces Sir Otes to follow the
other conquered knights to King Arthur.

PART VI.

Sir Lybius comes to a fair city and castle by a river-side,
beset round with pavilions or tents: he is informed, in the
castle is a beautiful lady besieged by a giant named Maugys,
who keeps the bridge, and will let none pass without doing
him homage: this Lybius refuses: a battle ensues; the giant
described: the several incidents of the battle; which lasts a
whole summer's day: the giant is wounded; put to flight;
slain. The citizens come out in procession to meet their de-
liverer: the lady invites him into her castle: falls in love
with him; and seduces him to her embraces. He forgets
the princess of Sinadone, and stays with this bewitching
lady a twelvemonth. This fair sorceress, like another Alcina,
intoxicates him with all kinds of sensual pleasure; and de-
tains him from the pursuit of honour.

PART VII.

Maid Ellen by chance gets an opportunity of speaking
to him; and upbraids him with his vice and folly: he is
filled with remorse, and escapes the same evening. At
length he arrives at the city and castle of Sinadone: is given
to understand that he must challenge the constable of the

art. Seld. and among Mr. Garrick's plays, K. vol. ix. — The Editor's MS. and the printed copies begin,

> Lordinge, and you wyl holde you styl.

The Cambridge MS. has it,

> Lystenyth, lordingis, gente and fre.

23. *Ipomydon* (or *Chylde Ipomydon*) is preserved among the Harl. MSS. 2252 (44). It is in distichs, and begins,

> Mekely, lordyngis, gentylle and fre.

In the library of Lincoln Cathedral, K k. 3. 10, is an old imperfect printed copy, wanting the whole first sheet A.

24. *The Squyr of Lowe Degre*, is one of those burlesqued by Chaucer in his Rhyme of Thopas[10]. — Mr. Garrick has a printed copy of this among his old plays, K. vol. ix. It begins,

> It was a squyer of lowe degre,
> That loved the kings daughter of Hungre.

25. *Historye of K. Richard Cure [Cœur] de Lyon*, [Impr. W. de Worde, 1528, 4to,] is preserved in the Bodleian library, c. 39, art. Selden. A fragment of it is also remaining in the Edinburgh MS. of old English poems; no. xxxvi. in 2 leaves. A large extract from this romance has been given already above, p. 16. Richard was the peculiar patron of Chivalry, and favourite of the old Minstrels and Troubadours. See Warton's Observ. vol. i. p. 29; vol. ii. p. 40.

26. Of the following I have only seen No. 27, but I believe they may all be referred to the class of romances.

The *Knight of Courtesy and the Lady of Faguel* (Bodl. lib. c. 39, art. Sheld. a printed copy). This Mr. Warton thinks is the story of Coucy's Heart, related in Fauchet, and in Howel's Letters [V. i. s. 6, l. 20. See Wart. Obs. v. ii. p. 40]. The Editor has seen a very beautiful old ballad on this subject in French.

27. The four following are all preserved in the MS. so

---

[10] This is alluded to by Shakspeare in his Henry V. (act. v.), where Fluellyn tells Pistol, he will make him a Squire of Low Degree, when he means to knock him down.

often referred to in the public library at Cambridge (690. Appendix to Bp. More's MSS. in Cat. MSS. tom. ii. p. 394), viz. *The Lay of Erle of Tholouse* (No. 27), of which the Editor hath also a copy from "Cod. MSS. Mus.Ashmol. Oxon." The first line of both is,

Jesus Chryste in Trynyte.

28. *Roberd Kynge of Cysyll* (or Sicily), shewing the fall of Pride. Of this there is also a copy among the Harl. MSS. 1703 (3) The Cambridge MS. begins,

Princis that be prowde in prese.

29. *Le bone Florence of Rome*, beginning thus:

As ferre as men ride or gone.

30. *Dioclesian the Emperour*, beginning,

Sum tyme ther was a noble man.

31. The two knightly brothers, *Amys and Amelion* (among the Harl. MSS. 2386, §. 42), is an old Romance of chivalry; as is also, I believe, the fragment of the *Lady Belesant, the Duke of Lombardy's fair daughter*, mentioned in the same article. See the Catalog. vol. ii.

32. In the Edinburgh MS. so often referred to (preserved in the Advocates' library, W. 4. 1), might probably be found some other articles to add to this list, as well as other copies of some of the pieces mentioned in it; for the whole volume contains not fewer than 37 Poems or Romances, some of them very long. But as many of them have lost the beginnings, which have been cut out for the sake of the illuminations; and as I have not had an opportunity of examining the MS. myself, I shall be content to mention only the articles that follow[1]: viz.

An old Romance about *Rouland* (not, I believe, the famous Paladine, but a champion named Rouland Louth; query), being in the volume, no. xxvii. in 5 leaves, and wants the beginning.

---

[1] Some of these I give, though mutilated and divested of their titles, because they may enable a curious inquirer to complete or improve other copies.

33. Another Romance, that seems to be a kind of continuation of this last, entitled *Otuel a Knight* (no. xxviii.), in 11 leaves and a half. The two first lines are,

> Herkneth both zinge and old.
> That willen heren of battailes bold.

34. *The King of Tars* (no. iv. in 5 leaves and a half; it is also in the Bodleian library, MS. Vernon, f. 304), beginning thus:

> Herkneth to me both eld and zing,
> For Maries love that swete thing.

35. A Tale or Romance (no. i. 2 leaves) that wants both beginning and end. The first lines now remaining are,

> Th Erl him graunted his will y-wis.   that the knicht him haden y told.
> The Baronnis that were of mikle pris.   befor him thay weren y-cald.

36. Another mutilated Tale or Romance (no. iii. 4 leaves) The first lines at present are,

> To Mr. Steward will y gon.   and tellen him the sothe of the
> Reseyved bestow sone anon.   gif zou will serve and with hir be.

37. A mutilated Tale or Romance (no. xi. in 13 leaves) The two first lines that occur are,

> That riche Dooke his fest gan hold
> With Erls and with Baronns bold.

I cannot conclude my account of this curious manuscript, without acknowledging that I was indebted to the friendship of the Rev. Dr. Blair, the ingenious Professor of Belles Lettres in the University of Edinburgh, for whatever I learned of its contents, and for the important additions it enabled me to make to the foregoing list.

To the preceding articles, two ancient metrical romances in the Scottish dialect may now be added, which are published in Pinkerton's *Scottish Poems*, reprinted from scarce editions, Lond. 1792, in 3 vols. 8vo, viz.

38. *Gawan and Gologras*, a Metrical Romance; from an edition printed at Edinburgh, 1508, 8vo, beginning,

> In the tyme of Arthur, as trew men me tald.

It is in stanzas of thirteen lines.

39. *Sir Gawan and Sir Galaron of Galloway*, a Metrical Romance, in the same stanzas as no. 38, from an ancient MS. beginning thus:

> In the tyme of Arthur an aunter[2] betydde
> By the Turnwathelan, as the boke tells;
> Whan he to Carlele was comen, and conqueror kyd, &c.

Both these (which exhibit the union of the old alliterative metre, with rhyme, &c., and in the termination of each stanza the short triplets of the *Turnament of Tottenham*) are judged to be as old as the time of our King Henry VI., being apparently the production of an old poet, thus mentioned by Dunbar, in his "Lament for the Deth of the Makkaris:"

> Clerk of Tranent eik he hes take,
> That made the aventers of Sir Gawane.

It will scarce be necessary to remind the reader, that *Turnewathelan* is evidently *Tearne-Wadling*, celebrated in the old ballad of the *Marriage of Sir Gawaine*. See p. 42, and no. xix. book iii. of this volume.

Many new references, and perhaps some additional articles might be added to the foregoing list from Mr. Warton's *History of English Poetry*, 3 vols. 4to, and from the Notes to Mr. Tyrwhitt's improved edition of Chaucer's *Canterbury Tales*, &c., in 5 vols. 8vo, which have been published since this Essay, &c. was first composed; but it will be sufficient once for all to refer the curious reader to those popular works.

The reader will also see many interesting particulars on the subject of these volumes, as well as on most points of general literature, in Sir John Hawkins's curious *History of Music*, &c., in 5 volumes, 4to; as also in Dr. Burney's *Hist.*, &c., in 4 vols. 4to.

---

[2] *i. e.* adventure.

END OF THE ESSAY.

I.

𝕮𝖍𝖊 𝕭𝖔𝖞 𝖆𝖓𝖉 𝖙𝖍𝖊 𝕸𝖆𝖓𝖙𝖑𝖊,

Is printed verbatim from the old MS. described in the Preface. The Editor believes it more ancient than it will appear to be at first sight; the transcriber of that manuscript having reduced the orthography and style in many instances to the standard of his own times.

The incidents of the *mantle* and the *knife* have not, that I can recollect, been borrowed from any other writer. The former of these evidently suggested to Spenser his conceit of Florimel's girdle, b. iv. c. 5, st. 3.

> That girdle gave the virtue of chaste love
> And wivehood true to all that did it beare ;
> But whosoever contrarie doth prove,
> Might not the same about her middle weare,
> But it would loose or else asunder teare.

So it happened to the false Florimel, st. 16, when

> —— being brought, about her middle small
> They thought to gird, as best it her became,
> But by no means they could it thereto frame,
> For ever as they fastned it, it loos'd
> And fell away, as feeling secret blame, &c.
> That all men wondred at the uncouth sight
> And each one thought as to their fancies came.
> But she herself did think it done for spight,
> And touched was with secret wrath and shame
> Therewith, as thing deviz'd her to defame:
> Then many other ladies likewise tride
> About their tender loynes to knit the same,
> But it would not on none of them abide,
> But when they thought it fast, eftsoones it was untide.

> Thereat all knights gan laugh and ladies lowre,
> Till that at last the gentle Amoret
> Likewise assayed to prove that girdle's powre.
> And having it about her middle set
> Did find it fit withouten breach or let,
> Whereat the rest gan greatly to envie.
> But Florimel exceedingly did fret,
> And snatching from her hand, &c.

As for the trial of the *horne*, it is not peculiar to our poet; it occurs in the old romance, entitled *Morte Arthur*, which was translated out of French in the time of King Edward IV., and first printed anno 1484. From that romance Ariosto is thought to have borrowed his tale of the *Enchanted Cup*, c. 42, &c. See Mr. Warton's Observations on the Faerie Queen, &c.

The story of the *horn* in Morte Arthur varies a good deal from this of our poet, as the reader will judge from the following extract: — "By the way they met with a knight that was sent from Morgan la Faye to king Arthur, and this knight had a fair horne all garnished with gold, and the horne had such a virtue, that there might no ladye or gentlewoman drinke of that horne, but if she were true to her husband: and if shee were false she should spill all the drinke, and if shee were true unto her lorde, shee might drink peaceably: and because of queene Guenever and in despite of Sir Launcelot du Lake, this horne was sent unto King Arthur." This horn is intercepted and brought unto another king named Marke, who is not a whit more fortunate than the British hero; for he makes "his qeene drinke thereof, and an hundred ladies moe, and there were but foure ladies of all those that drank cleane," of which number the said queen proves not to be one. [Book ii. chap. 22, ed. 1632.]

In other respects the two stories are so different, that we have just reason to suppose this ballad was written before that romance was translated into English.

As for Queen Guenever, she is here represented no otherwise than in the old histories and romances. Holinshed observes, that "she was evil reported of, as noted of incontinence and breach of faith to hir husband." Vol. i. p. 93.

⁎ Such readers as have no relish for pure antiquity, will find a more modern copy of this ballad at the end of the volume.

In the third day of may,
To Carleile did come
A kind curteous child,
That cold much of wisdome.

A kirtle and a mantle   5
This child had uppon,
With 'brouches' and ringes
Full richelye bedone.

He had a sute of silke
About his middle drawne;   10
Without he cold of curtesye
He thought itt much shame.

God speed thee, king Arthur,
Sitting at thy meate:
And,the goodly queene Guénever,   15
I cannott her forgett.

I tell you, lords, in this hall;
I hett you all to 'heede;'
Except you be the more surer
Is you for to dread.   20

He plucked out of his 'poterner,'
And longer wold not dwell,
He pulled forth a pretty mantle,
Betweene two nut-shells.

Have thou here, king Arthur;   25
Have thou heere of mee:
Give itt to thy comely queene
Shapen as itt is alreadye.

Itt shall never become that wiffe,
That hath once done amisse.   30

V. 7, branches. MS.   V. 18, heate. MS.   V. 21, poterver. MS.

Then every knight in the kings court
Began to care for 'his.'

Forth came dame Guénever;
To the mantle shee her 'hied;'
The ladye shee was newfangle,   35
But yett shee was affrayd.

When shee had taken the mantle;
She stoode as shee had beene madd:
It was from the top to the toe
As sheeres had itt shread.   40

One while was it 'gule;'
Another while was itt greene;
Another while was it wadded:
Ill itt did her beseeme.

Another while was it blacke   45
And bore the worst hue:
By my troth, quoth king Arthur,
I thinke thou be not true.

Shee threw downe the mantle,
That bright was of blee;   50
Fast with a rudd redd,
To her chamber can shee flee.

She curst the weaver, and the walker,
That clothe that had wrought;
And bade a vengeance on his crowne,   55
That hither hath itt brought.

I had rather be in a wood,
Under a greene tree;
Then in king Arthurs court
Shamed for to bee.   60

V. 32, his wiffe. MS.   V. 34, bided. MS.   V. 41, gaule. MS.

Kay called forth his ladye,
And bade her come neere;
Saies, Madam, and thou be guiltye,
I pray thee hold thee there.

Forth came his ladye   65
Shortlye and anon;
Boldlye to the mantle
Then is shee gone.

When she had tane the mantle,
And cast it her about;   70
Then was shee bare
'Before all the rout.'

Then every knight,
That was in the kings court,
Talked, laughed, and showted   75
Full oft att that sport.

Shee threw downe the mantle,
That bright was of blee;
Fast, with a red rudd,
To her chamber can shee flee.   80

Forth came an old knight
Pattering ore a creede,
And he proferred to this little boy
Twenty markes to his meede;

And all the time of the Christmasse 85
Willinglye to ffeede;
For why this mantle might
Doe his wiffe some need.

When she had tane the mantle,
Of cloth that was made,   90

V. 75, lauged. MS.

Shee had no more left on her,
But a tassell and a threed:
Then every knight in the kings court
Bade evill might shee speed.

Shee threw downe the mantle,   95
That bright was of blee;
And fast, with a redd rudd,
To her chamber can shee flee.

Craddocke called forth his ladye,
And bade her come in;   100
Saith, Winne this mantle, ladye,
With a litle dinne.

Winne this mantle, ladye,
And it shal be thine,
If thou never did amisse   105
Since thou wast mine.

Forth came Craddockes ladye
Shortlye and anon;
But boldlye to the mantle
Then is shee gone.   110

When she had tane the mantle,
And cast it her about,
Upp att her great toe
It began to crinkle and crowt:
Shee said, bowe downe, mantle,   115
And shame me not for nought.

Once I did amisse,
I tell you certainlye,
When I kist Craddockes mouth
Under a greene tree;   120
When I kist Craddockes mouth
Before he marryed mee.

When shee had her shreeven,
And her sines shee had tolde;
The mantle stoode about her   125
Right as shee wold:

Seemelye of coulour
Glittering like gold:
Then every knight in Arthurs court
Did her behold.   130

Then spake dame Guénever
To Arthur our king;
She hath tane yonder mantle
Not with right, but with wronge.

See you not yonder woman,   135
That maketh her self soe 'cleane?'
I have seene tane out of her bedd
Of men fiveteene;

Priests, clarkes, and wedded men
From her bedeene: 140
Yett shee taketh the mantle,
And maketh her self cleane.

Then spake the little boy,
That kept the mantle in hold;
Sayes, king, chasten thy wiffe,   145
Of her words shee is to bold:

Shee is a bitch and a witch,
And a whore bold:
King, in thine owne hall
Thou art a cuckold.   150

The little boy stoode
Looking out a dore;

V. 134, wright. MS.   V. 136, cleare. MS.   V. 140, by deene. MS.

'And there as he was lookinge
He was ware of a wyld bore.'

He was ware of a wyld bore,   155
Wold have werryed a man:
He pulld forth a wood kniffe,
Fast thither that he ran:
He brought in the bores head,
And quitted him like a man.   160

He brought in the bores head,
And was wonderous bold:
He said there was never a cuckolds kniffe
Carve itt that cold.

Some rubbed their knives   165
Uppon a whetstone:
Some threw them under the table,
And said they had none.

King Arthur, and the child
Stood looking upon them;   170
All their knives edges
Turned backe againe.

Craddocke had a little knive
Of iron and of steele;
He britled the bores head   175
Wonderous weele;
That every knight in the kings court
Had a morssell.

The little boy had a horne,
Of red gold that ronge: 180
He said, there was noe cuckolde
Shall drinke of my horne;
But he shold it sheede
Either behind or beforne.

V. 170, them upon. MS.   V. 175, or birtled. MS.

Some shedd on their shoulder, 185
And some on their knee;
He that cold not hitt his mouthe,
Put it in his eye:
And he that was a cuckold
Every man might him see. 190

Craddocke wan the horne,
And the bores head:
His ladie wan the mantle
Unto her meede.
Everye such a lovely ladye 195
God send her well to speede.

II.

The Marriage of Sir Gawaine,

Is chiefly taken from the fragment of an old ballad in the
Editor's MS., which he has reason to believe more ancient
than the time of Chaucer, and what furnished that bard with
his *Wife of Bath's Tale*. The original was so extremely
mutilated, half of every leaf being torn away, that without
large supplements, &c. it was deemed improper for this col-
lection: these it has therefore received, such as they are.
They are not here particularly pointed out, because the
Fragment itself will now be found printed at the end of this
volume.

PART THE FIRST.

King Arthur lives in merry Carleile,
  And seemely is to see;
And there with him queene Guenever,
  That bride soe bright of blee.

And there with him queene Guenever, 5
  That bride so bright in bowre:

And all his barons about him stoode,
  That were both stiffe and stowre.

The king a royale Christmasse kept,
  With mirth and princelye cheare;   10
To him repaired many a knighte,
  That came both farre and neare.

And when they were to dinner sette,
  And cups went freely round:
Before them came a fair damsèlle,   15
  And knelt upon the ground.

A boone, a boone, O kinge Arthùre,
  I beg a boone of thee;
Avenge me of a carlish knighte,
  Who hath shent my love and mee.   20

At Tearne-Wadling[1] his castle stands,
  Near to that lake so fair,
And proudlye rise the battlements,
  And streamers deck the air.

Noe gentle knighte, nor ladye gay,   25
  May pass that castle-wall:
But from that foule discurteous knighte,
  Mishappe will them befalle.

Hee's twice the size of common men,
  Wi' thewes, and sinewes stronge,   30
And on his backe he bears a clubbe,
  That is both thicke and longe.

---

[1] *Tearne-Wadling* is the name of a small lake near Hesketh in Cumberland, on the road from Penrith to Carlisle. There is a tradition, that an old castle once stood near the lake, the remains of which were not long since visible. *Tearn*, in the dialect of that country, signifies a small lake, and is still in use.

This grimme baròne 'twas our harde happe,
  But yester morne to see;
When to his bowre he bare my love,   35
  And sore misused mee.

And when I told him, king Arthùre
  As lyttle shold him spare;
Goe tell, sayd hee, that cuckold kinge,
  To meete mee if he dare.   40

Upp then sterted king Arthùre,
  And sware by hille and dale,
He ne'er wolde quitt that grimme baròne,
  Till he had made him quail.

Goe fetch my sword Excalibar: 45
  Goe saddle mee my steede;
Nowe, by my faye, that grimme baròne
  Shall rue this ruthfulle deede.

And when he came to Tearne Wadlinge
  Benethe the castle walle: 50
"Come forth; come forth; thou proude baròne,
  Or yielde thyself my thralle."

On magicke grounde that castle stoode,
  And fenc'd with many a spelle:
Noe valiant knighte could tread thereon,   55
  But straite his courage felle.

Forth then rush'd that carlish knight,
  King Arthur felte the charme:
His sturdy sinewes lost their strengthe,
  Downe sunke his feeble arme: 60

Nowe yield thee, yield thee, kinge Arthùre,
  Now yield thee, unto mee:
Or fighte with mee, or lose thy lande,
  Noe better termes maye bee,

Unlesse thou sweare upon the rood,   65
   And promise on thy faye,
Here to returne to Tearne-Wadling,
   Upon the new-yeare's daye:

And bringe me worde what thing it is
   All women moste desyre: 70
This is thy ransome, Arthur, he sayes,
   Ile have noe other hyre.

King Arthur then helde up his hande,
   And sware upon his faye,
Then tooke his leave of the grimme barone,   75
   And faste hee rode awaye.

And he rode east, and he rode west,
   And did of all inquyre,
What thing it is all women crave,
   And what they most desyre   80

Some told him riches, pompe, or state;
   Some rayment fine and brighte;
Some told him mirthe; some flatterye;
   And some a jollye knighte.

In letters all king Arthur wrote,   85
   And seal'd them with his ringe:
But still his minde was helde in doubte,
   Each tolde a different thinge.

As ruthfulle he rode over a more,
   He saw a ladye sette   90
Betweene an oke, and a greene holléye,
   All clad in red[2] scarlette.

[2] This was a common phrase in our old writers; so Chaucer, in his
Prologue to the Cant. Tales, says of the Wife of Bath:
        Her hosen were of fyne scarlet red.

What when gaye ladyes goe with their lordes   125
    To drinke the ale and wine;
Alas! then I must hide myself,
    I must not goe with mine?

"My faire ladyè, sir Gawaine sayd,
    I yield me to thy skille;   130
Because thou art mine owne ladyè
    Thou shalt have all thy wille."

Nowe blessed be thou, sweete Gawàine,
    And the daye that I thee see;
For as thou seest mee at this time,   135
    Soe shall I ever bee.

My father was an aged knighte,
    And yet it chanced soe,
He tooke to wife a false ladyè,
    Whiche broughte me to this woe.   140

Shee witch'd mee, being a faire yonge maide,
    In the greene forèst to dwelle;
And there to abide in lothlye shape,
    Most like a fiend of helle.

Midst mores and mosses; woods, and wilds;   145
    To lead a lonesome life:
Till some yong faire and courtlye knighte
    Wolde marrye me to his wife:

Nor fully to gaine mine owne trewe shape,
    Such was her devilish skille;   150
Until he wolde yielde to be rul'd by mee,
    And let mee have all my wille.

She witchd my brother to a carlish boore,
    And made him stiffe and stronge;
And built him a bowre on magicke grounde,   155
    To live by rapine and wronge.

But now the spelle is broken throughe,
And wronge is turnde to righte;
Henceforth I shall bee a fair ladyè,
And hee be a gentle knighte.   160

*_**

III.

King Ryence's Challenge.

This song is more modern than many of those which fol-
low it, but is placed here for the sake of the subject. It was
sung before Queen Elizabeth at the grand entertainment at
Kenilworth Castle in 1575, and was probably composed for
that occasion. In a letter describing those festivities it is
thus mentioned: "A Minstral came forth with a sollem song,
warranted for story out of K. Arthur's acts, whereof I gat a
copy, and is this:

"So it fell out on a Pentecost," &c.

After the song the narrative proceeds: "At this the
Minstrell made a pause and a curtezy for Primus Passus.
More of the song is thear, but I gatt it not."

The story in *Morte Arthur*, whence it is taken, runs as
follows: "Came a messenger hastely from king Ryence of
North Wales, — saying, that king Ryence had discomfited
and overcomen eleaven kings, and everiche of them did him
homage, and that was this: they gave him their beards cleane
flayne off, — wherefore the messenger came for king Arthur's
beard, for king Ryence had purfeled a mantell with kings
beards, and there lacked for one a place of the mantell, where-
fore he sent for his beard, or else he would enter into his lands,
and brenn and slay, and never leave till he have thy head
and thy beard. Well, said king Arthur, thou hast said thy
message, which is the most villainous and lewdest message
that ever man heard sent to a king. Also thou mayest see
my beard is full young yet for to make a purfell of, but tell
thou the king that — or it be long he shall do to me homage

on both his knees, or else he shall leese his head." [B. i. c. 24. See also the same Romance, b. i. c. 92.]

The thought seems to be originally taken from Jeff. Monmouth's Hist. b. x. c. 3, which is alluded to by Drayton in his Poly-Olb. Song iv., and by Spenser in Faer. Queen, vi. 1 13, 15. See Warton's Observations on Spenser, vol. ii. page 223.

The following text is composed of the best readings selected from three different copies. The first in Enderbie's Cambria Triumphans, p. 197. The second in the Letter above mentioned. And tho third inserted in MS. in a copy of Morte Arthur, 1632, in the Bodl. library.

Stow tells us, that king Arthur kept his round table at "diverse places, but especially at Carlion, Winchester, and Camalet, in Somersetshire." This Camalet, "sometimes a famous towne or castle, is situate on a very high tor or hill," &c. [See an exact description in Stow's Annals, ed. 1631, p. 55.]

As it fell out on a Pentecost day,
   King Arthur at Camelot kept his court royall,
With his faire queene dame Guenever the gay;
   And many bold barons sitting in hall;
   With ladies attired in purple and pall;
And heraults in hewkes, hooting on high,
Cryed *Largesse, Largesse, Chevaliers tres-hardie*[1].

A doughty dwarfe to the uppermost deas
   Right pertlye gan pricke, kneeling on knee;
With steven fulle stoute amids all the preas,
   Sayd, Nowe sir king Arthur, God save thee, and see!
   Sir Ryence of North-gales greeteth well thee,
And bids thee thy beard anon to him send,
Or else from thy jaws he will it off rend.

---

[1] *Largesse, Largesse.* The heralds resounded these words as oft as they received the bounty of the knights. See *Mémoires de la Chevalerie*, tom. i. p. 99. — The expression is still used in the form of installing knights of the garter.

For his robe of state is a rich scarlet mantle,
 With eleven kings beards bordered[2] about,
And there is room lefte yet in a kantle,
 For thine to stande, to make the twelfth out:
 This must be done, be thou never so stout;
This must be done, I tell thee no fable,
Maugre the teethe of all thy round table.

When this mortal message from his mouthe past,
 Great was the noyse bothe in hall and in bower:
The king fum'd; the queene screecht; ladies were aghast;
 Princes puff'd; barons blustred; lords began lower;
 Knights stormed; squires startled, like steeds in a stower:
Pages and yeomen yell'd out in the hall,
Then in came sir Kay, the 'king's' seneschal.

Silence, my soveraignes, quoth this courteous knight,
 And in that stound the stowre began still:
'Then' the dwarfe's dinner full deerely was dight;
 Of wine and wassel he had his wille:
 And, when he had eaten and drunken his fill,
An hundred pieces of fine coyned gold
Were given this dwarf for his message bold.

But say to sir Ryence, thou dwarf, quoth the king,
 That for his bold message I do him defye;
And shortlye with basins and pans will him ring
 Out of North-gales; where he and I
 With swords, and not razors, quickly shall trye,
Whether he, or king Arthur will prove the best barbor;
And therewith he shook his good sword Escalàbor.

   * * * * *

*** Strada, in his Prolusions, has ridiculed the story of the giant's mantle, made of the beards of kings.

[2] *i. e.* set round the border, as furs are now round the gowns of magistrates.

IV.

King Arthur's Death.

A FRAGMENT.

THE subject of this ballad is evidently taken from the old
romance *Morte Arthur*, but with some variations, especially
in the concluding stanzas; in which the author seems rather
to follow the traditions of the old Welsh bards, who "be-
lieved that King Arthur was not dead, but conveied awaie
by the Fairies into some pleasant place, where he should
remaine for a time, and then returne againe and reign in as
great authority as ever." — Holinshed, b. v. c. 14; or, as it is
expressed in an old Chronicle printed at Antwerp 1493, by
Ger. de Leew, "The Bretons supposen, that he [K. Arthur]
— shall come yet and conquere all Bretaigne, for certes this
is the prophicye of Merlyn: He sayd, that his deth shall be
doubteous; and sayd soth, for men thereof yet have doubte,
and shullen for ever more, — for men wyt not whether that
he lyveth or is dede." See more ancient testimonies in
Selden's Notes on Poly Olbion, Song iii.

This fragment, being very incorrect and imperfect in the
original MS., hath received some conjectural emendations,
and even a supplement of three or four stanzas composed
from the romance of *Morte Arthur*.

* * * * *

On Trinitye Mondaye in the morne,
   This sore battayle was doom'd to bee;
Where manye a knighte cry'd, Well-awaye!
   Alacke, it was the more pittie.

Ere the first crowinge of the cocke,   5
   When as the kinge in his bed laye,
He thoughte sir Gawaine to him came[1],
   And there to him these wordes did saye.

[1] Sir Gawaine had been killed at Arthur's landing on his return from
abroad. See the next ballad, ver. 73.

Nowe, as you are mine unkle deare,
   And as you prize your life, this daye   10
O meet not with your foe in fighte;
   Putt off the battayle, if yee maye.

For sir Launcelot is nowe in Fraunce,
   And with him many an hardye knighte:
Who will within this moneth be backe,   15
   And will assiste yee in the fighte.

The kinge then call'd his nobles all,
   Before the breakinge of the daye;
And tolde them howe sir Gawaine came,
   And there to him these wordes did saye.   20

His nobles all this counsayle gave,
   That earlye in the morning, hee
Shold send awaye an herauld at armes,
   To aske a parley faire and free.

Then twelve good knightes king Arthur chose,   25
   The best of all that with him were:
To parley with the foe in field,
   And make with him agreement faire.

The king he charged all his hoste,
   In readinesse there for to bee: 30
But noe man sholde noe weapon sturre,
   Unlesse a sword drawne they shold see.

And Mordred on the other parte,
   Twelve of his knights did likewise bringe;
The best of all his companye,   35
   To hold the parley with the kinge.

Sir Mordred alsoe charged his hoste,
   In readinesse there for to bee;
But noe man sholde noe weapon sturre,
   But if a sworde drawne they shold see.   40

For he durste not his unkle truste,
   Nor he his nephewe, sothe to tell:
Alacke! it was a woefulle case,
   As ere in Christentye befelle.

But when they were together mette,   45
   And both to faire accordance broughte;
And a month's league betweene them sette,
   Before the battayle sholde be foughte;

An addere crept forth of a bushe,
   Stunge one o' th' king's knightes on the knee: 50
Alacke! it was a woefulle chance,
   As ever was in Christentie.

When the knighte found him wounded sore,
   And sawe the wilde-worm hanginge there;
His sworde he from his scabberde drewe: 55
   A piteous case, as ye shall heare.

For when the two hostes sawe the sworde,
   They joyned battayle instantlye;
Till of soe manye noble knightes,
   On one side there were left but three.   60

For all were slain that durst abide,
   And but some fewe that fled awaye:
Ay mee! it was a bloodye fielde,
   As ere was foughte on a summer's daye.

Upon king Arthur's own partyè,   65
   Onlye himselfe escaped there,
And Lukyn duke of Gloster free,
   And the king's butler Bedevere.

And when the king beheld his knightes,
   All dead and scattered on the molde: 70

Ver. 41, 42, the folio MS. reads father . . . . sonne.

The teares fast trickled downe his face;
  That manlye face in fight so bolde.

Nowe reste yee all, brave knights, he said,
  Soe true and faithful to your trust:
And must yee then, ye valiant hearts,   75
  Be lefte to moulder into dust?

Most loyal have yee been to mee,
  Most true and faithful unto deathe:
And, oh! to rayse yee up againe,
  How freelye could I yield my breathe!   80

But see, the traitor's yet alive,
  Lo where hee stalkes among the deade!
Nowe bitterlye he shall abye:
  And vengeance fall upon his head.

O staye, my liege, then sayd the duke;   85
  O staye for love and charitie:
Remember what the vision spake,
  Nor meete your foe, if it may bee.

O, staye mee not, thou worthye wight,
  This debt my loyal knights I owe: 90
Betide me life, betide me death,
  I will avenge them of their foe.

Then straite he grasp'd his trustye speare,
  And on his horse then mounted hee:
As his butler holpe him to his horse,   95
  His bowels gushed to his knee.

Alas! then sayd the noble king,
  That I should live this sight to see!
To see this good knight here be slaine,
  All for his love in helping mee!   100

He put his speare into his reste,
   And to sir Mordred loud gan crye;
Nowe sette thyself upon thy guarde,
   For, traitor, nowe thy death is nye.

Sir Mordred lifted up his sworde,   105
   And fierce to meet the king ran hee:
The king his speare he through him thrust;
   A fathom thorow his bodìe.

When Mordered felt the stroke of death,
   And found that he was wounded soe;   110
He thruste himselfe upon the speare,
   And strucke the king a deadlye blowe.

Then grimmlye dyed sir Mordered,
   Presentlye upon that tree:
And bloody streames ranne from the kinge   115
   Ere to the duke returned hee.

Sir Lukyn then he thus bespake,
   Sir knighte, thou hast been faithfulle tryde,
Nowe take my sword Excalibar[2],
   That hangs so freelye by my syde: 120

O take my sword Excalibar,
   And there into the river throwe:
For here, henceforth, benethe this tree,
   All use of weapons I foregoe.

And fare thee well, thou trustye sword,   125
   A better neer had valiant knighte,
With thee full ofte, and many a daye,
   Have I withstood my foe in fighte.

With this good fauchion in my hande,
   Oft have I reapd the bloody feelde: 130

---

[2] More commonly called *Caliburn*. In the folio MS. *Escalberd*.

But nowe the fatalle houre is come,
　　That never more I may thee weelde

The duke to the river side he went,
　　And there his owne sword in threwe he:
But he kept back Excalibar,   135
　　He kept it back in privitie.

For all of coleyne was the blade;
　　And all the hilte of precious stone:
And ever alacke! then sayd the knighte,
　　Must such a sword awaye be throwne?   140

Then backe he came unto the kinge,
　　Who sayd, Sir Lukyn, what did yee see?
Nothing my liege, save that the winde
　　Blewe oer the waters faire and free.

O goe againe, then said the kinge,   145
　　O good sir Lukyn, goe againe:
Into the rivere throwe my sword,
　　Nor keepe me lingering here in paine.

The duke then to the river went,
　　And the kings scabberd in threwe hee: 150
But hee kept backe Excalibar,
　　And hid it undernethe a tree.

Then backe he came to tell the kinge,
　　Who sayde, Sir Lukyn, sawe ye oughte?
Nothinge, my liege, save that the winde   155
　　Nowe with the angrye waters fought.

O Lukyn, Lukyn, said the kinge,
　　Twice haste thou dealt deceytfullye:
Alacke, whom may wee ever truste,
　　When suche a knighte soe false can bee?   160

Who for their deeds and martiall feates,
   As bookes done yett record,
Amongst all other nations
   Wer feared through the world.   20

And in the castle off Tyntagill
   King Uther mee begate
Of Agyana a bewtyous ladye,
   And come of 'hie' estate.

And when I was fifteen yeere old,   25
   Then was I crowned kinge:
All Brittaine that was att an uprore,
   I did to quiett bringe.

And drove the Saxons from the realme,
   Who had opprest this land;   30
All Scotland then throughe manly feates
   I conquered with my hand.

Ireland, Denmarke, Norwaye,
   These countryes wan I all;
Iseland, Gotheland, and Swetheland;   35
   And made their kings my thrall.

I conquered all Gallya,
   That now is called France;
And slew the hardye Froll in feild
   My honor to advance.   40

And the ugly gyant Dynabus
   Soe terrible to vewe,
That in Saint Barnards mount did lye,
   By force of armes I slew:

ʃV. 23. She is named *Igerna* in the old Chronicles.   V. 24, his. MS.
V. 39, Froland field. MS. Froll, according to the Chronicles, was a Roman
knight, governor of Gaul.   V. 41, Danibus. MS.

And Lucyus the emperour of Rome   45
  I brought to deadly wracke;
And a thousand more of noble knightes
  For feare did turne their backe:

Five kinges of 'paynims' I did kill
  Amidst that bloody strife;   50
Besides the Grecian emperour
  Who alsoe lost his liffe.

Whose carcasse I did send to Rome
  Cladd poorlye on a beere;
And afterward I past Mount-Joye   55
  The next approaching yeere.

Then I came to Rome, where I was mett
  Right as a conquerour,
And by all the cardinalls solempnelye
  I was crowned an emperour.   60

One winter there I made abode:
  Then word to mee was brought
Howe Mordred had oppressd the crowne:
  What treason he had wrought

Att home in Brittaine with my queene;   65
  Therefore I came with speede
To Brittaine backe, with all my power,
  To quitt that traiterous deede:

And soone at Sandwiche I arrivde,
  Where Mordred me withstoode: 70
But yett at last I landed there,
  With effusion of much blood.

For there my nephew sir Gawaine dyed,
  Being wounded in that sore,

V. 49, of Pavye. MS.

The whiche sir Lancelot in fight   75
   Had given him before.

Thence chased I Mordered away,
   Who fledd to London right,
From London to Winchester, and
   To Cornewalle took his flyght.   80

And still I him pursued with speed
   Till at the last wee mett:
Wherby an appointed day of fight
   Was there agreed and sett.

Where we did fight, of mortal life   85
   Eche other to deprive,
Till of a hundred thousand men
   Scarce one was left alive.

There all the noble chivalrye
   Of Brittaine tooke their end.   90
O see how fickle is their state
   That doe on feates depend!

There all the traiterous men were slaine,
   Not one escapte away;
And there dyed all my vallyant knightes.   95
   Alas! that woefull day!

Two and twenty yeere I ware the crowne
   In honor and great fame;
And thus by death was suddenlye
   Deprived of the same.   100

V. 92, perhaps fates.

VI.

𝔄 Dyttie to Ḩey Doѡne.

COPIED from an old MS. in the Cotton library [Vesp. A. 25], entitled "Divers things of Hen. viij's time."

WHO sekes to tame the blustering winde,
　Or causse the floods bend to his wyll,
Or els against dame nature's kinde
　To 'change' things frame by cunning skyll:
That man I thinke bestoweth paine,　　　　　　5
Thoughe that his laboure be in vaine.

Who strives to breake the sturdye steele,
　Or goeth about to staye the sunne;
Who thinks to causse an oke to reele,
　Which never can by force be done:　　　　　　10
That man likewise bestoweth paine,
Thoughe that his laboure be in vaine.

Who thinks to stryve against the streame,
　And for to sayle without a maste;
Unlesse he thinks perhapps to faine,　　　　　　15
　His travell ys forelorne and waste;
And so in cure of all his paine,
His travell ys his cheffest gaine.

So he lykewise, that goes about
　To please eche eye and every eare,　　　　　　20
Had nede to have withouten doubt
　A golden gyft with him to beare;
For evyll report shall be his gaine,
Though he bestowe both toyle and paine

Ver. 4, causse. MS.

God grant eche man one to amend; 25
  God send us all a happy place;
And let us pray unto the end,
  That we may have our princes grace:
Amen, amen! so shall we gaine
A dewe reward for all our paine. 30

VII.

Glasgerion.

An ingenious friend thinks that the following old ditty
(which is printed from the Editor's folio MS.) may possibly
have given birth to the Tragedy of *The Orphan*, in which
Polidore intercepts Monimia's intended favours to Castalio.

See what is said concerning the hero of this song (who is
celebrated by Chaucer under the name of Glaskyrion), in the
Essay prefixed to vol. i., note (i), part iv. (2.)

Glasgerion was a kings owne sonne,
  And a harper he was goode:
He harped in the kings chambere,
  Where cuppe and caudle stoode.

And soe did hee in the queens chambere, 5
  Till ladies waxed 'glad.'
And then bespake the kinges daughter;
  And these wordes thus shee sayd.

Strike on, strike on, Glasgèrion,
  Of thy striking doe not blinne: 10
Theres never a stroke comes oer thy harpe,
  But it glads my hart withinne.

Ver. 6, wood. MS.

Faire might he fall, ladye, quoth hee,
    Who taught you nowe to speake!
I have loved you, ladye, seven longe yeere   15
    My minde I neere durst breake.

But come to my bower, my Glasgeriòn,
    When all men are att rest:
As I am a ladie true of my promise,
    Thou shalt bee a welcome guest.   20

Home then came Glasgèrion,
    A glad man, lord! was hee.
And, come thou hither, Jacke my boy;
    Come hither unto mee.

For the kinges daughter of Normandye   25
    Hath granted mee my boone:
And att her chambere must I bee
    Beffore the cocke have crowen.

O master, master, then quoth hee,
    Lay your head downe on this stone: 30
For I will waken you, master deere,
    Afore it be time to gone.

But up then rose that lither ladd,
    And hose and shoone did on:
A coller he cast upon his necke,   35
    Hee seemed a gentleman.

And when he came to the ladyes chambere,
    He thrild upon a pinn [1].
The lady was true of her promise,
    And rose and lett him inn.   40

V. 16, harte. MS.

[1] This is elsewhere expressed '*twirled the pin*,' or '*tirled at the pin*,' [see
b. ii. s. vi. v. 3,] and seems to refer to the turning round the button on the
outside of a door, by which the latch rises, still used in cottages.

He did not take the lady gaye
   To boulster nor to bed:
'Nor thoughe hee had his wicked wille,
   A single word he sed.'

He did not kisse that ladyes mouthe,   45
   Nor when he came, nor yode:
And sore that ladye did mistrust,
   He was of some churls bloud.

But home then came that lither ladd,
   And did off his hose and shoone;   50
And cast the coller from off his necke:
   He was but a churlès sonne.

Awake, awake, my deere master,
   The cock hath well-nigh crowen.
Awake, awake, my master deere,   55
   I hold it time to be gone.

For I have saddled your horse, mastèr,
   Well bridled I have your steede:
And I have served you a good breakfast:
   For thereof ye have need.   60

Up then rose good Glasgeriòn,
   And did on hose and shoone;
And cast a coller about his necke:
   For he was a kinge his sonne.

And when he came to the ladyes chambere,   65
   He thrilled upon the pinne:
The ladye was more than true of promise,
   And rose and let him inn.

O whether have you left with me
   Your bracelet or your glove?   70
Or are you returned backe againe
   To know more of my love?

Glasgèrion swore a full great othe,
　　By oake, and ashe, and thorne;
Ladye, I was never in your chambère,　　　　75
　　Sith the time that I was borne.

O then it was your lither foot-page,
　　He hath beguiled mee.
Then shee pulled forth a little pen-knìffe,
　　That hanged by her knee:　　　　80

Sayes, there shall never noe churlès blood
　　Within my bodye spring:
No churlès blood shall eer defile
　　The daughter of a kinge.

Home then went Glasgèrion,　　　　85
　　And woe, good lord, was hee.
Sayes, come thou hither, Jacke my boy,
　　Come hither unto mee.

If I had killed a man to night,
　　Jacke, I would tell it thee:　　　　90
But if I have not killed a man to night,
　　Jacke, thou hast killed three.

And he puld out his bright browne sword,
　　And dryed it on his sleeve,
And he smote off that lìther ladds head,　　　　95
　　Who did his ladye grieve.

He sett the swords poynt till his brest,
　　The pummil untill a stone:
Throw the falsenesse of that lither ladd,
　　These three lives were all gone.　　　　100

V. 77, litle. MS.　　　　V. 100, werne all. MS.

VIII.

𝔒𝔩𝔡 𝔕𝔬𝔟𝔦𝔫 𝔬𝔣 𝔓𝔬𝔯𝔱𝔦𝔫𝔤𝔞𝔩𝔢.

FROM an ancient copy in the Editor's folio MS., which was
judged to require considerable corrections.

In the former edition, the hero of this piece had been
called Sir Robin, but that title not being in the MS. is now
omitted.

————

LET never again soe old a man
    Marrye soe yonge a wife,
As did old Robin of Portingale;
    Who may rue all the dayes of his life.

For the mayors daughter of Lin, god wott,   5
    He chose her to his wife,
And thought with her to have lived in love,
    But they fell to hate and strife.

They scarce were in their wed-bed laid,
    And scarce was hee asleepe,   10
But upp shee rose, and forth shee goes,
    To the steward, and gan to weepe.

Sleepe you, wake you, faire sir Gyles?
    Or be you not within?
Sleepe you, wake you, faire sir Gyles,   15
    Arise and let me inn.

O, I am waking, sweete, he said,
    Sweete ladye, what is your will?
I have unbethought me of a wile
    How my wed-lord weell spill.   20

Ver. 19, unbethought [properly *onbethought*]; this word is still used in the
Midland counties in the same sense as *bethought*. .

Twenty-four good knights, shee sayes,
    That dwell about this towne,
Even twenty-four of my next cozèns,
    Will helpe to dinge him downe.

All that beheard his litle foote-page,   25
    As he watered his masters steed;
And for his masters sad perille
    His verry heart did bleed.

He mourned, sighed, and wept full sore;
    I sweare by the holy roode   30
The teares he for his master wept
    Were blent water and bloude.

And that beheard his deare mastèr
    As he stood at his garden pale:
Sayes, Ever alacke, my litle foot-page,   35
    What causes thee to wail?

Hath any one done to thee wronge
    Any of thy fellowes here?
Or is any of thy good friends dead,
    That thou shedst manye a teare?   40

Or, if it be my head bookes-man,
    Aggrieved he shal bee:
For no man here within my howse,
    Shall doe wrong unto thee.

O, it is not your head bookes-man,   45
    Nor none of his degree;
But, on to-morrow ere it be noone
    All deemed to die are yee.

And of that bethank your head stewàrd,
    And thank your gay ladye.   50

V. 32, blend. MS.   V. 47, or to-morrow. MS.

If this be true, my litle foot-page,
  The heyre of my land thoust bee.

If it be not true, my dear mastèr,
  No good death let me die.
If it be not true, thou litle foot-page,   55
  A dead corse shalt thou lie.

O call now downe my faire ladye,
  O call her downe to mee:
And tell my ladye gay how sicke,
  And like to die I bee.   60

Downe then came his ladye faire,
  All clad in purple and pall:
The rings that were on her fingèrs,
  Cast light throughout the hall.

What is your will, my owne wed-lord?   65
  What is your will with mee?
O see, my ladye deere, how sicke,
  And like to die I bee.

And thou be sicke, my own wed-lord,
  Soe sore it grieveth me: 70
But my five maydens and myselfe
  Will 'watch thy' bedde for thee.

And at the waking of your first sleepe,
  We will a hott drinke make:
And at the waking of your 'next' sleepe,   75
  Your sorrowes we will slake.

He put a silk cote on his backe,
  And mail of manye a fold:
And hee putt a steele cap on his head,
  Was gilt with good red gold.   80

V. 56, bec. MS.   V. 72, make the. MS.   V. 75, first. MS.

He layd a bright browne sword by his side,
    And another att his feete:
'And twentye good knights he placed at hand,
    To watch him in his sleepe.'

And about the middle time of the night,   85
    Came twentye-four traitours inn:
Sir Giles he was the foremost man,
    The leader of that ginn.

Old Robin with his bright browne sword,
    Sir Gyles head soon did winn: 90
And scant of all those twenty-four,
    Went out one quick agenn.

None save only a litle foot page,
    Crept forth at a window of stone:
And he had two armes when he came in,   95
    And he went back with one.

Upp then came that ladie gaye
    With torches burning bright:
She thought to have brought sir Gyles a drinke,
    Butt she found her owne wedd knight.   100

The first thinge that she stumbled on
    It was sir Gyles his foote:
Sayes, Ever alacke, and woe is mee!
    Here lyes my sweete hart-roote.

The next thinge that she stumbled on   105
    It was sir Gyles his heade:
Sayes, Ever, alacke, and woe is mee!
    Heere lyes my true love deade.

Hee cutt the pappes beside her brest,
    And didd her body spille;   110
He cutt the eares beside her heade,
    And bade her love her fille.

He called then up his litle foot-page,
   And made him there his heyre;
And sayd, henceforth my worldlye goodes   115
   And countrye I forsweare.

He shope the crosse on his right shoulder,
   Of the white 'clothe' and the redde[1],
And went him into the holy land,
   Wheras Christ was quicke and dead.   120

V. 118, neshe. MS.

[1] Every person who went on a CROISADE to the Holy Land, usually wore
a cross on his upper garment, on the right shoulder, as a badge of his pro-
fession. Different nations were distinguished by crosses of different colours:
the English wore white, the French red, &c. This circumstance seems to
be confounded in the ballad. [V. Spelman, Gloss.]

☞ In the foregoing piece, Giles, steward to a rich old
merchant trading to Portugal, is qualified with the title of
Sir, not as being a knight, but rather, I conceive, as having
received an inferior order of priesthood.

IX.

Child Waters.

Child is frequently used by our old writers as a title. It is
repeatedly given to Prince Arthur in the *Faerie Queen:* and
the son of a king is in the same poem called *Child Tristram*
[b. v. c. 11. st. 8, 13, — b. vi. c. 2. st. 36, — ibid. c. 8. st. 15].
In an old ballad quoted in Shakspeare's *King Lear*, the hero
of Ariosto is called *Child Roland*. Mr. Theobald supposes
this use of the word was received along with their romances
from the Spaniards, with whom *Infante* signifies a *Prince*.
A more eminent critic tells us, that "in the old times of
chivalry, the noble youth, who were candidates for knight-
hood, during the time of their probation were called *Infans*,
Varlets, *Damoysels*, *Bacheliers*. The most noble of the youth

were particularly called *Infans*." [Vide Warb. Shakesp.] A
late commentator on Spenser observes, that the Saxon word
cniht knight, signifies also a *Child*. [See Upton's Gloss. to
the *Faerie Queen*.]

The Editor's MS. collection, whence the following piece
is taken, affords several other ballads, wherein the word
Child occurs as a title: but in none of these it signifies *Prince*.
See the song entitled *Gil Morrice* in this volume.

It ought to be observed that the word *Child*, or *Chield*, is
still used in North Britain to denominate a man, commonly
with some contemptuous character affixed to him, but some-
times to denote man in general.

Childe Waters in his stable stoode
 And stroakt his milke-white steede:
To him a fayre yonge ladye came
 As ever ware womans weede.

Sayes, Christ you save, good Childe Waters: 5
 Sayes, Christ you save, and see:
My girdle of gold that was too longe,
 Is now too short for mee.

And all is with one childe of yours,
 I feele sturre at my side: 10
My gowne of greene it is too straighte;
 Before, it was too wide.

If the childe be mine, faire Ellen, he sayd,
 Be mine as you tell mee;
Then take you Cheshire and Lancashire both, 15
 Take them your owne to bee.

If the childe be mine, faire Ellen, he sayd,
 Be mine, as you doe sweare:
Then take you Cheshire and Lancashire both,
 And make that childe your heyre. 20

Shee sayes, I had rather have one kisse,
   Childe Waters, of thy mouth;
Than I wolde have Cheshire and Lancashire both
   That lye by north and southe.

And I had rather have one twinklìng,   25
   Childe Waters, of thine ee:
Then I wolde have Cheshire and Lancashire both,
   To take them mine owne to bee.

To morrowe, Ellen, I must forth ryde
   Farr into the north countree;   30
The fayrest ladye that I can finde,
   Ellen, must goe with mee.

'Thoughe I am not that ladye fayre,
   Yet let me go with thee:'
And ever I pray you, Childe Watèrs,   35
   Your foot-page let me bee.

If you will my foot-page bee, Ellèn,
   As you doe tell to mee;
Then you must cut your gowne of greene,
   An inch above your knee: 40

Soe must you doe your yellowe lockes,
   An inch above your ee:
You must tell no man what is my name;
   My footpage then you shall bee.

Shee, all the long daye Childe Waters rode,   45
   Ran barefoote by his syde;
Yet was he never soe courteous a knighte,
   To say, Ellen, will you ryde?

Shee, all the long daye Childe Waters rode,
   Ran barefoote thorow the broome;   50
Yet was hee never soe courteous a knighte,
   To say, put on your shoone.

Ride softlye, shee sayd, O Childe Waters,
  Why doe you ryde so fast?
The childe, which is no mans but thine,   55
  My bodye itt will brast.

Hee sayth, seest thou yond water, Ellen,
  That flows from banke to brimme. —
I trust in God, O Childe Waters,
  You never will see [1] me swimme.   60

But when shee came to the water syde,
  She sayled to the chinne:
Nowe the Lord of heaven be my speede,
  For I must learne to swimme.

The salt waters bare up her clothes;   65
  Our Ladye bare up her chinne:
Childe Waters was a woe man, good Lord,
  To see faire Ellen swimme.

And when shee over the water was
  Shee then came to his knee: 70
Hee sayd, Come hither, thou fayre Ellèn,
  Loe yonder what I see.

Seest thou not yonder hall, Ellèn?
  Of redd gold shines the yate:
Of twenty foure faire ladyes there   75
  The fairest is my mate.

Seest thou not yonder hall, Ellèn?
  Of redd golde shines the towre:
There are twenty four fayre ladyes there,
  The fayrest is my paramoure.   80

I see the hall now, Childe Waters,
  Of redd golde shines the yate:

[1] *i. e.* permit, suffer, &c.

God give you good now of yourselfe,
   And of your worthye mate.

I see the hall now, Childe Waters,   85
   Of redd golde shines the towre:
God give you good now of yourselfe,
   And of your paramoure.

There twenty four fayre ladyes were
   A playing at the ball: 90
And Ellen the fayrest ladye there,
   Must bring his steed to the stall.

There twenty four fayre ladyes were,
   A playinge at the chesse;
And Ellen the fayrest ladye there,   95
   Must bring his horse to gresse.

And then bespake Childe Waters sister,
   These were the wordes sayd shee:
You have the prettyest page, brothèr,
   That ever I did see.   100

But that his bellye it is soe bigge,
   His girdle stands soe hye:
And ever I pray you, Childe Watèrs,
   Let him in my chamber lye.

It is not fit for a little foot page,   105
   That has run throughe mosse and myre,
To lye in the chamber of any ladye,
   That weares soe riche attyre.

It is more meete for a little foot page,
   That has run throughe mosse and myre,   110
To take his supper upon his knee,
   And lye by the kitchen fyre.

Ver. 84, worldlye. MS.

Now when they had supped every one,
    To bedd they tooke theyr waye:
He sayd, come hither, my little foot-page,   115
    And hearken what I saye.

Goe thee downe into yonder towne,
    And lowe into the streete;
The fayrest ladye that thou canst finde,
    Hyre in mine armes to sleepe,   120
And take her up in thine armes twaine,
    For filing[2] of her feete.

Ellen is gone into the towne:
    And lowe into the streete:
The fayrest ladye that shee colde finde,   125
    She hyred in his armes to sleepe;
And tooke her up in her armes twayne,
    For filing of her feete.

I praye you nowe, good Childe Waters,
    Let mee lye at your feete: 130
For there is noe place about this house,
    Where I may 'saye a sleepe.

'He gave her leave, and fair Ellèn
    'Down at his beds feet laye:'
This done the nighte drove on apace,   135
    And when it was neare the daye,

Hee sayd, Rise up, my little foot-page,
    Give my steede corne and haye;
And give him nowe the good black oats,
    To carry mee better awaye.   140

Up then rose the fayre Ellèn
    And gave his steede corne and haye:

V. 132, i. e. essay, attempt.

[2] i. e. defiling. See Warton's Observ. vol. ii. p. 158.

And soe shee did the good black oates,
   To carry him the better awaye.

She leaned her back to the manger side,   145
   And grievouslye did groane:
Shee leaned her back to the manger side,
   And there shee made her moane.

And that beheard his mother deare,
   Shee heard 'her woefull woe,'   150
Shee sayd, Rise up, thou Childe Watèrs,
   And into thy stable goe.

For in thy stable is a ghost,
   That grievouslye doth grone:
Or else some woman laboures with childe,   155
   Shee is soe woe-begone.

Up then rose Childe Waters soone,
   And did on his shirte of silke;
And then he put on his other clothes,
   On his bodye as white as milke.   160

And when he came to the stable dore,
   Full still there hee did stand,
That hee mighte heare his fayre Ellèn,
   Howe shee made her monànd.

She sayd, Lullabye, mine own dear childe,   165
   Lullabye, deare childe, deare:
I wolde thy father were a kinge,
   Thy mothere layd on a biere.

Peace nowe, hee sayd, good faire Ellèn,
   Bee of good cheere, I praye;   170
And the bridale and the churchinge bothe
   Shall bee upon one daye.

V. 164, *i. e.* moaning, bemoaning, &c.

X.

Phillida and Corydon.

THIS sonnet is given from a small quarto MS. in the Editor's possession, written in the time of Queen Elizabeth. Another copy of it, containing some variations, is reprinted in the *Muses Library*, p. 295, from an ancient miscellany entitled *England's Helicon*, 1600, 4to. The author was Nicholas Breton, a writer of some fame in the reign of Elizabeth, who also published an interlude entitled "An old man's lesson and a young man's love," 4to, and many other little pieces in prose and verse, the titles of which may be seen in Winstanley, Ames' Typog. and Osborne's Harl. Catalog., &c. He is mentioned with great respect by Meres, in his second part of *Wit's Commonwealth*, 1598, f. 283, and is alluded to in Beaumont and Fletcher's *Scornful Lady*, act ii., and again in *Wit without Money*, act iii. See Whalley's Ben Jonson, vol. iii. p. 103.

The present edition is improved by a copy in *England's Helicon*, edit. 1614, 8vo.

IN the merrie moneth of Maye,
In a morne by break of daye,
With a troope of damselles playing
Forthe 'I yode' forsooth a maying:

When anon by a wood side,   5
Where that Maye was in his pride,
I espied all alone
Phillida and Corydon.

Much adoe there was, god wot;
He wold love, and she wold not.   10
She sayde, never man was trewe;
He sayes, none was false to you.

Ver. 4, the wode. MS.

He sayde, hee had lovde her longe:
She sayes, love should have no wronge.
Corydon wold kisse her then: 15
She sayes, maydes must kisse no men,

Tyll they doe for good and all.
When she made the shepperde call
All the heavens to wytnes truthe,
Never loved a truer youthe.   20

Then with manie a prettie othe,
Yea and nay, and faithe and trothe;
Suche as seelie shepperdes use
When they will not love abuse;

Love, that had bene long deluded,   25
Was with kisses sweete concluded;
And Phillida with garlands gaye
Was made the lady of the Maye.

———

⁎ The foregoing little Pastoral of *Phillida and Corydon*
is one of the songs in "The Honourable Entertainment gieven
to the Queenes Majestie in Progresse at Elvetham in Hamp-
shire, by the R. H. the Earle of Hertford, 1591," 4to. [Printed
by Wolfe. No name of author.] See in that pamphlet,

"The thirde daies Entertainment.

"On Wednesday morning about 9 o'clock, as her Majestie
opened a casement of her gallerie window, ther were 3 ex-
cellent musicians, who being disguised in auncient country
attire, did greet her with a pleasant song of Corydon and
Phillida, made in 3 parts of purpose. The song, as well for
the worth of the dittie, as the aptnesse of the note therto ap-
plied, it pleased her Highnesse after it had been once sung
to command it againe, and highly to grace it with her
cheerefull acceptance and commendation.

"The Plowman's Song.
"In the merrie month of May," &c.

The splendour and magnificence of Elizabeth's reign is no where more strongly painted than in these little diaries of some of her summer excursions to the houses of her nobility; nor could a more acceptable present be given to the world, than a republication of a select number of such details as this of the entertainment at Elvetham, that at Killingworth, &c. &c., which so strongly mark the spirit of the times, and present us with scenes so very remote from modern manners.

☞ Since the above was written, the public hath been gratified with a most complete work on the foregoing subject, entitled, *The Progresses and Public Processions of Queen Elizabeth*, &c. By John Nichols, F. A. S. Edinb. and Perth, 1788, 2 vols. 4to.

XI.

Little Musgrave and Lady Barnard.

This ballad is ancient, and has been popular; we find it quoted in many old plays. See Beaum. and Fletcher's *Knight of the Burning Pestle*, 4to, 1613, act v. *The Varietie*, a comedy, 12mo, 1649, act iv., &c. In Sir William Davenant's play, *The Witts*, act iii., a gallant thus boasts of himself:

"Limber and sound! besides I sing Musgrave,
And for Chevy-chace no lark comes near me."

In the Pepys Collection, vol. iii. p. 314, is an imitation of this old song, in thirty-three stanzas, by a more modern pen, with many alterations, but evidently for the worse.

This is given from an old printed copy in the British Museum, with corrections; some of which are from a fragment in the Editor's folio MS. It is also printed in Dryden's Collection of Miscellaneous Poems.

As it fell out on a highe holye daye,
 As many bee in the yeare,
When young men and maides together do goe,
 Their masses and mattins to heare,

Little Musgràve came to the church door,   5
 The priest was at the mass;
But he had more mind of the fine womèn,
 Then he had of our Ladyes grace.

And some of them were clad in greene,
 And others were clad in pall;   10
And then came in my lord Barnardes wife,
 The fairest among them all.

Shee cast an eye on little Musgràve
 As bright as the summer sunne:
O then bethought him little Musgràve,   15
 This ladyes heart I have wonne.

Quoth she, I have loved thee, little Musgràve,
 Fulle long and manye a daye.
So have I loved you, ladye faire,
 Yet word I never durst saye.   20

I have a bower at Bucklesford-Bury, [1],
 Full daintilye bedight,
If thoult wend thither, my little Musgràve,
 Thoust lig in mine armes all night.

Quoth hee, I thanke yee, ladye faire,   25
 This kindness yee shew to mee;
And whether it be to my weale or woe,
 This night will I lig with thee.

All this beheard a litle foot-page,
 By his ladyes coach as he ranne: 30

---

[1] Bucklefield-berry. fol. MS.

Quoth he, thoughe I am my ladyes page,
  Yet Ime my lord Barnardes manne.

My lord Barnàrd shall knowe of this,
  Although I lose a limbe.
And ever whereas the bridges were broke,   35
  He layd him downe to swimme.

Asleep or awake, thou lord Barnàrd,
  As thou art a man of life,
Lo! this same night at Bucklesford-Bury
  Little Musgrave's abed with thy wife.   40

If it be trew, thou litle foote-page,
  This tale thou hast told to mee,
Then all my lands in Bucklesford-Bury
  I freelye will give to thee.

But and it be a lye, thou litle foot-page,   45
  This tale thou hast told to mee,
On the highest tree in Bucklesford-Bury
  All hanged shalt thou bee.

Rise up, rise up, my merry men all,
  And saddle me my good steede;   50
This night must I to Bucklesford-bury;
  God wott, I had never more neede.

Then some they whistled, and some they sang,
  And some did loudlye saye,
Whenever lord Barnardes horne it blewe,   55
  Awaye, Musgràve, away.

Methinkes I heare the throstle cocke,
  Methinkes I heare the jaye,
Methinkes I heare lord Barnards horne:
  I would I were awaye.   60

Lye still, lye still, thou little Musgràve,
    And huggle me from the cold;
For it is but some shephardes boye
    A whistling his sheepe to the fold.

Is not thy hawke upon the pearche,   65
    Thy horse eating corne and haye?
And thou a gaye lady within thine armes:
    And wouldst thou be awaye?

By this lord Barnard was come to the dore,
    And lighted upon a stone: 70
And he pulled out three silver keyes,
    And opened the dores eche one.

He lifted up the coverlett,
    He lifted up the sheete;
How now, how now, thou little Musgràve,   75
    Dost find my gaye ladye sweete?

I find her sweete, quoth little Musgràve,
    The more is my griefe and paine;
Ide gladlye give three hundred poundes
    That I were on yonder plaine.   80

Arise, arise, thou little Musgràve,
    And put thy cloathes nowe on,
It shall never be said in my countree,
    That I killed a naked man.

I have two swordes in one scabbàrde,   85
    Full deare they cost my purse;
And thou shalt have the best of them,
    And I will have the worse.

The first stroke that little Musgrave strucke,
    He hurt lord Barnard sore;   90

V. 64, Is whistling sheepe ore the mold. fol. MS.

The next stroke that lord Barnard strucke,
    Little Musgrave never strucke more.

With that bespake the ladye faire,
    In bed whereas she laye,
Althoughe thou art dead, my little Musgràve,   95
    Yet for thee I will praye:

And wishe well to thy soule will I,
    So long as I have life;
So will I not do for thee, Barnàrd,
    Thoughe I am thy wedded wife.   100

He cut her pappes from off her brest;
    Great pitye it was to see,
The drops of this fair ladyes bloode
    Run trickling downe her knee.

Wo worth, wo worth ye, my merrye men all,   105
    You never were borne for my goode:
Why did you not offer to stay my hande,
    When you sawe me wax so woode?

For I have slaine the fairest sir knighte,
    That ever rode on a steede;   110
So have I done the fairest lady,
    That ever ware womans weede.

A grave, a grave, lord Barnard cryde,
    To putt these lovers in;
But lay my ladye o' the upper hande,   115
    For shee comes o' the better kin.

☞ That the more modern copy is to be dated about the middle of the last century, will be readily conceived from the tenour of the concluding stanza, viz.

    "This sad Mischief by Lust was wrought:
       Then let us call for Grace,
    That we may shun the wicked vice,
       And fly from Sin a-pace."

XII.

The Ew-Bughts Marion.

A SCOTTISH SONG.

THIS sonnet appears to be ancient: that and its simplicity
of sentiment have recommended it to a place here.

———————

WILL ze gae to the ew-bughts, Marion,
  And wear in the sheip wi' mee?
The sun shines sweit, my Marion,
  But nae half sae sweit as thee.
O Marion's a bonnie lass;   5
  And the blyth blinks in her ee:
And fain wad I marrie Marion,
  Gin Marion wad marrie mee.

Theire's gowd in zour garters, Marion;
  And siller on zour white hauss-bane[1]:   10
Fou faine wad I kisse my Marion
  At eene quhan I cum hame.
Theire's braw lads in Earnslaw, Marion,
  Quha gape and glowr wi' their ee
At kirk, quhan they see my Marion;   15
  Bot nane of them lues like mee.

Ive nine milk-ews, my Marion,
  A cow and a brawney quay;
Ise gie tham au to my Marion,
  Just on her bridal day.   20
And zees get a grein sey apron,
  And waistcote o' London broun;
And wow bot ze will be vaporing
  Quhaneir ze gang to the toun.

[1] *Hauss-bane, i. e.* the neck-bone. Marion had probably a silver locket
on, tied close to her neck with a riband, an usual ornament in Scotland.
where a sore throat is called "*a sair hause*," properly *halse.*

Ime yong and stout, my Marion,   25
   None dance lik mee on the greine;
And gin ze forsak me, Marion,
   Ise een gae draw up wi' Jeane.
Sae put on zour pearlins, Marion,
   And kirtle oth' cramasie,   30
And sune as my chin has nae haire on,
   I sall cum west, and see zee.

XIII.

Ĉḥe Ḳnigḥt anḍ Sḥepḥerḍ's Ḍaugḥter.

THIS ballad (given from an old black-letter copy, with some corrections) was popular in the time of Queen Elizabeth, being usually printed with her picture before it, as Hearne informs us in his preface to *Gul. Newbrig. Hist.* Oxon. 1719, 8vo, vol. i. p. lxx. It is quoted in Fletcher's comedy of *The Pilgrim*, act iv. sc. 1.

THERE was a shepherds daughter,
   Came tripping on the waye;
And there by chance a knighte shee mett,
   Which caused her to staye.

Good morrowe to you, beauteous maide,   5
   These words pronounced hee:
O I shall dye this daye, he sayd,
   If Ive not my wille of thee.

The Lord forbid, the maide replyde,
   That you shold waxe so wode!   10
'But for all that shee could do or saye,
   He wold not be withstood.'

Sith you have had your wille of mee,
   And put me to open shame,

Now, if you are a courteous knighte,   15
 Tell me what is your name?

Some do call mee Jacke, sweet heart,
 And some do call mee Jille;
But when I come to the kings fair courte
 They calle me Wilfulle Wille.   20

He sett his foot into the stirrup,
 And awaye then he did ride;
She tuckt her girdle about her middle,
 And ranne close by his side.

But when she came to the brode watèr, 25
 She sett her brest and swamme;
And when she was got out againe,
 She tooke to her heels and ranne.

He never was the courteous knighte,
 To saye, faire maide, will ye ride? 30
And she was ever too loving a maide
 To saye, sir knighte abide.

When she came to the kings faire courte,
 She knocked at the ring;
So readye was the king himself   35
 To let this faire maide in.

Now Christ you save, my gracious liege,
 Now Christ you save and see,
You have a knighte within your courte
 This daye hath robbed mee.   40

What hath he robbed thee of, sweet heart?
 Of purple or of pall?
Or hath he took thy gaye gold ring
 From off thy finger small?

He hath not robbed mee, my liege,   45
  Of purple nor of pall:
But he hath gotten my maiden head,
  Which grieves mee worst of all.

Now if he be a batchelor,
  His bodye Ile give to thee;   50
But if he be a married man,
  High hanged he shall bee.

He called downe his merrye men all,
  By one, by two, by three;
Sir William used to bee the first,   55
  But nowe the last came hee.

He brought her downe full fortye pounde,
  Tyed up withinne a glove:
Faire maid, Ile give the same to thee;
  Go, seeke thee another love.   60

O Ile have none of your gold, she sayde,
  Nor Ile have none of your fee;
But your faire bodye I must have,
  The king hath granted mee.

Sir William ranne and fetchd her then   65
  Five hundred pound in golde,
Saying, faire maide, take this to thee,
  Thy fault will never be tolde.

Tis not the gold that shall mee tempt,
  These words then answered shee,   70
But your own bodye I must have,
  The king hath granted mee.

Ver. 50. His bodye Ile give to thee. This was agreeable to the feudal customs: the lord had a right to give a wife to his vassals. See Shakspeare's *All's well that ends well.*

Would I had dranke the water cleare,
    When I did drinke the wine,
Rather than any shepherds brat   75
    Shold bee a ladye of mine!

Would I had drank the puddle foule,
    When I did drink the ale,
Rather than ever a shepherds brat
    Shold tell me such a tale!   80

A shepherds brat even as I was,
    You mote have let mee bee,
I never had come to the kings faire courte,
    To crave any love of thee.

He sett her on a milk-white steede,   85
    And himself upon a graye;
He hung a bugle about his necke,
    And soe they rode awaye.

But when they came unto the place,
    Where marriage-rites were done,   90
She proved herself a dukes daughtèr,
    And he but a squires sonne.

Now marrye me, or not, sir knight,
    Your pleasure shall be free:
If you make me ladye of one good towne,   95
    Ile make you lord of three.

Ah! cursed bee the gold, he sayd,
    If thou hadst not been trewe,
I shold have forsaken my sweet love,
    And have changed her for a newe.   100

And now their hearts being linked fast,
    They joyned hand in hande:
Thus he had both purse, and person **too,**
    And all at his commande.

XIV.

The Shepherd's Address to his Muse.

THIS poem, originally printed from the small MS. volume
mentioned above in no. x., has been improved by a more
perfect copy in *England's Helicon*, where the author is dis-
covered to be N. Breton.

GOOD Muse, rocke me aslepe
    With some sweete harmony:
This wearie eyes is not to kepe
    Thy wary company.

Sweet Love, begon a while,   5
    Thou seest my heavines:
Beautie is borne but to beguyle
    My harte of happines.

See how my little flocke,
    That lovde to feede on highe,   10
Doe headlonge tumble downe the rocke,
    And in the valley dye.

The bushes and the trees,
    That were so freshe and greene,
Doe all their deintie colors leese,   15
    And not a leafe is seene.

The blacke birde and the thrushe,
    That made the woodes to ringe,
With all the rest, are now at hushe,
    And not a note they singe.   20

Swete Philomele, the birde
    That hath the heavenly throte,
Doth nowe, alas! not once afforde
    Recordinge of a note.

The flowers have had a frost,   25
   The herbs have loste their savoure;
And Phillida the faire hath lost
   'For me her wonted' favour.

Thus all these careful sights
   So kill me in conceit: 30
That now to hope upon delights,
   It is but meere deceite.

And therefore, my sweete Muse,
   That knowest what helpe is best,
Doe nowe thy heavenlie conninge use   35
   To sett my harte at rest:

And in a dreame bewraie
   What fate shal be my frende;
Whether my life shall still decaye,
   Or when my sorrowes ende.   40

XV.

Lord Thomas and Fair Ellinor,

Is given (with corrections) from an ancient copy in black-letter in the Pepys collection, entitled, "A tragical ballad on the unfortunate love of lord Thomas and fair Ellinor, together with the downfall of the browne girl." In the same collection may be seen an attempt to modernize this old song, and reduce it to a different measure: a proof of its popularity.

Lord Thomas he was a bold forrestèr,
   And a chaser of the kings deere:
Faire Ellinor was a fine womàn,
   And Lord Thomas he loved her deare.

Come riddle my riddle, dear mother, he sayd,   5
    And riddle us both as one;
Whether I shall marrye with faire Ellinòr,
    And let the browne girl alone?

The browne girl she has got houses and lands,
    Faire Ellinor she has got none,   10
And therefore I charge thee on my blessìng,
    To bring me the browne girl home.

And as it befelle on a high holidaye,
    As many there are beside,
Lord Thomas he went to faire Ellinòr,   15
    That should have been his bride.

And when he came to faire Ellinors bower,
    He knocked there at the ring,
And who was so readye as faire Ellinòr,
    To lett lord Thomas withinn.   20

What newes, what newes, lord Thomas, she sayd?
    What newes dost thou bring to mee?
I am come to bid thee to my weddíng,
    And that is bad newes for thee.

O God forbid, lord Thomas, she sayd,   25
    That such a thing should be done;
I thought to have been the bride my selfe,
    And thou to have been the bridegrome.

Come riddle my riddle, dear mother, she sayd,
    And riddle it all in one;   30
Whether I shall goe to lord Thomas his wedding,
    Or whether shall tarry at home?

There are manye that are your friendes, daughtèr,
    And manye a one your foe,

Ver. 29. It should probably be, Reade me, read, &c., *i. e.* Advise me, advise.

Therefore I charge you on my blessing,   35
　　To lord Thomas his wedding don't goe.

There are manye that are my friendes, mothèr;
　　But were every one my foe,
Betide me life, betide me death,
　　To lord Thomas his wedding I'ld goe.   40

She cloathed herself in gallant attire,
　　And her merrye men all in greene;
And as they rid through every towne,
　　They took her to be some queene.

But when she came to lord Thomas his gate,   45
　　She knocked there at the ring;
And who was so readye as lord Thomàs,
　　To lett faire Ellinor in.

Is this your bride? fair Ellinor sayd,
　　Methinks she looks wonderous browne;   50
Thou mightest have had as faire a womàn,
　　As ever trod on the grounde.

Despise her not, fair Ellin, he sayd,
　　Despise her not unto mee;
For better I love thy little fingèr,   55
　　Than all her whole bodèe.

This browne bride had a little penknife,
　　That was both long and sharpe,
And betwixt the short ribs and the long,
　　She prick'd faire Ellinor's harte.   60

O Christ thee save, lord Thomas, hee sayd,
　　Methinks thou lookst wonderous wan;
Thou usedst to look with as fresh a colòur,
　　As ever the sun shone on.

Oh, art thou blind, lord Thomas? she sayd,   65
    Or canst thou not very well see?
Oh! dost thou not see my owne hearts bloode
    Run trickling down my knee.

Lord Thomas he had a sword by his side;
    As he walked about the halle,   70
He cut off his brides head from her shoulders,
    And threw it against the walle.

He set the hilte against the grounde,
    And the point against his harte.
There never three lovers together did meete,   75
    That sooner againe did parte.

*** The reader will find a Scottish song on a similar subject to this, below (book iii. no. iv.) entitled, *Lord Thomas and Lady Annet.*

XVI.

Cupid and Campaspe.

This elegant little sonnet is found in the third act of an old play, entitled, *Alexander and Campaspe*, written by John Lilye, a celebrated writer in the time of Queen Elizabeth. That play was first printed in 1591; but this copy is given from a later edition.

Cupid and my Campaspe playd
At cardes for kisses; Cupid payd:
He stakes his quiver, bow and arrows,
His mothers doves, and teame of sparrows;
Loses them too; then down he throws
The coral of his lippe, the rose
Growing on's cheek, (but none knows how,)

With these, the crystal of his browe,
And then the dimple of his chinne;
All these did my Campaspe winne.
At last he set her both his eyes,
She won, and Cupid blind did rise.
   O Love! has she done this to thee?
   What shall, alas! become of mee?

XVII.

The Lady turned Serving-Man,

Is given from a written copy, containing some improvements (perhaps modern ones) upon the popular ballad, entitled, "The famous flower of Serving-men; or, the Lady turned Serving-man."

You beauteous ladyes, great and small,
I write unto you one and all,
Whereby that you may understand
What I have suffered in the land.

I was by birth a lady faire,   5
An ancient barons only heire,
And when my good old father dyed,
Then I became a young knightes bride.

And there my love built me a bower,
Bedeck'd with many a fragrant flower;   10
A braver bower you ne'er did see
Then my true-love did build for mee.

And there I livde a ladye gay,
Till fortune wrought our loves decay;
For there came foes so fierce a band,   15
That soon they over-run the land.

7*

They came upon us in the night,
And brent my bower, and slew my knight;
And trembling hid in mans array,
I scant with life escap'd away.   20

In the midst of this extremitie,
My servants all did from me flee:
Thus was I left myself alone,
With heart more cold than any stone.

Yet though my heart was full of care,   25
Heaven would not suffer me to dispaire,
Wherefore in haste I chang'd my name
From faire Elise, to sweet Williame:

And therewithall I cut my haire,
Resolv'd my man's attire to weare;   30
And in my beaver, hose and band,
I travell'd far through many a land.

At length all wearied with my toil,
I sate me downe to rest awhile;
My heart it was so fill'd with woe,   35
That downe my cheeke the teares did flow.

It chanc'd the king of that same place
With all his lords a hunting was,
And seeing me weepe, upon the same
Askt who I was, and whence I came.   40

Then to his grace I did replye,
I am a poore and friendlesse boye,
Though nobly borne, nowe forc'd to bee
A serving-man of lowe degree.

Stand up, faire youth, the king reply'd,   45
For thee a service I'll provyde:
But tell me first what thou canst do;
Thou shalt be fitted thereunto.

Wilt thou be usher of my hall,
To wait upon my nobles all?   50
Or wilt be taster of my wine,
To 'tend on me when I shall dine?

Or wilt thou be my chamberlaine,
About my person to remaine?
Or wilt thou be one of my guard,   55
And I will give thee great reward?

Chuse, gentle youth, said he, thy place.
Then I reply'd, If it please your grace
To shew such favour unto mee,
Your chamberlaine I faine would bee 60

The king then smiling gave consent,
And straitwaye to his court I went;
Where I behavde so faithfullie,
That hee great favour showd to mee.

Now marke what fortune did provide; 65
The king he would a hunting ride
With all his lords and noble traine,
Sweet William must at home remaine.

Thus being left alone behind,
My former state came in my mind: 70
I wept to see my mans array:
No longer now a ladye gay.

And meeting with a ladyes vest,
Within the same myself I drest;
With silken robes, and jewels rare, 75
I deckt me, as a ladye faire:

And taking up a lute straitwaye,
Upon the same I strove to play;
And sweetly to the same did sing,
As made both hall and chamber ring. 80

"My father was as brave a lord,
As ever Europe might afford;
My mother was a lady bright;
My husband was a valiant knight:

"And I myself a ladye gay,　　　　　　　　85
Bedeckt with gorgeous rich array;
The happiest lady in the land
Had not more pleasure at command.

"I had my musicke every day
Harmonious lessons for to play;　　　　　90
I had my virgins fair and free
Continually to wait on mee.

"But now, alas! my husband's dead,
And all my friends are from me fled,
My former days are past and gone,　　　95
And I am now a serving-man."

And fetching many a tender sigh,
As thinking no one then was nigh,
In pensive mood I laid me lowe,
My heart was full, the tears did flowe.　100

The king, who had a huntinge gone,
Grewe weary of his sport anone,
And leaving all his gallant traine,
Turn'd on the sudden home againe:

And when he reach'd his statelye tower,　105
Hearing one sing within his bower,
He stopt to listen, and to see
Who sung there so melodiouslie.

Thus heard he everye word I sed,
And saw the pearlye teares I shed,　　　110
And found to his amazement there,
Sweete William was a ladye faire.

Then stepping in, Faire ladye, rise,
And dry, said he, those lovelye eyes,
For I have heard thy mournful tale, 115
The which shall turne to thy availe.

A crimson dye my face orespred,
I blusht for shame, and hung my head,
To find my sex and story knowne,
When as I thought I was alone. 120

But to be briefe, his royall grace
Grewe so enamour'd of my face,
The richest gifts he proffered mee,
His mistress if that I would bee.

Ah! no, my liege, I firmlye sayd, 125
I'll rather in my grave be layd,
And though your grace hath won my heart,
I ne'er will act soe base a part.

Faire ladye, pardon me, sayd hee,
Thy virtue shall rewarded bee, 130
And since it is soe fairly tryde
Thou shalt become my royal bride.

Then strait to end his amorous strife,
He tooke sweet William to his wife.
The like before was never seene, 135
A serving-man became a queene.

⁎

XVIII.

Gil Morrice,

A SCOTTISH BALLAD.

THE following piece hath run through two editions in
Scotland: the second was printed at Glasgow in 1755, 8vo.
Prefixed to them both is an advertisement, setting forth that

the preservation of this poem was owing to "a lady, who
favoured the printers with a copy, as it was carefully col-
lected from the mouths of old women and nurses;" and
"any reader that can render it more correct or complete,"
is desired to oblige the public with such improvements.   In
consequence of this advertisement, sixteen additional verses
have been produced and handed about in manuscript, which
are here inserted in their proper places: (these are from ver.
109 to ver. 121, and from ver. 124 to ver. 129, but are, per-
haps, after all, only an ingenious interpolation).

As this poem lays claim to a pretty high antiquity, we
have assigned it a place among our early pieces: though,
after all, there is reason to believe it has received very con-
siderable modern improvements: for in the Editor's ancient
MS. collection is a very old imperfect copy of the same
ballad: wherein, though the leading features of the story
are the same, yet the colouring here is so much improved
and heightened, and so many additional strokes are thrown
in, that it is evident the whole has undergone a revisal.

N. B. The Editor's MS. instead of *lord Barncrd*, has *John
Stewart;* and instead of *Gil Morrice*, *Child Maurice*, which
last is probably the original title.   See above, p. 75.

GIL MORRICE was an erlès son,
  His name it waxed wide;
It was nae for his great richés,
  Nor zet his mickle pride;
Bot it was for a lady gay,   5
  That livd on Carron side.

Quhair sall I get a bonny boy,
  That will win hose and shoen;
That will gae to lord Barnard's ha';
  And bid his lady cum?   10
And ze maun rin my errand, Willie;
  And ze may rin wi' pride;

Ver. 11, something seems wanting here.

Quhen other boys gae on their foot,
  On horse-back ze sall ride.

O no! Oh no! my master dear!   15
  I dare nae for my life;
I'll no gae to the bauld baròns,
  For to triest furth his wife.
My bird Willie, my boy Willie;
  My dear Willie, he sayd: 20
How can ze strive against the stream?
  For I sall be obeyd.

Bot, O my master dear! he cryd,
  In grene wod ze're zour lain;
Gi owre sic thochts, I walde ze rede,   25
  For fear ze should be tain.
Haste, haste, I say, gae to the ha',
  Bid hir cum here wi speid:
If ze refuse my heigh command,
  Ill gar zour body bleid.   30

Gae bid hir take this gay mantèl,
  'Tis a' gowd bot the hem;
Bid hir cum to the gude grene wode,
  And bring nane bot hir lain:
And there it is, a silken sarke,   35
  Hir ain hand sewd the sleive;
And bid hir cum to Gill Morice,
  Speir nae bauld barons leave.

Yes, I will gae zour black errand,
  Though it be to zour cost;   40
Sen ze by me well nae be warn'd,
  In it ze sall find frost.
The baron he is a man of might,
  He neir could bide to taunt,

V. 32 and 68, perhaps, 'bout the hem.

As ze will see before its nicht,   45
   How sma' ze hae to vaunt.

And sen I maun zour errand rin
   Sae sair against my will,
I'se make a vow and keip it trow,
   It sall be done for ill.   50
And quhen he came to broken brigue,
   He bent his bow and swam:
And quhen he came to grass growing,
   Set down his feet and ran.

And quhen he came to Barnards ha',   55
   Would neither chap nor ca':
Bot set his bent bow to his breist,
   And lichtly lap the wa'.
He wauld nae tell the man his errand,
   Though he stude at the gait;   60
Bot straiht into the ha' he cam,
   Quhair they were set at meit.

Hail! hail! my gentle sire and dame!
   My message winna waite;
Dame, ze·maun to the gude grene wod   65
   Before that it be late.
Ze're bidden tak this gay mantèl,
   Tis a' gowd bot the hem;
Zou maun gae to the gude grene wode,
   Ev'n by your sel alane.   70

And there it is, a silken sarke,
   Your ain hand sewd the sleive;
Ze maun gae speik to Gill Morice:
   Speir nae bauld barons leave.
The lady stamped wi' hir foot,   75
   And winked wi' her ee;

V. 58. Could this be the wall of the castle?

Bot a' that she coud say or do,
  Forbidden he wad nae bee.

Its surely to my bow'r-womàn;
  It neir could be to me,   80
I brocht it to lord Barnards lady;
  I trow that ze be she.
Then up and spack the wylie nurse,
  (The bairn upon hir knee)
If it be cum frae Gill Morice,   85
  It's deir welcum to mee.

Ze leid, ze leid, ze filthy nurse,
  Sae loud I heird ze lee;
I brocht it to lord Barnards lady;
  I trow ze be nae shee.   90

Then up and spack the bauld baròn,
  An angry man was hee;
He's tain the table wi' his foot,
  Sae has he wi' his knee;
Till siller cup and 'mazer[1]' dish   95
  In flinders he gard flee.

Gae bring a robe of zour clidìng,
  That hings upon the pin;
And I'll gae to the gude grene wode,
  And speik wi' zour lemmàn.   100
O bide at hame, now lord Barnàrd,
  I warde ze bide at hame;
Neir wyte a man for violence,
  That neir wate ze wi' nane.

Gil Morice sate in gude grene wode,   105
  He whistled and he sang:

V. 88, perhaps, loud say I heire.

[1] i. e. a drinking cup of maple; other edit. read ezar.

O what mean a' the folk comìng,
   My mother tarries lang.
His hair was like the threeds of gold,
   Drawne frae Minerva's loome: 110
His lipps like roses drapping dew,
   His breath was a' perfume.

His browe was like the mountain snae
   Gilt by the morning beam:
His cheeks like living roses glow: 115
   His een like azure stream.
The boy was clad in robes of grene,
   Sweete as the infant spring:
And like the mavis on the bush,
   He gart the vallies ring.   120

The baron came to the grene wode,
   Wi' mickle dule and care,
And there he first spied Gill Morìce,
   Kameing his zellow hair,
That sweetly wavd around his face,   125
   That face beyond compare:
He sang sae sweet it might dispel
   A' rage but fell despair.

Nae wonder, nae wonder, Gill Morìce,
   My lady loed thee weel,   130
The fairest part of my bodie
   Is blacker than thy heel.
Zet neir the less now, Gill Morìce,
   For a' thy great beautiè,
Ze's rew the day ze eir was born;   135
   That head sall gae wi' me.

V. 128. So Milton, —
      Vernal delight and joy: able to drive
      All sadness but despair.
                          B. iv. v. 155.

Now he has drawn his trusty brand,
   And slaited on the strae;
And thro' Gill Morice' fair body
   He's gar cauld iron gae.   140
And he has tain Gill Morice' head
   And set it on a speir;
The meanest man in a' his train
   Has gotten that head to bear.

And he has tain Gill Morice up,   145
   Laid him across his steid,
And brocht him to his painted bowr,
   And laid him on a bed.
The lady sat on castil wa',
   Beheld baith dale and doun;   150
And there she saw Gill Morice' head
   Cum trailing to the toun.

Far better I loe that bluidy head,
   Both and that zellow hair,
Than lord Barnard, and a' his lads,   155
   As they lig here and thair.
And she has tain her Gill Morice,
   And kissd baith mouth and chin:
I was once as fow of Gill Morrice,
   As the hip is o' the stean.   160

I got ze in my father's house,
   Wi' mickle sin and shame;
I brocht thee up in gude grene wode,
   Under the heavy rain.
Oft have I by thy cradle sitten,   165
   And fondly seen thee sleip;
But now I gae about thy grave,
   The saut tears for to weip.

And syne she kissd his bluidy cheik,
   And syne his bluidy chin: 170

O better I loe my Gill Morice
    Than a' my kith and kin!
Away, away, ze ill womàn,
    And an il deith mait ze dee:
Gin I had kend he'd bin zour son,   175
    He'd neir bin slain for mee.

Obraid me not, my lord Barnard!
    Obraid me not for shame!
Wi' that saim speir O pierce my heart!
    And put me out o' pain.   180
Since nothing bot Gill Morice head
    Thy jelous rage could quell,
Let that saim hand now tak hir life,
    That neir to thee did ill.

To me nae after days nor nichts   185
    Will eir be saft or kind;
I'll fill the air with heavy sighs,
    And greet till I am blind.
Enough of blood by me's bin spilt,
    Seek not zour death frae me;   190
I rather lourd it had been my sel
    Than eather him or thee.

With waefo wae I hear zour plaint;
    Sair, sair I rew the deid,
That eir this cursed hand of mine   195
    Had gard his body bleid.
Dry up zour tears, my winsome dame,
    Ze neir can heal the wound;
Ze see his head upon the speir,
    His heart's blude on the ground.   200

I curse the hand that did the deid,
    The heart that thocht the ill;
The feet that bore me wi' sik speid,
    The comely zouth to kill

I'll ay lament for Gill Morice,   205
   As gin he were mine ain;
I'll neir forget the dreiry day
   On which the zouth was slain.

*** This little pathetic tale suggested the plot of the tragedy of *Douglas*.

Since it was first printed, the Editor has been assured that the foregoing ballad is still current in many parts of Scotland, where the hero is universally known by the name of *Child Maurice*, pronounced by the common people *Cheild* or *Cheeld*, which occasioned the mistake.

It may be proper to mention, that other copies read ver. 110, thus:

"Shot frae the golden sun."

And ver. 116, as follows:

"His een like azure sheene."

END OF THE FIRST BOOK.

RELIQUES

OF

ANCIENT POETRY.

&c.

SERIES THE THIRD.
BOOK II.

I.

𝕿𝖍𝖊 𝕷𝖊𝖌𝖊𝖓𝖉 𝖔𝖋 𝕾𝖎𝖗 𝕲𝖚𝖞,

Contains a short summary of the exploits of this famous champion, as recorded in the old story-books, and is commonly entitled, "A pleasant song of the valiant deeds of chivalry atchieved by that noble knight sir Guy of Warwick, who, for the love of fair Phelis, became a hermit, and dyed in a cave of craggy rocke, a mile distant from Warwick."

The history of Sir Guy, though now very properly resigned to children, was once admired by all readers of wit and taste: for taste and wit had once their childhood. Although of English growth, it was early a favourite with other nations: it appeared in French in 1525, and is alluded to in the old Spanish romance of *Tirante el Blanco*, which, it is believed, was written not long after the year 1430. See advertisement to the French translation, 2 vols. 12mo.

The original whence all these stories are extracted, is a very ancient romance in old English verse, which is quoted by Chaucer as a celebrated piece even in his time, (viz.

"Men speken of romances of price,
　Of Horne childe and Ippotis,
　　Of Bevis, and sir Guy," &c.　　R. of Thop.)

and was usually sung to the harp at Christmas dinners
and brideales, as we learn from Puttenham's *Art of Poetry*,
4to, 1589.

This ancient romance is not wholly lost. An imperfect
copy in black letter, "Imprynted at London — for Wylliam
Copland," in 34 sheets, 4to, without date, is still preserved
among Mr. Garrick's collection of old plays. As a speci-
men of the poetry of this antique rhymer, take his descrip-
tion of the dragon mentioned in verse 105 of the following
ballad:

"A messenger came to the king.
　Syr king, he sayd, lysten me now,
　For bad tydinges I bring you,
　In Northumberlande there is no man,
　But that they be slayne everychone:
　For there dare no man route,
　By twenty myle rounde aboute,
　For doubt of a fowle dragon,
　That sleath men and beastes downe.
　He is blacke as any cole,
　Rugged as a rough fole;
　His bodye from the navill upwarde
　No man may it pierce it is so harde;
　His neck is great as any summere;
　He renneth as swift as any distrere;
　Pawes he hath as a lyon:
　All that he toucheth he sleath dead downe.
　Great winges he hath to flight,
　That is no man that bare him might.
　There may no man fight him agayne,
　But that he sleath him certayne:
　For a fowler beast then is he,
　Y wis of none never heard ye."

Sir William Dugdale is of opinion that the story of Guy
is not wholly apocryphal, though he acknowledges the
monks have sounded out his praises too hyperbolically. In
particular, he gives the duel fought with the Danish cham-
pion as a real historical truth, and fixes the date of it in the
year 926, ætat. Guy 67. See his Warwickshire.

The following is written upon the same plan as ballad v.
book i., but which is the original, and which the copy, can-
not be decided.   This song is ancient, as may be inferred
from the idiom preserved in the margin, ver. 94. 102: and
was once popular, as appears from Fletcher's *Knight of the
Burning Pestle*, act ii., sc. ult.

It is here published from an ancient MS. copy in the
Editor's old folio volume collated with two printed ones, one
of which is in black letter in the Pepys collection.

WAS ever knight for ladyes sake
   Soe tost in love, as I sir Guy
For Phelis fayre, that lady bright
   As ever man beheld with eye?

She gave me leave myself to try,   5
   The valiant knight with sheeld and speare,
Ere that her love shee wold grant me;
   Which made me venture far and neare.

Then proved I a baron bold,
   In deeds of armes the doughtyest knight   10
That in those dayes in England was,
   With sworde and speare in feild to fight.

An English man I was by birthe:
   In faith of Christ a christyan true:
The wicked lawes of infidells   15
   I sought by prowesse to subdue.

'Nine' hundred twenty yeere and odde
   After our Saviour Christ his birth,
When king Athèlstone wore the crowne,
   I lived heere upon the earth.   20

Ver. 9, The proud sir Guy. P.C.   V. 17, Two hundred. MS. and P.C.

Sometime I was of Warwicke erle,
   And, as I sayd, of very truth
A ladyes love did me constraine
   To seeke strange ventures in my youth.

To win me fame by feates of armes   25
   In strange and sundry heathen lands;
Where I atchieved for her sake
   Right dangerous conquests with my hands.

For first I sayled to Normandye,
   And there I stoutlye wan in fight   30
The emperours daughter of Almaine,
   From manye a vallyant worthye knight.

Then passed I the seas to Greece
   To helpe the emperour in his right;
Against the mightye souldans hoaste   35
   Of puissant Persians for to fight.

Where I did slay of Sarazens,
   And heathen pagans, manye a man;
And slew the souldans cozen deere,
   Who had to name doughtye Coldràn.   40

Eskeldered a famous knight
   To death likewise I did pursue:
And Elmayne king of Tyre alsoe,
   Most terrible in fight to viewe.

I went into the souldans hoast,   45
   Being thither on embassage sent,
And brought his head awaye with mee;
   I having slaine him in his tent.

There was a dragon in that land
   Most fiercelye mett me by the waye   50
As hee a lyon did pursue,
   Which I myself did alsoe slay.

8*

Then soon I past the seas from Greece,
   And came to Pavye land aright:
Where I the duke of Pavye killed,   55
   His hainous treason to requite.

To England then I came with speede,
   To wedd faire Phelis lady bright:
For love of whome I travelled farr
   To try my manhood and my might.   60

But when I had espoused her,
   I stayd with her but fortye dayes,
Ere that I left this ladye faire,
   And went from her beyond the seas.

All cladd in gray, in pilgrim sort,   65
   My voyage from her I did take
Unto the blessed Holy-land,
   For Jesus Christ my Saviours sake.

Where I erle Jonas did redeeme,
   And all his sonnes, which were fifteene,   70
Who with the cruell Sarazens,
   In prison for long time had beene.

I slew the giant Amarant
   In battel fiercelye hand to hand:
And doughty Barknard killed I,   75
   A treacherous knight of Pavye land

Then I to England came againe,
   And here with Colbronde fell I fought:
An ugly gyant which the Danes
   Had for their champion hither brought.   80

I overcame him in the feild,
   And slewe him soone right valliantlye;
Whereby this land I did redeeme
   From Danish tribute utterlye.

And afterwards I offered upp   85
    The use of weapons solemnlye
At Winchester, whereas I fought,
    In sight of manye far and nye.

'But first,' near Winsor, I did slaye
    A bore of passing might and strength;   90
Whose like in England never was
    For hugenesse both in bredth and length.

Some of his bones in Warwicke yett
    Within the castle there doe lye:
One of his sheeld-bones to this day   95
    Hangs in the citye of Coventrye.

On Dunsmore heath I alsoe slewe
    A monstrous wyld and cruell beast,
Calld the Dun-cow of Dunsmore heath;
    Which manye people had opprest.   100

Some of her bones in Warwicke yett
    Still for a monument doe lye;
And there expos'd to lookers viewe
    As wonderous strange, they may espye.

A dragon in Northumberland   105
    I alsoe did in fight destroye,
Which did bothe man and beast oppresse,
    And all the countrye sore annoye.

At length to Warwicke I did come,
    Like pilgrim poore, and was not knowne;   110
And there I lived a hermitts life
    A mile and more out of the towne.

Where with my hands I hewed a house
    Out of a craggy rocke of stone;

V. 94, 102, doth lye. MS.

And lived like a palmer poore   115
  Within that cave myself alone:

And daylye came to begg my bread
  Of Phelis att my castle gate;
Not knowne unto my loved wiffe,
  Who dailye mourned for her mate.   120

Till att the last I fell sore sicke,
  Yea sicke soe sore that I must dye;
I sent to her a ring of golde,
  By which shee knewe me presentlye.

Then shee repairing to the cave   125
  Before that I gave up the ghost;
Herself closd up my dying eyes:
  My Phelis faire, whom I lovd most.

Thus dreadful death did me arrest,
  To bring my corpes unto the grave;   130
And like a palmer dyed I,
  Wherby I sought my soule to save.

My body that endured this toyle,
  Though now it be consumed to mold;
My statue faire engraven in stone,   135
  In Warwicke still you may behold.

II.

Guy and Amarant.

THE Editor found this poem in his ancient folio manuscript
among the old ballads; he was desirous, therefore, that it
should still accompany them; and as it is not altogether de-
void of merit, its insertion here will be pardoned.

Although this piece seems not imperfect, there is reason
to believe that it is only a part of a much larger poem, which

contained the whole history of Sir Guy: for, upon comparing
it with the common story-book, 12mo, we find the latter to
be nothing more than this poem reduced to prose: which is
only effected by now and then altering the rhyme, and
throwing out some few of the poetical ornaments. The dis-
guise is so slight, that it is an easy matter to pick complete
stanzas in any page of that book.

The author of this poem has shown some invention.
Though he took the subject from the old romance quoted
before, he has adorned it afresh, and made the story entirely
his own.

Guy journeyes towards that sanctifyed ground,
   Whereas the Jewes fayre citye sometime stood,
Wherin our Saviours sacred head was crownd,
   And where for sinfull man he shed his blood:
To see the sepulcher was his intent,   5
The tombe that Joseph unto Jesus lent.

With tedious miles he tyred his wearye feet,
   And passed desart places full of danger,
At last with a most woefull wight[1] did meet,
   A man that unto sorrow was noe stranger: 10
For he had fifteen sonnes, made captives all
To slavish bondage, in extremest thrall.

A gyant called Amarant detaind them,
   Whom noe man durst encounter for his strength:
Who in a castle, which he held, had chaind them: 15
   Guy questions, where? and understands at length
The place not farr. — Lend me thy sword, quoth hee,
Ile lend my manhood all thy sonnes to free.

With that he goes, and lays upon the dore,
   Like one that sayes, I must, and will come in: 20

---

[1] Erle Jonas, mentioned in the foregoing ballad.

The gyant never was soe rowz'd before:
  For noe such knocking at his gate had bin:
Soe takes his keyes, and clubb, and cometh out
Staring with ireful countenance about.

Sirra, quoth hee, what busines hast thou heere?   25
  Art come to feast the crowes about my walls?
Didst never heare, noe ransome can him cleere,
  That in the compasse of my furye falls:
For making me to take a porters paines,
With this same clubb I will dash out thy braines.   30

Gyant, quoth Guy, y'are quarrelsome I see,
  Choller and you seem very neere of kin:
Most dangerous at the clubb belike you bee;
  I have bin better armd, though nowe goe thin;
But shew thy utmost hate, enlarge thy spight,   35
Keene is my weapon, and shall doe me right

Soe draws his sword, salutes him with the same
  About the head, the shoulders, and the side:
Whilst his erected clubb doth death proclaime,
  Standinge with huge Colossus' spacious stride,   40
Putting such vigour to his knotty beame,
That like a furnace he did smoke extreame.

But on the ground he spent his strokes in vaine,
  For Guy was nimble to avoyde them still,
And ever ere he heav'd his clubb againe,   45
  Did brush his plated coat against his will:
Att such advantage Guy wold never fayle,
To bang him soundlye in his coate of mayle.

Att last through thirst the gyant feeble grewe,
  And sayd to Guy, As thou'rt of humane race,   50
Shew itt in this, give natures wants their dewe,
  Let me but goe, and drinke in yonder place:
Thou canst not yeeld to 'me' a smaller thing,
Than to graunt life, thats given by the spring.

I graunt thee leave, quoth Guye, goe drink thy last,   55
  Go pledge the dragon, and the salvage bore[2]:
Succeed the tragedyes that they have past,
  But never thinke to taste cold water more:
Drinke deepe to Death and unto him carouse:
Bid him receive thee in his earthen house.   60

Soe to the spring he goes, and slakes his thirst:
  Takeing the water in extremely like
Some wracked shipp that on a rocke is burst,
  Whose forced hulke against the stones does stryke;
Scooping it in soe fast with both his hands,   65
That Guy admiring to behold it stands.

Come on, quoth Guy, let us to worke againe,
  Thou stayest about thy liquor overlong;
The fish, which in the river doe remaine,
  Will want thereby: thy drinking doth them wrong: 70
But I will see their satisfaction made,
With gyants blood they must, and shall be payd.

Villaine, quoth Amarant, Ile crush thee streight;
  Thy life shall pay thy daring toungs offence:
This clubb, which is about some hundred weight,   75
  Is deathes commission to dispatch thee hence:
Dresse thee for ravens dyett I must needes;
And breake thy bones, as they were made of reedes.

Incensed much by these bold pagan bostes,
  Which worthye Guy cold ill endure to heare,   80
He hewes upon those bigg supporting postes,
  Which like two pillars did his body beare:
Amarant for those wounds in choller growes
And desperatelye att Guy his clubb he throwes:

Ver. 64, bulke. MS. and ᴘ.co.

[2] Which Guy had slain before.

Which did directly on his body light,   85
   Soe violent, and weighty there-withall,
That downe to ground on sudden came the knight;
   And, ere he cold recover from the fall,
The gyant gott his clubb againe in fist,
And aimd a stroke that wonderfullye mist.   90

Traytor, quoth Guy, thy falshood Ile repay,
   This coward act to intercept my bloode.
Sayes Amarant, Ile murther any way,
   With enemyes all vantages are good:
O could I poyson in thy nostrills blowe,   95
Besure of it I wold dispatch thee soe.

Its well, said Guy, thy honest thoughts appeare,
   Within that beastlye bulke where devills dwell;
Which are thy tenants while thou livest heare,
   But will be landlords when thou comest in hell: 100
Vile miscreant, prepare thee for their den,
Inhumane monster, hatefull unto men.

But breathe thy selfe a time, while I goe drinke,
   For flameing Phœbus with his fyerye eye
Torments me soe with burning heat, I thinke   105
   My thirst wolde serve to drinke an ocean drye:
Forbear a litle, as I delt with thee.
Quoth Amarant, Thou hast noe foole of mee.

Noe, sillye wretch, my father taught more witt,
   How I shold use such enemyes as thou;   110
By all my gods I doe rejoice at itt,
   To understand that thirst constraines thee now:
For all the treasure, that the world containes,
One drop of water shall not coole thy vaines.

Releeve my foe! why, 'twere a madmans part: 115
   Refresh an adversarye to my wrong!

If thou imagine this, a child thou art:
  Noe, fellow, I have known the world too long
To be soe simple: now I know thy want,
  A minutes space of breathing I'll not grant.   120

And with these words heaving aloft his clubb
  Into the ayre, he swings the same about:
Then shakes his lockes, and doth his temples rubb,
  And, like the Cyclops, in his pride doth strout:
Sirra, says hee, I have you at a lift,   125
Now you are come unto your latest shift.

Perish forever: with this stroke I send thee
  A medicine, that will doe thy thirst much good:
Take noe more care for drinke before I end thee,
  And then wee'll have carouses of thy blood: 130
Here's at thee with a butcher's downright blow,
To please my furye with thine overthrow.

Infernall, false, obdurate feend, said Guy,
  That seemst a lumpe of crueltye from hell;
Ungratefull monster, since thou dost deny   135
  The thing to mee wherin I used thee well:
With more revenge, than ere my sword did make,
On thy accursed head revenge Ile take.

Thy gyants longitude shall shorter shrinke,
  Except thy sun-scorcht skin be weapon proof: 140
Farewell my thirst; I doe disdaine to drinke;
  Streames keepe your waters to your owne behoof;
Or let wild beasts be welcome thereunto;
With those pearle drops I will not have to do.

Here, tyrant, take a taste of my good-will,   145
  For thus I doe begin my bloodye bout:
You cannot chuse but like the greeting ill;
  It is not that same clubb will beare you out;
And take this payment on thy shaggye crowne —
A blowe that brought him with a vengeance downe.   150

Then Guy sett foot upon the monsters brest,
   And from his shoulders did his head divide;
Which with a yawninge mouth did gape, unblest;
   Noe dragons jawes were ever seene soe wide
To open and to shut, till life was spent.   155
Then Guy tooke keyes, and to the castle went,

Where manye woefull captives he did find,
   Which had beene tyred with extremityes;
Whom he in freindly manner did unbind,
   And reasoned with them of their miseryes: 160
Eche told a tale with teares, and sighes, and cryes,
All weeping to him with complaining eyes.

There tender ladyes in darke dungeons lay,
   That were surprised in the desart wood,
And had noe other dyett everye day,   165
   But flesh of humane creatures for their food:
Some with their lovers bodyes had beene fed,
And in their wombes their husbands buryed.

Now he bethinkes him of his being there,
   To enlarge the wronged brethren from their woes: 170
And, as he searcheth, doth great clamours heare,
   By which sad sound's direction on he goes,
Untill he findes a darksome obscure gate,
Arm'd strongly ouer all with iron plate.

That he unlockes, and enters, where appeares   175
   The strangest object that he ever saw;
Men that with famishment of many years,
   Were like deathes picture, which the painters draw!
Divers of them were hanged by eche thombe;
Others head-downward: by the middle some.   180

With diligence he takes them from the walle,
   With lybertye their thraldome to acquaint:

Then the perplexed knight their father calls,
   And sayes, Receive thy sonnes though poore and faint:
I promisd you their lives, accept of that;   185
But did not warrant you they shold be fat.

The castle I doe give thee, heere's the keyes,
   Where tyranye for many yeeres did dwell:
Procure the gentle tender ladyes ease,
   For pittyes sake, use wronged women well: 190
Men easilye revenge the wrongs men do;
But poore weake women have not strength thereto.

The good old man, even overjoyed with this,
   Fell on the ground, and wold have kist Guys feete:
Father, quoth he, refraine soe base a kiss,   195
   For age to honor youth I hold unmeete:
Ambitious pryde hath hurt mee all it can,
I goe to mortifie a sinfull man.

⁎ The foregoing poem on *Guy and Amarant* has been
discovered to be a fragment of "The famous historie of Guy
earle of Warwicke, by Samuel Rowlands, London, printed
by J. Bell, 1649," 4to, in xii. cantos, beginning thus:
   "When dreadful Mars in armour every day.
Whether the edition in 1649 was the first, is not known, but
the author, Sam. Rowlands, was one of the minor poets
who lived in the reigns of Queen Elizabeth and James I.,
and perhaps later. His other poems are chiefly of the re-
ligious kind, which makes it probable that the history of
Guy was one of his earliest performances. There are extant
of his, (1) "The betraying of Christ, Judas in dispaire, the
seven words of our Saviour on the crosse, with other poems
on the passion, &c. 1598," 4to. [Ames Typ. p. 428.] (2.) "A
Theatre of delightful Recreation, Lond. printed for A. John-
son, 1605," 4to. (Penes editor.) This is a book of poems on
subjects chiefly taken from the Old Testament. (3.) "Me-

mory of Christ's miracles, in verse. Lond. 1618," 4to. (4.)
"Heaven's glory, earth's vanity, and hell's horror." Lond.
1638, 8vo. [These two in Bod. Cat.]

In the present edition, the foregoing poem has been much
improved from the printed copy.

III.

The Auld Good-Man.

A SCOTTISH SONG.

I have not been able to meet with a more ancient copy of
this humorous old song, than that printed in *The Tea-Table
Miscellany*, &c., which seems to have admitted some corrup-
tions.

Late in an evening forth I went
  A little before the sun gade down,
And there I chanc't, by accident,
  To light on a battle new begun:
A man and his wife wer fawn in a strife,   5
  I canna weel tell ye how it began;
But aye she wail'd her wretched life,
  Cryeng, Evir alake, mine auld goodman!

HE.

Thy auld goodman, that thou tells of,
  The country kens where he was born,   10
Was but a silly poor vagabond,
  And ilka ane leugh him to scorn:
For he did spend and make an end
  Of gear 'his fathers nevir' wan;
He gart the poor stand frae the door,   15
  Sae tell nae mair of thy auld goodman.

SHE.

My heart, alake! is liken to break,
  Whan I think on my winsome John,

His blinkan ee, and gait sae free,
  Was naithing like thee, thou dosend drone;   20
Wi' his rosie face, and flaxen hair,
  And skin as white as ony swan,
He was large and tall, and comely withall;
  Thou'lt nevir be like mine auld goodman.

HE.

Why dost thou plein? I thee maintein;   25
  For meal and mawt thou disna want:
But thy wild bees I canna please,
  Now whan our gear gins to grow scant:
Of houshold stuff thou hast enough;
  Thou wants for neither pot nor pan;   30
Of sicklike ware he left thee bare;
  Sae tell nae mair of thy auld goodman

SHE.

Yes I may tell, and fret my sell,
  To think on those blyth days I had,
Whan I and he together ley   35
  In armes into a well-made bed:
But now I sigh and may be sad,
  Thy courage is cauld, thy colour wan,
Thou falds thy feet, and fa's asleep;
  Thou'lt nevir be like mine auld goodman.   40

Then coming was the night sae dark,
  And gane was a' the light of day:
The carle was fear'd to miss his mark,
  And therefore wad nae longer stay:
Then up he gat, and ran his way,   45
  I trowe, the wife the day she wan;
And aye the owreword of the fray
  Was, Evir alake! mine auld goodman.

IV.

ꜰair Margaret and Sweet William.

Tʜɪs seems to be the old song quoted in Fletcher's *Knight of the Burning Pestle*, acts ii. and iii.; although the six lines there preserved are somewhat different from those in the ballad, as it stands at present. The reader will not wonder at this, when he is informed that this is only given from a modern printed copy picked up on a stall. Its full title is, "Fair Margaret's Misfortune; or, Sweet William's frightful dreams on his wedding-night, with the sudden death and burial of those noble lovers."

The lines preserved in the play are this distich,

> "You are no love for me, Margaret,
>   I am no love for you."

And the following stanza,

> "When it was grown to dark midnight,
>   And all were fast asleep,
> In came Margarets grimly ghost
>   And stood at Williams feet."

These lines have acquired an importance by giving birth to one of the most beautiful ballads in our own or any language. See the song entitled *Margaret's Ghost*, at the end of this volume.

Since the first edition some improvements have been in-serted, which were communicated by a lady of the first distinction, as she had heard this song repeated in her infancy.

———————

> As it fell out on a long summer's day
>   Two lovers they sat on a hill;
> They sat together that long summer's day,
>   And could not talk their fill.

> I see no harm by you, Margarèt,   5
>   And you see none by mee:
> Before to-morrow at eight o' the clock
>   A rich wedding you shall see.

Fair Margaret sat in her bower-windòw,
   Combing her yellow hair,   10
There she spyed sweet William and his bride,
   As they were a riding near.

Then down she layd her ivory combe,
   And braided her hair in twain:
She went alive out of her bower,   15
   But ne'er came alive in't again.

When day was gone, and night was come,
   And all men fast asleep,
Then came the spirit of fair Marg'ret,
   And stood at Williams feet.   20

Are you awake, sweet William? shee said;
   Or, sweet William, are you asleep?
God give you joy of your gay bride-bed,
   And me of my winding sheet.

When day was come, and night was gone,   25
   And all men wak'd from sleep,
Sweet William to his lady sayd,
   My dear, I have cause to weep.

I dreamt a dream, my dear ladyè,
   Such dreames are never good: 30
I dreamt my bower was full of red 'wine,'
   And my bride-bed full of blood.

Such dreams, such dreams, my honoured Sir,
   They never do prove good;
To dream thy bower was full of red 'wine,'   35
   And thy bride-bed full of blood.

He called up his merry men all,
   By one, by two, and by three;

Ver. 31, 35, swine. P. CC.

Saying, I'll away to fair Marg'ret's bower,
  By the leave of my ladiè.   40

And when he came to fair Marg'ret's bower,
  He knocked at the ring;
And who so ready as her seven brethrèn
  To let sweet William in.

Then he turned up the covering-sheet,   45
  Pray let me see the dead;
Methinks she looks all pale and wan,
  She hath lost her cherry red.

I'll do more for thee, Margarèt,
  Than any of thy kin;   50
For I will kiss thy pale wan lips,
  Though a smile I cannot win.

With that bespake the seven brethrèn,
  Making most piteous mone:
You may go kiss your jolly brown bride,   55
  And let our sister alone.

If I do kiss my jolly brown bride,
  I do but what is right;
I neer made a vow to yonder poor corpse
  By day, nor yet by night.   60

Deal on, deal on, my merry men all,
  Deal on your cake and your wine[1],
For whatever is dealt at her funeral to-day,
  Shall be dealt to-morrow at mine.

Fair Margaret dyed to-day, to-day,   65
  Sweet William dyed the morrow:
Fair Margaret dyed for pure true love,
  Sweet William dyed for sorrow.

---

[1] Alluding to the dole anciently given at funerals.

Margaret was buryed in the lower chancèl,
  And William in the higher;   70
Out of her brest there sprang a rose,
  And out of his a briar.

They grew till they grew unto the church top,
  And then they could grow no higher;
And there they tyed in a true lovers knot,   75
  Which made all the people admire.

Then came the clerk of the parish,
  As you the truth shall hear,
And by misfortune cut them down,
  Or they had now been there.   80

V.

Barbara Allen's Cruelty.

GIVEN, with some corrections, from an old black-letter
copy entitled, "Barbara Allen's cruelty, or the young man's
tragedy."

In Scarlet towne, where I was borne,
  There was a faire maid dwellin,
Made every youth crye, Wel-awaye!
  Her name was Barbara Allen.

All in the merrye month of May,   5
  When greene buds they were swellin,
Yong Jemmye Grove on his death-bed lay,
  For love of Barbara Allen.

He sent his man unto her then,
  To the town where shee was dwellin;   10
You must come to my master deare,
  Giff your name be Barbara Allen.

9*

For death is printed on his face,
    And ore his hart is stealin:
Then haste away to comfort him,   15
    O lovelye Barbara Allen.

Though death be printed on his face,
    And ore his harte is stealin,
Yet little better shall he bee
    For bonny Barbara Allen.   20

So slowly, slowly, she came up,
    And slowly she came nye him;
And all she sayd, when there she came,
    Yong man, I think y'are dying.

He turnd his face unto her strait,   25
    With deadlye sorrow sighing;
O lovely maid, come pity mee,
    Ime on my death-bed lying.

If on your death-bed you doe lye,
    What needs the tale you are tellin: 30
I cannot keep you from your death;
    Farewell, sayd Barbara Allen.

He turnd his face unto the wall,
    As deadlye pangs he fell in:
Adieu! adieu! adieu to you all,   35
    Adieu to Barbara Allen.

As she was walking ore the fields,
    She heard the bell a knellin;
And every stroke did seem to saye,
    Unworthy Barbara Allen.   40

She turnd her bodye round about,
    And spied the corps a coming:
Laye down, laye down the corps, she sayd,
    That I may look upon him.

With scornful eye she looked downe,   45
  Her cheeke with laughter swellin;
Whilst all her friends cryd out amaine,
  Unworthye Barbara Allen.

When he was dead, and laid in grave,
  Her harte was struck with sorrowe,   50
O mother, mother, make my bed,
  For I shall dye to-morrowe.

Hard-harted creature him to slight,
  Who loved me so dearlye:
O that I had beene more kind to him,   55
  When he was alive and neare me!

She, on her death-bed as she laye,
  Beg'd to be buried by him;
And sore repented of the daye,
  That she did ere denye him.   60

Farewell, she sayd, ye virgins all,
  And shun the fault I fell in:
Henceforth take warning by the fall
  Of cruel Barbara Allen.

*_**

VI.

Sweet William's Ghost.

A SCOTTISH BALLAD.

FROM Allan Ramsay's *Tea-Table Miscellany*. The concluding stanza of this piece seems modern.

THERE came a ghost to Margaret's door,
  With many a grievous grone,
And ay he tirled at the pin;
  But answer made she none.

Is this my father Philip?   5
    Or is't my brother John?
Or is't my true love Willie,
    From Scotland new come home?

'Tis not thy father Philip;
    Nor yet thy brother John: 10
But tis thy true love Willie
    From Scotland new come home.

O sweet Margret! O dear Margret!
    I pray thee speak to mee:
Give me my faith and troth, Margret,   15
    As I gave it to thee.

Thy faith and troth thou'se nevir get,
    'Of me shalt nevir win,'
Till that thou come within my bower,
    And kiss my cheek and chin.   20

If I should come within thy bower,
    I am no earthly man:
And should I kiss thy rosy lipp,
    Thy days will not be lang.

O sweet Margret, O dear Margret,   25
    I pray thee speak to mee:
Give me my faith and troth, Margret,
    As I gave it to thee.

Thy faith and troth thou'se nevir get,
    'Of me shalt nevir win,'   30
Till thou take me to yon kirk yard,
    And wed me with a ring.

My bones are buried in a kirk yard
    Afar beyond the sea,
And it is but my sprite, Margret,   35
    That's speaking now to thee.

She stretched out her lilly-white hand,
   As for to do her best:
Hae there your faith and troth, Willie,
   God send your soul good rest.   40

Now she has kilted her robes of green,
   A piece below her knee:
And a' the live-lang winter night
   The dead corps followed shee.

Is there any room at your head, Willie?   45
   Or any room at your feet?
Or any room at your side, Willie,
   Wherein that I may creep?

There's nae room at my head, Margret,
   There's nae room at my feet,   50
There's no room at my side, Margret,
   My coffin is made so meet.

Then up and crew the red red cock,
   And up then crew the gray:
Tis time, tis time, my dear Margret,   55
   That 'I' were gane away.

No more the ghost to Margret said,
   But, with a grievous grone,
Evanish'd in a cloud of mist,
   And left her all alone.   60

O stay, my only true love, stay,
   The constant Margret cried:
Wan grew her cheeks, she clos'd her een,
   Stretch'd her saft limbs, and died.

VII.

Sir John Grehme and Barbara Allan.

A SCOTTISH BALLAD.

PRINTED, with a few conjectural emendations, from a written copy.

IT was in and about the Martinmas time,
  When the greene leaves wer a fallan:
That Sir John Grehme o' the west countrye,
  Fell in luve wi' Barbara Allan.

He sent his man down throw the towne,   5
  To the plaice wher she was dwellan:
O haste and cum to my maister deare,
  Gin ye bin Barbara Allan.

O hooly, hooly raise she up,
  To the plaice wher he was lyan;   10
And whan she drew the curtain by,
  Young man, I think ye're dyan[1].

O its I'm sick, and very very sick,
  And its a' for Barbara Allan.
O the better for me ye'se never be,   15
  Though your harts blude wer spillan.

Remember ye nat in the tavern, sir,
  Whan ye the cups wer fillan;
How ye made the healths gae round and round,
  And slighted Barbara Allan?   20

He turn'd his face unto the wa',
  And death was with him dealan;

---

[1] An ingenious friend thinks the rhymes *dyand* and *lyand* ought to be transposed; as the taunt, 'Young man, I think ye're lyand,' would be very characteristical.

Adiew! adiew! my dear friends a',
  Be kind to Barbara Allan.

Then hooly, hooly raise she up,   25
  And hooly, hooly left him;
And sighan said, she could not stay,
  Since death of life had reft him.

She had not gane a mile but twa,
  Whan she heard the deid-bell knellan;   30
And everye jow the deid-bell geid,
  Cried, Wae to Barbara Allan!

O mither, mither, mak my bed,
  O mak it saft and narrow:
Since my love died for me to day,   35
  Ise die for him to morrowe.

⁎

VIII.

The Bailiff's Daughter of Islington.

From an ancient black-letter copy in the Pepys collection,
with some improvements communicated by a lady as she had
heard the same recited in her youth. The full title is, "True
love requited; or, the Bailiff's daughter of Islington."
Islington in Norfolk is probably the place here meant.

There was a youthe, and a well-beloved youthe,
  And he was a squires son:
He loved the bayliffes daughter deare,
  That lived in Islington.

Yet she was coye, and would not believe
  That he did love her soe,
Noe nor at any time would she
  Any countenance to him showe.

But when his friendes did understand
   His fond and foolish minde,   10
They sent him up to faire London
   An apprentice for to binde.

And when he had been seven long yeares,
   And never his love could see:
Many a teare have I shed for her sake,   15
   When she little thought of mee.

Then all the maids of Islington
   Went forth to sport and playe,
All but the bayliffes daughter deare;
   She secretly stole awaye.   20

She pulled off her gowne of greene,
   And put on ragged attire,
And to faire London she would go
   Her true love to enquire.

And as she went along the high road,   25
   The weather being hot and drye,
She sat her downe upon a green bank,
   And her true love came riding bye.

She started up, with a colour soe redd,
   Catching hold of his bridle-reine;   30
One penny, one penny, kind sir, she sayd,
   Will ease me of much paine.

Before I give you one penny, sweet-heart,
   Praye tell me where you were borne.
At Islington, kind sir, sayd shee,   35
   Where I have had many a scorne.

I prythee, sweet-heart, then tell to mee,
   O tell me, whether you knowe
The bayliffes daughter of Islington.
   She is dead, sir, long agoe.   40

If she be dead, then take my horse,
    My saddle and bridle also;
For I will into some farr countrye,
    Where noe man shall me knowe.

O staye, O staye, thou goodlye youthe,   45
    She standeth by thy side;
She is here alive, she is not dead,
    And readye to be thy bride

O farewell grief, and welcome joye,
    Ten thousand times therefore;   50
For nowe I have founde mine owne true love,
    Whom I thought I should never see more.

IX.

The Willow Tree.

A PASTORAL DIALOGUE.

FROM the small black-letter collection, entitled, "The
Golden Garland of princely Delights;" collated with two
other copies, and corrected by conjecture.

WILLY.

How now, shepherde, what meanes that?
Why that willowe in thy hat?
Why thy scarffes of red and yellowe
Turn'd to branches of greene willowe?

CUDDY.

They are chang'd, and so am I;   5
Sorrowes live, but pleasures die:
Phillis hath forsaken mee,
Which makes me weare the willowe-tree.

WILLY.

Phillis! shee that lov'd thee long?
Is shee the lass hath done thee wrong?   10
Shee that lov'd thee long and best,
Is her love turned to a jest?

CUDDY.

Shee that long true love profest,
She hath robb'd my heart of rest:
For she a new love loves, not mee;   15
Which makes me wear the willowe-tree.

WILLY.

Come then, shepherde, let us joine,
Since thy happ is like to mine:
For the maid I thought most true
Mee hath also bid adieu.   20

CUDDY.

Thy hard happ doth mine appease,
Companye doth sorrowe ease:
Yet, Phillis, still I pine for thee,
And still must weare the willowe-tree.

WILLY.

Shepherde, be advis'd by mee,   25
Cast off grief and willowe-tree:
For thy grief brings her content,
She is pleas'd if thou lament.

CUDDY.

Herdsman, I'll be rul'd by thee,
There lyes grief and willowe-tree: 30
Henceforth I will do as they,
And love a new love every day.

∗

X.

The Lady's Fall,

Is given (with corrections) from the Editor's ancient folio
MS. collated with two printed copies in black-letter; one in
the British Museum, the other in the Pepys collection. Its
old title is, "A lamentable ballad of the Lady's fall." To
the tune of *In pescod time*, &c. The ballad here referred to
is preserved in the *Muses Library*, 8vo, p. 281. It is an alle-
gory or vision, entitled, *The Shepherd's Slumber*, and opens
with some pretty rural images, viz.

> "In pescod time when hound to horn
> Gives eare till buck be kil'd,
> And little lads with pipes of corne
> Sate keeping beasts a-field,
>
> "I went to gather strawberries
> By woods and groves full fair," &c.

MARKE well my heavy dolefull tale,
    You loyall lovers all,
And heedfully beare in your brest
    A gallant ladyes fall.
Long was she wooed, ere shee was wonne   5
    To lead a wedded life,
But folly wrought her overthrowe
    Before shee was a wife.

Too soone, alas! shee gave consent
    And yeelded to his will,   10
Though he protested to be true,
    And faithfull to her still.
Shee felt her body altered quite,
    Her bright hue waxed pale,
Her lovelye cheeks chang'd color white,   15
    Her strength began to fayle.

Soe that with many a sorrowful sigh,
  This beauteous ladye milde,
With greeved hart, perceived herselfe
  To have conceived with childe.   20
Shee kept it from her parents sight
  As close as close might bee,
And soe put on her silken gowne
  None might her swelling see.

Unto her lover secretly   25
  Her greefe she did bewray,
And, walking with him hand in hand,
  These words to him did say:
Behold, quoth shee, a maids distresse
  By love brought to thy bowe,   30
Behold I goe with childe by thee,
  Tho none thereof doth knowe.

The little babe springs in my wombe
  To heare its fathers voyce,
Lett it not be a bastard called,   35
  Sith I made thee my choyce:
Come, come, my love, perform thy vowe
  And wed me out of hand;
O leave me not in this extreme
  Of griefe, alas! to stand.   40

Think on thy former promises,
  Thy oathes and vowes eche one;
Remember with what bitter teares
  To mee thou madest thy moane.
Convay me to some secrett place,   45
  And marry me with speede;
Or with thy rapyer end my life,
  Ere further shame proceede.

Alacke! my beauteous love, quoth hee,
  My joye, and only dear;   50

Which way can I convay thee hence,
  When dangers are so near?
Thy friends are all of hye degree,
  And I of meane estate;
Full hard it is to gett thee forthe   55
  Out of thy fathers gate.

Dread not thy life to save my fame,
  For, if thou taken bee,
My selfe will step betweene the swords,
  And take the harme on mee: 60
Soe shall I scape dishonor quite;
  And if I should be slaine,
What could they say, but that true love
  Had wrought a ladyes bane.

But feare not any further harme;   65
  My selfe will soe devise,
That I will ryde away with thee
  Unknowen of mortall eyes:
Disguised like some pretty page
  Ile meete thee in the darke,   70
And all alone Ile come to thee
  Hard by my fathers parke.

And there, quoth hee, Ile meete my deare
  If God soe lend me life,
On this day month without all fayle   75
  I will make thee my wife.
Then with a sweet and loving kisse,
  They parted presentlye,
And att their partinge brinish teares
  Stoode in eche others eye.   80

Att length the wished day was come,
  On which this beauteous mayu,
With longing eyes, and strange attire,
  For her true lover stayd.

When any person shee espyed   85
   Come ryding ore the plaine,
She hop'd it was her owne true love:
   But all her hopes were vaine.

Then did shee weepe and sore bewayle
   Her most unhappy fate;   90
Then did shee speake these woefull words,
   As succourlesse she sate;
O false, forsworne, and faithlesse man,
   Disloyall in thy love,
Hast thou forgott thy promise past,   95
   And wilt thou perjured prove?

And hast thou now forsaken mee
   In this my great distresse,
To end my dayes in open shame,
   Which thou mightst well redresse?   100
Woe worth the time I eer believ'd
   That flattering tongue of thine:
Wold God that I had never seene
   The teares of thy false eyne.

And thus with many a sorrowful sigh,   105
   Homewards shee went againe;
Noe rest came in her waterye eyes,
   Shee felt such privye paine.
In travail strong shee fell that night,
   With many a bitter throwe;   110
What woefull paines shee then did feel,
   Doth eche good woman knowe.

Shee called up her waiting mayd,
   That lay at her bedds feete,
Who musing at her mistress woe,   115
   Began full fast to weepe.
Weepe not, said shee, but shutt the dores
   And windowes round about,

Let none bewray my wretched state,
 But keepe all persons out. 120

O mistress, call your mother deare,
 Of women you have neede,
And of some skilfull midwifes helpe,
 That better may you speed.
Call not my mother for thy life, 125
 Nor fetch no woman here;
The midwifes helpe comes all too late,
 My death I doe not feare.

With that the babe sprang from her wombe
 No creature being nye, 130
And with one sighe, which brake her hart,
 This gentle dame did dye.
The lovely litle infant younge,
 The mother being dead,
Resigned its new received breath 135
 To him that had it made.

Next morning came her own true love,
 Affrighted at the newes,
And he for sorrow slew himselfe,
 Whom eche one did accuse. 140
The mother with her new borne babe,
 Were laide both in one grave:
Their parents overworne with woe,
 No joy thenceforth cold have.

Take heed, you dayntye damsells all, 145
 Of flattering words beware,
And to the honour of your name
 Have an especial care.
Too true, alas! this story is,
 As many one can tell: 150
By others harmes learne to be wise,
 And you shall do full well.

—————

XI.

Waly Waly, Love be Bonny.

A SCOTTISH SONG.

This is a very ancient song, but we could only give it from a modern copy. Some editions, instead of the four last lines in the second stanza, have these, which have too much merit to be wholly suppressed:

> "Whan cockle shells turn siller bells,
> And muscles grow on every tree,
> When frost and snaw sall warm us aw',
> Than sall my love prove true to me."
> See the *Orpheus Caledonius*, &c.

Arthur's-seat, mentioned in verse 17, is a hill near Edinborough; at the bottom of which is St. Anthony's well.

O WALY waly up the bank,
  And waly waly down the brae,
And waly waly yon burn side,
  Where I and my love wer wont to gae.
I leant my back unto an aik,   5
  I thought it was a trusty tree;
But first it bow'd, and syne it brak,
  Sae my true love did lichtly me.

O waly waly, gin love be bonny,
  A little time while it is new;   10
But when its auld, it waxeth cauld,
  And fades awa' like morning dew.
O wherfore shuld I busk my head?
  Or wherfore shuld I kame my hair?
For my true love has me forsook,   15
  And says he'll never loe me mair.

Now Arthur-seat sall be my bed,
  The sheets shall neir be fyl'd by me:

Saint Anton's well sall be my drink,
    Since my true love has forsaken me.   20
Marti'mas wind, when wilt thou blaw,
    And shake the green leaves aff the tree?
O gentle death, whan wilt thou cum?
    For of my life I am wearìe.

Tis not the frost, that freezes fell,   25
    Nor blawing snaws inclemencie;
'Tis not sic cauld, that makes me cry,
    But my loves heart grown cauld to me.
Whan we came in by Glasgowe town,
    We were a comely sight to see,   30
My love was cled in black velvet,
    And I my sell in cramasìe.

But had I wist, before I kisst,
    That love had been sae ill to win;
I had lockt my heart in a case of gowd,   35
    And pinnd it with a siller pin.
And, oh! if my young babe were born,
    And set upon the nurses knee,
And I my sell were dead and gane!
    For a maid again Ise never be.   40

XII.
The Wanton Wife of Bath.

From an ancient copy in black-print, in the Pepys collection. Mr. Addison has pronounced this an excellent ballad: See the Spectator, No. 248.

In Bath a wanton wife did dwelle,
    As Chaucer he doth write;
Who did in pleasure spend her dayes,
    And many a fond delight.

Upon a time sore sicke she was   5
   And at the length did dye;
And then her soul at heaven gate,
   Did knocke most mightilye.

First Adam came unto the gate:
   Who knocketh there? quoth hee.   10
I am the wife of Bath, she sayd,
   And faine would come to thee.

Thou art a sinner, Adam sayd,
   And here no place shalt have.
And so art thou, I trowe, quoth shee,   15
   'And eke a' doting knave.

I will come in, in spight, she sayd,
   Of all such churles as thee;
Thou wert the causer of our woe,
   Our paine and misery;   20

And first broke Gods commandiments,
   In pleasure of thy wife.
When Adam heard her tell this tale,
   He ranne away for life.

Then downe came Jacob at the gate,   25
   And bids her packe to hell,
Thou false deceiving knave, quoth she,
   Thou mayst be there as well.

For thou deceiv'dst thy father deare,
   And thine own brother too.   30
Away 'slunk' Jacob presently,
   And made no more adoo.

She knockes again with might and maine,
   And Lot he chides her straite.

Ver. 16. Now gip you. P.

How now, quoth she, thou drunken ass,   35
   Who bade thee here to prate?

With thy two daughters thou didst lye,
   On them two bastardes got.
And thus most tauntingly she chaft
   Against poor silly Lot.   40

Who calleth there, quoth Judith then,
   With such shrill sounding notes?
This fine minkes surely came not here,
   Quoth she, for cutting throats.

Good Lord, how Judith blush'd for shame,   45
   When she heard her say soe!
King David hearing of the same,
   He to the gate would goe.

Quoth David, who knockes there so loud,
   And maketh all this strife?   50
You were more kinde, good Sir, she sayd,
   Unto Uriah's wife.

And when thy servant thou didst cause
   In battle to be slaine:
Thou causedst far more strife than I,   55
   Who would come here so faine.

The woman's mad, quoth Solomon,
   That thus doth taunt a king.
Not half so mad as you, she sayd,
   I trowe, in manye a thing.   60

Thou hadst seven hundred wives at once,
   For whom thou didst provide;
And yet, god wot, three hundred whores
   Thou must maintaine beside:

And they made thee forsake thy God,   65
    And worship stockes and stones;
Besides the charge they put thee to
    In breeding of young bones.

Hadst thou not bin beside thy wits,
    Thou wouldst not thus have ventur'd;   70
And therefore I do marvel much,
    How thou this place hast enter'd.

I never heard, quoth Jonas then,
    So vile a scold as this.
Thou whore-son run-away, quoth she,   75
    Thou diddest more amiss.

'They say,' quoth Thomas, womens tongues
    Of aspen-leaves are made.
Thou unbelieving wretch, quoth she,
    All is not true that's sayd.   80

When Mary Magdalen heard her then,
    She came unto the gate.
Quoth she, good woman, you must think
    Upon your former state.

No sinner enters in this place   85
    Quoth Mary Magdalene.   Then
'Twere ill for you, fair mistress mine,
    She answered her agen:

You for your honestye, quoth she,
    Had once been ston'd to death;   90
Had not our Saviour Christ come by,
    And written on the earth.

It was not by your occupation,
    You are become divine:

Ver. 77. I think. P.

I hope my soul in Christ his passion,   95
   Shall be as safe as thine.

Uprose the good apostle Paul,
   And to this wife he cryed,
Except thou shake thy sins away,
   Thou here shalt be denyed.   100

Remember, Paul, what thou hast done,
   All through a lewd desire:
How thou didst persecute God's church,
   With wrath as hot as fire.

Then up starts Peter at the last,   105
   And to the gate he hies:
Fond fool, quoth he, knock not so fast,
   Thou weariest Christ with cries.

Peter, said she, content thyselfe,
   For mercye may be won,   110
I never did deny my Christ,
   As thou thyselfe hast done.

When as our Saviour Christ heard this,
   With heavenly angels bright,
He comes unto this sinful soul,   115
   Who trembled at his sight.

Of him for mercye she did crave.
   Quoth he, thou hast refus'd
My profferd grace, and mercy both,
   And much my name abus'd.   120

Sore have I sinned, Lord, she sayd,
   And spent my time in vaine,
But bring me like a wandring sheepe
   Into thy flocke againe.

O Lord my God, I will amend 125
   My former wicked vice:
The thief for one poor silly word,
   Past into paradise.

My lawes and my commandiments,
   Saith Christ, were knowne to thee; 130
But of the same in any wise,
   Not yet one word did yee.

I grant the same, O Lord, quoth she;
   Most lewdly did I live:
But yet the loving father did 135
   His prodigal son forgive.

So I forgive thy soul, he sayd,
   Through thy repenting crye:
Come enter then into my joy,
   I will not thee denye. 140

XIII.

The Bride's Burial.

FROM two ancient copies in black-letter: one in the Pepys
collection, the other in the British Museum.

To the tune of *The Lady's Fall.*

COME mourne, come mourne with mee,
   You loyall lovers all;
Lament my loss in weeds of woe,
   Whom griping grief doth thrall.

Like to the drooping vine, 5
   Cut by the gardener's knife,
Even so my heart, with sorrow slaine,
   Doth bleed for my sweet wife.

By death, that grislye ghost,
  My turtle dove is slaine,   10
And I am left, unhappy man,
  To spend my dayes in paine.

Her beauty late so bright,
  Like roses in their prime,
Is wasted like the mountain snowe,   15
  Before warme Phebus' shine.

Her faire red colour'd cheeks
  Now pale and wan; her eyes,
That late did shine like crystal stars,
  Alas, their light it dies: 20

Her pretty lilly hands,
  With fingers long and small,
In colour like the earthlye claye,
  Yea, cold and stiff withall.

When as the morning-star   25
  Her golden gates had spred,
And that the glittering sun arose
  Forth from fair Thetis' bed;

Then did my love awake,
  Most like a lilly-flower,   30
And as the lovely queene of heaven,
  So shone shee in her bower.

Attired was shee then
  Like Flora in her pride,
Like one of bright Diana's nymphs,   35
  So look'd my loving bride.

And as fair Helen's face
  Did Grecian dames besmirche,
So did my dear exceed in sight
  All virgins in the church.   40

When we had knitt the knott
  Of holy wedlock-band,
Like alabaster joyn'd to jett,
  So stood we hand in hand;

Then lo! a chilling cold   45
  Strucke every vital part,
And griping grief, like pangs of death,
  Seiz'd on my true love's heart.

Down in a swoon she fell,
  As cold as any stone;   50
Like Venus picture lacking life,
  So was my love brought home.

At length her rosye red,
  Throughout her comely face,
As Phœbus beames with watry cloudes   55
  Was cover'd for a space.

When with a grievous groane,
  And voice both hoarse and drye,
Farewell, quoth she, my loving friend,
  For I this daye must dye;   60

The messenger of God
  With golden trumpe I see,
With manye other angels more,
  Which sound and call for mee

Instead of musicke sweet,   65
  Go toll my passing-bell;
And with sweet flowers strow my grave,
  That in my chamber smell.

Strip off my bride's arraye,
  My cork shoes from my feet;   70
And, gentle mother, be not coye
  To bring my winding-sheet.

My wedding dinner drest,
  Bestowe upon the poor,
And on the hungry, needy, maimde,   75
  Now craving at the door.

Instead of virgins yong,
  My bride-bed for to see,
Go cause some cunning carpenter
  To make a chest for mee.   80

My bride laces of silk
  Bestowd, for maidens meet,
May fitly serve, when I am dead,
  To tye my hands and feet.

And thou, my lover true,   85
  My husband and my friend,
Let me intreat thee here to staye,
  Until my life doth end.

Now leave to talk of love,
  And humblye on your knee,   90
Direct your prayers unto God:
  But mourn no more for mee.

In love as we have livde,
  In love let us depart;
And I, in token of my love,   95
  Do kiss thee with my heart.

O staunch those bootless teares,
  Thy weeping tis in vaine:
I am not lost, for wee in heaven
  Shall one daye meet againe.   100

With that shee turn'd aside,
  As one dispos'd to sleep,
And like a lamb departed life:
  Whose friends did sorely weep.

Her true love seeing this,   105
    Did fetch a grievous groane,
As tho' his heart would burst in twaine,
    And thus he made his moane.

O darke and dismal daye,
    A daye of grief and care,   110
That hath bereft the sun so bright,
    Whose beams refresht the air.

Now woe unto the world,
    And all that therein dwell,
O that I were with thee in heaven,   115
    For here I live in hell.

And now this lover lives
    A discontented life,
Whose bride was brought unto the grave
    A maiden and a wife.   120

A garland fresh and faire
    Of lillies there was made,
In sign of her virginitye,
    And on her coffin laid.

Six maidens all in white,   125
    Did beare her to the ground:
The bells did ring in solemn sort,
    And made a dolefull sound.

In earth they laid her then,
    For hungry wormes a preye;   130
So shall the fairest face alive
    At length be brought to claye.

XIV.

Dulcina.

GIVEN from two ancient copies, one in black-print, in the Pepys collection, the other in the Editor's folio MS. Each of these contained a stanza not found in the other. What seemed the best readings were selected from both.

This song is quoted as very popular in Walton's *Compleat Angler*, chap. ii. It is more ancient than the ballad of *Robin-Good-Fellow* printed below, which yet is supposed to have been written by Ben Jonson.

As at noone Dulcina rested
  In her sweete and shady bower,
Came a shepherd, and requested
  In her lapp to sleepe an hour.
     But from her looke   5
     A wounde he tooke
  Soe deepe, that for a further boone
     The nymph he prayes.
     Wherto shee sayes,
  Forgoe me now, come to me soone.   10

But in vayne shee did conjure him
  To depart her presence soe;
Having a thousand tongues to allure him,
  And but one to bid him goe:
     Where lipps invite,   15
     And eyes delight,
  And cheekes, as fresh as rose in june,
     Persuade delay;
     What boots, she say,
  Forgoe me now, come to me soone?   20

He demands what time for pleasure
  Can there be more fit than now:

She sayes, night gives love that leysure,
  Which the day can not allow.
    He sayes, the sight   25
    'Improves delight.
  'Which she denies: Nights mirkie noone
    In Venus' playes
    Makes bold, shee sayes:
  Forgoc me now, come to mee soone.   30

But what promise or profession
  From his hands could purchase scope?
Who would sell the sweet possession
  Of suche beautye for a hope?
    Or for the sight   35
    Of lingering night
  Foregoe the present joyes of noone?
    Though ne'er soe faire
    Her speeches were,
  Forgoe me now, come to me soone.   40

How, at last, agreed these lovers?
  Shee was fayre, and he was young:
The tongue may tell what th' eye discovers;
  Joyes unseene are never sung.
    Did shee consent,   45
    Or he relent;
  Accepts he night, or grants shee noone;
    Left he her a mayd,
    Or not; she sayd
  Forgoe me now, come to me soone   50

XV.

The Lady Isabella's Tragedy.

THIS ballad is given from an old black-letter copy in the
Pepys collection, collated with another in the British Mu-
seum, H. 263, folio. It is there entitled, "The Lady Isabella's

Tragedy, or the Step-Mother's Cruelty; being a relation of a
lamentable and cruel murther, committed on the body of the
lady Isabella, the only daughter of a noble Duke, &c.   To
the tune of *The Lady's Fall*." To some copies are annexed
eight more modern stanzas, entitled, "The Dutchess's and
Cook's Lamentation."

THERE was a lord of worthy fame,
    And a hunting he would ride,
Attended by a noble traine
    Of gentrye by his side.

And while he did in chase remaine,   5
    To see both sport and playe;
His ladye went, as she did feigne,
    Unto the church to praye.

This lord he had a daughter deare,
    Whose beauty shone so bright,   10
She was belov'd, both far and neare,
    Of many a lord and knight.

Fair Isabella was she call'd,
    A creature faire was shee;
She was her fathers only joye;   15
    As you shall after see.

Therefore her cruel step-mothèr
    Did envye her so much,
That daye by daye she sought her life,
    Her malice it was such.   20

She bargain'd with the master-cook,
    To take her life awaye:
And taking of her daughters book,
    She thus to her did saye.

Go home, sweet daughter, I thee praye,   25
 Go hasten presentlie:
And tell unto the master-cook
 These wordes that I tell thee.

And bid him dresse to dinner streight
 That faire and milk-white doe,   30
That in the park doth shine so bright,
 There's none so faire to showe.

This ladye fearing of no harme,
 Obey'd her mothers will;
And presentlye she hasted home,   35
 Her pleasure to fulfill.

She streight into the kitchen went,
 Her message for to tell;
And there she spied the master-cook,
 Who did with malice swell.   40

Nowe, master-cook, it must be soe,
 Do that which I thee tell:
You needes must dresse the milk-white doe,
 Which you do knowe full well.

Then streight his cruell bloodye hands,   45
 He on the ladye layd;
Who quivering and shaking stands,
 While thus to her he sayd:

Thou art the doe that I must dresse;
 See here, behold my knife;   50
For it is pointed presently
 To ridd thee of thy life.

O then, cried out the scullion-boye,
 As loud as loud might bee:
O save her life, good master-cook,   55
 And make your pyes of mee!

For pityes sake do not destroye
 My ladye with your knife;
You know shee is her father's joye,
 For Christes sake save her life.   60

I will not save her life, he sayd,
 Nor make my pyes of thee;
Yet if thou dost this deed bewraye,
 Thy butcher I will bee.

Now when this lord he did come home 65
 For to sit downe and eat;
He called for his daughter deare,
 To come and carve his meat.

Now sit you downe, his ladye sayd,
 O sit you downe to meat: 70
Into some nunnery she is gone;
 Your daughter deare forget.

Then solemnlye he made a vowe,
 Before the companie:
That he would neither eat nor drinke, 75
 Until he did her see.

O then bespake the scullion-boye,
 With a loud voice so hye:
If now you will your daughter see,
 My lord, cut up that pye: 80

Wherein her fleshe is minced small,
 And parched with the fire;
All caused her by her step-mothèr,
 Who did her death desire.

And cursed bee the master-cook, 85
 O cursed may he bee!
I proffered him my own heart's blood,
 From death to set her free.

Then all in blacke this lord did mourne;
   And for his daughters sake,   90
He judged her cruell step-mothèr
   To be burnt at a stake.

Likewise he judg'd the master-cook
   In boiling lead to stand;
And made the simple scullion-boye   95
   The heire of all his land.

XVI.

A Hue and Cry after Cupid.

THIS song is a kind of translation of a pretty poem of
Tasso's, called *Amore fuggitivo*, generally printed with his
Aminta, and originally imitated from the first Idyllium of
Moschus.

It is extracted from Ben Jonson's Masque at the marriage
of Lord Viscount Hadington, on Shrove-Tuesday, 1608. One
stanza, full of dry mythology, is here omitted, as it had been
dropt in a copy of this song printed in a small volume, called
Le Prince d'Amour. Lond. 1660, 8vo.

BEAUTIES, have yee seen a toy,
Called Love, a little boy,
Almost naked, wanton, blinde;
Cruel now, and then as kinde?
If he bee amongst yee, say: 5
He is Venus' run away.

Shee, that will but now discover
Where the winged wag doth hover,
Shall to-night receive a kisse,
How and where herselfe would wish: 10
But who brings him to his mother
Shall have that kisse, and another

Markes he hath about him plentie;
You may know him among twentie:
All his body is a fire,   15
And his breath a flame entire:
Which, being shot, like lightning, in,
Wounds the heart, but not the skin.

Wings he hath, which though yee clip,
He will leape from lip to lip,   20
Over liver, lights, and heart;
Yet not stay in any part.
And, if chance his arrow misses,
He will shoot himselfe in kisses.

He doth beare a golden bow,   25
And a quiver hanging low,
Full of arrowes, which outbrave
Dian's shafts; where, if he have
Any head more sharpe than other,
With that first he strikes his mother.   30

Still the fairest are his fuell,
When his daies are to be cruell;
Lovers hearts are all his food,
And his baths their warmest bloud:
Nought but wounds his hand doth season,   35
And he hates none like to Reason.

Trust him not: his words, though sweet,
Seldome with his heart doe meet:
All his practice is deceit:
Everie gift is but a bait: 40
Not a kisse but poyson beares;
And most treason's in his teares.

Idle minutes are his raigne;
Then the straggler makes his gaine,
                                            11*

By presenting maids with toyes   45
And would have yee thinke hem joyes;
'Tis the ambition of the elfe
To have all childish as himselfe.

If by these yee please to know him,
Beauties, be not nice, but show him.   50
Though yee had a will to hide him,
Now, we hope, yee'le not abide him,
Since yee heare this falser's play,
And that he is Venus' run-away.

XVII.

The King of France's Daughter.

THE story of this ballad seems to be taken from an incident in the domestic history of Charles the Bald, king of France. His daughter Judith was betrothed to Ethelwulph king of England: but before the marriage was consummated, Ethelwulph died, and she returned to France; whence she was carried off by Baldwin, Forester of Flanders; who, after many crosses and difficulties, at length obtained the king's consent to their marriage, and was made Earl of Flanders. This happened about A. D. 863. — See Rapin, Henault, and the French historians.

The following copy is given from the Editor's ancient folio MS. collated with another in black-letter in the Pepys collection, entitled, "An excellent Ballad of a prince of England's courtship to the king of France's daughter, &c. To the tune of *Crimson Velvet.*"

Many breaches having been made in this old song by the hand of time, principally (as might be expected) in the quick returns of the rhyme, an attempt is here made to repair them.

In the dayes of old,
  When faire France did flourish,
Storyes plaine have told,
  Lovers felt annoye.
The queene a daughter bare,   5
  Whom beautye's queene did nourish:
She was lovelye faire,
  She was her fathers joye.
A prince of England came,
Whose deeds did merit fame,   10
  But he was exil'd, and outcast:
Love his soul did fire,
Shee granted his desire,
  Their hearts in one were linked fast
Which when her father proved,   15
Sorelye he was moved,
  And tormented in his minde.
  He sought for to prevent them;
And, to discontent them,
  Fortune cross'd these lovers kinde.   20

When these princes twaine
  Were thus barr'd of pleasure,
Through the kinges disdaine,
  Which their joyes withstoode:
The lady soone prepar'd   25
  Her jewells and her treasure:
Having no regard
  For state and royall bloode;
In homelye poore array
She went from court away,   30
  To meet her joye and hearts delight;
Who in a forrest great
Had taken up his seat,
  To wayt her coming in the night
But, lo! what sudden danger   35
To this princely stranger

Chanced, as he sate alone!
By outlawes he was robbed,
And with ponyards stabbed,
   Uttering many a dying grone.   40

The princesse, arm'd by love,
  And by chaste desire,
All the night did rove
  Without dread at all:
Still unknowne she past   45
  In her strange attire;
Coming at the last
  Within echoes call, —
You faire woods, quoth shee.
Honoured may you bee,   50
  Harbouring my hearts delight;
Which encompass here
My joye and only deare,
  My trustye friend, and comelye knight.
Swecte, I come unto thee,   55
Sweete, I come to woo thee
  That thou mayst not angry bee
For my long delaying;
For thy curteous staying
  Soone amendes Ile make to thee.   60

Passing thus alone
  Through the silent forest,
Many a grievous grone,
  Sounded in her eares:
She heard one complayne   65
  And lament the sorest,
Seeming all in payne,
  Shedding deadly teares.
Farewell, my deare, quoth hee,
Whom I must never see;   70

For why my life is att an end,
Through villaines crueltye:
For thy sweet sake I dye,
  To show I am a faithfull friend.
Here I lye a bleeding,   75
While my thoughts are feeding
  On the rarest beautye found.
O hard happ, that may be!
Little knowes my ladye
  My heartes blood lyes on the ground.   80

With that a grone he sends
  Which did burst in sunder
All the tender bands
  Of his gentle heart.
She, who knewe his voice,   85
  At his wordes did wonder;
All her former joyes
  Did to griefe convert.
Strait she ran to see,
Who this man shold bee,   90
  That soe like her love did seeme:
Her lovely lord she found
Lye slaine upon the ground,
  Smear'd with gore a ghastlye streame.
Which his lady spying,   95
Shrieking, fainting, crying,
  Her sorrows could not uttered bee:
Fate, she cryed, too cruell:
For thee — my dearest jewell,
  Would God! that I had dyed for thee.   100

His pale lippes, alas!
  Twentye times she kissed,
And his face did wash
  With her trickling teares:

Every gaping wound   105
   Tenderlye she pressed,
And did wipe it round
   With her golden haires.
Speake, fair love, quoth shee,
Speake, faire prince, to mee,   110
   One sweete word of comfort give:
Lift up thy deare eyes,
Listen to my cryes,
   Thinke in what sad griefe I live.
All in vaine she sued,   115
All in vaine she wooed,
   The prince's life was fled and gone,
There stood she still mourning,
Till the suns retourning,
   And bright day was coming on.   120

In this great distresse
   Weeping, wayling ever,
Oft shee cryed, alas!
   What will become of mee?
To my fathers court   125
   I returne will never:
But in lowlye sort
   I will a servant bee.
While thus she made her mone,
Weeping all alone,   130
   In this deepe and deadlye feare:
A for'ster all in greene,
Most comelye to be seene,
   Ranging the woods did find her there.
Moved with her sorrowe,   135
Maid, quoth hee, good morrowe,
   What hard happ has brought thee here?
Harder happ did never
Two kinde hearts dissever:
   Here lies slaine my brother deare.   140

Where may I remaine,
　Gentle for'ster, shew me,
'Till I can obtaine
　A service in my neede?
Paines I will not spare:　　　　　　　145
　This kinde favour doe mee,
It will ease my care;
　Heaven shall be thy meede.
The for'ster all amazed,
On her beautye gazed,　　　　　　　150
　Till his heart was set on fire
If, faire maid, quoth hee,
You will goe with mee,
　You shall have your hearts desire.
He brought her to his mother,　　　　155
And above all other
　He sett forth this maidens praise.
Long was his heart inflamed,
At length her love he gained,
　And fortune crown'd his future dayes.　160

Thus unknowne he wedde
　With a kings faire daughter:
Children seven they had,
　Ere she told her birth.
Which when once he knew,　　　　　165
　Humblye he besought her,
He to the world might shew
　Her rank and princelye worth.
He cloath'd his children then,
(Not like other men)　　　　　　　170
　In partye-colours strange to see:
The right side cloth of gold,
The left side to behold,
　Of woollen cloth still framed hee[1].

[1] This will remind the reader of the livery and device of Charles Brandon, a private gentleman, who married the Queen-dowager of France, sister

Men thereatt did wonder;   175
Golden fame did thunder
  This strange deede in every place;
The king of France came thither,
It being pleasant weather,
  In those woods the hart to chase.   180

The children then they bring,
  So their mother will'd it,
Where the royall king
  Must of force come bye:
Their mothers riche array,   185
  Was of crimson velvet:
Their fathers all of gray,
  Seemelye to the eye.
Then this famous king,
Noting every thing,   190
  Askt how he durst be so bold
To let his wife soe weare,
And decke his children there
  In costly robes of pearl and gold.
The forrester replying,   195
And the cause descrying[2],
  To the king these words did say,
Well may they, by their mother,
Weare rich clothes with other,
  Being by birth a princesse gay.   200

The king aroused thus,
  More heedfullye beheld them,

of Henry VIII. At a tournament which he held at his wedding, the trap-
pings of his horse were half cloth of gold, and half frieze, with the following
motto:
            "Cloth of Gold, do not despise,
              Tho' thou art matcht with Cloth of Frize;
              Cloth of Frize, be not too bold,
              Tho' thou art matcht with Cloth of Gold."
See Sir W. Temple's Misc. vol. iii. p. 356.
            [2] *i. e.* describing. See Gloss.

Till a crimson blush
　His remembrance crost.
The more I fix my mind　　　　　　　　　205
　On thy wife and children,
The more methinks I find
　The daughter which I lost.
Falling on her knee,
I am that child, quoth shee;　　　　　　210
　Pardon mee, my soveraine liege.
The king perceiving this,
His daughter deare did kiss,
　While joyfull teares did stopp his speeche.
With his traine he tourned,　　　　　　　215
And with them sojourned.
　Strait he dubb'd her husband knight;
Then made him erle of Flanders,
And chiefe of his commanders:
　Thus were their sorrowes put to flight.　220

***

XVIII.

The Sweet Neglect.

THIS little madrigal (extracted from Ben Jonson's *Silent
Woman*, act i. sc. 1, first acted in 1609) is in imitation of a
Latin poem printed at the end of the variorum edit. of Pe-
tronius, beginning, "*Semper munditias, semper Basilissa,
decoras,*" &c.　See Whalley's Ben Jonson, vol. ii. p. 420.

STILL to be neat, still to be drest,
As you were going to a feast:
Still to be poud'red, still perfum'd:
Lady, it is to be presum'd,
Though art's hid causes are not found,　　　5
All is not sweet, all is not sound.

Give me a looke, give me a face,
That makes simplicitie a grace;
Robes loosely flowing, haire as free:
Such sweet neglect more taketh me,　　　　　　10
Than all th' adulteries of art,
That strike mine eyes, but not my heart.

XIX.

The Children in the Wood.

THE subject of this very popular ballad (which has been set in so favourable a light by the *Spectator*, No. 85) seems to be taken from an old play, entitled, "Two lamentable Tragedies; the one of the murder of Maister Beech, a chandler in Thames-streete, &c. The other of a young child murthered in a wood by two ruffins, with the consent of his unkle. By Rob. Yarrington, 1601, 4to." Our ballad-maker has strictly followed the play in the description of the father and mother's dying charge: in the uncle's promise to take care of their issue: his hiring two ruffians to destroy his ward, under pretence of sending him to school: their choosing a wood to perpetrate the murder in: one of the ruffians relenting, and a battle ensuing, &c. In other respects he has departed from the play. In the latter, the scene is laid in Padua: there is but one child, which is murdered by a sudden stab of the unrelenting ruffian: he is slain himself by his less bloody companion; but ere he dies he gives the other a mortal wound: the latter living just long enough to impeach the uncle; who, in consequence of this impeachment, is arraigned and executed by the hand of justice, &c. Whoever compares the play with the ballad, will have no doubt but the former is the original: the language is far more obsolete, and such a vein of simplicity runs through the whole performance, that, had the ballad been written first, there is no doubt but every circumstance of it would have been received into the drama: whereas this was probably built on some Italian novel.

Printed from two ancient copies, one of them in black-letter in the Pepys collection. Its title at large is, — "The Children in the Wood: or, the Norfolk Gentleman's Last Will and Testament: to the tune of *Rogero*, &c."

Now ponder well, you parents deare,
   These wordes, which I shall write;
A doleful story you shall heare,
   In time brought forth to light.
A gentleman of good account   5
   In Norfolke dwelt of late,
Who did in honour far surmount
   Most men of his estate.

Sore sicke he was, and like to dye,
   No helpe his life could save;   10
His wife by him as sicke did lye,
   And both possest one grave.
No love between these two was lost,
   Each was to other kinde,
In love they liv'd, in love they dyed,   15
   And left two babes behinde:

The one a fine and pretty boy,
   Not passing three yeares olde;
The other a girl more young than he,
   And fram'd in beautyes molde.   20
The father left his little son,
   As plainlye doth appeare,
When he to perfect age should come,
   Three hundred poundes a yeare.

And to his little daughter Jane   25
   Five hundred poundes in gold,

To be paid downe on marriage-day,
  Which might not be controll'd:
But if the children chance to dye,
  Ere they to age should come,   30
Their uncle should possesse their wealth;
  For so the wille did run.

Now, brother, said the dying man,
  Look to my children deare;
Be good unto my boy and girl,   35
  No friendes else have they here:
To God and you I recommend
  My children deare this daye;
But little while be sure we have
  Within this world to staye.   40

You must be father and mother both,
  And uncle all in one;
God knowes what will become of them,
  When I am dead and gone.
With that bespake their mother deare,   45
  O brother kinde, quoth shee,
You are the man must bring our babes
  To wealth or miserie:

And if you keep them carefully,
  Then God will you reward;   50
But if you otherwise should deal,
  God will your deedes regard.
With lippes as cold as any stone,
  They kist their children small:
God bless you both, my children deare;   55
  With that the teares did fall.

These speeches then their brother spake
  To this sicke couple there,
The keeping of your little ones,
  Sweet sister, do not feare: 60

God never prosper me nor mine,
  Nor aught else that I have,
If I do wrong your children deare,
  When you are layd in grave.

The parents being dead and gone,   65
  The children home he takes,
And bringes them straite unto his house,
  Where much of them he makes.
He had not kept these pretty babes
  A twelvemonth and a daye,   70
But, for their wealth, he did devise
  To make them both awaye.

He bargain'd with two ruffians strong,
  Which were of furious mood,
That they should take these children young,   75
  And slaye them in a wood.
He told his wife an artful tale,
  He would the children send
To be brought up in faire Londòn,
  With one that was his friend.   80

Away then went those pretty babes,
  Rejoycing at that tide,
Rejoycing with a merry minde,
  They should on cock-horse ride.
They prate and prattle pleasantly,   85
  As they rode on the waye,
To those that should their butchers be,
  And work their lives decaye:

So that the pretty speeche they had,
  Made Murder's heart relent;   90
And they that undertooke the deed,
  Full sore did now repent.
Yet one of them more hard of heart,
  Did vowe to do his charge,

Because the wretch, that hired him,   95
   Had paid him very large.

The other won't agree thereto,
   So here they fall to strife;
With one another they did fight,
   About the childrens life: 100
And he that was of mildest mood,
   Did slaye the other there,
Within an unfrequented wood;
   The babes did quake for feare!

He took the children by the hand,   105
   Teares standing in their eye,
And bad them straitwaye follow him,
   And look they did not crye:
And two long miles he ledd them on,
   While they for food complaine: 110
Staye here, quoth he, I'll bring you bread,
   When I come back againe.

These pretty babes, with hand in hand,
   Went wandering up and downe:
But never more could see the man   115
   Approaching from the town:
Their prettye lippes with black-berries,
   Were all besmeared and dyed,
And when they sawe the darksome night,
   They sat them downe and cryed.   120

Thus wandered these poor innocents,
   Till deathe did end their grief,
In one anothers armes they dyed,
   As wanting due relief:
No burial 'this' pretty 'pair'   125
   Of any man receives,

Ver. 125, these .. babes. PPC.

Till Robin-red-breast piously
   Did cover them with leaves.

And now the heavy wrathe of God
   Upon their uncle fell;   130
Yea, fearfull fiends did haunt his house,
   His conscience felt an hell:
His barnes were fir'd, his goodes consum'd,
   His landes were barren made,
His cattle dyed within the field,   135
   And nothing with him stayd.

And in a voyage to Portugal
   Two of his sonnes did dye;
And to conclude, himselfe was brought
   To want and miserye: 140
He pawn'd and mortgaged all his land
   Ere seven yeares came about.
And now at length this wicked act
   Did by this meanes come out:

The fellowe, that did take in hand   145
   These children for to kill,
Was for a robbery judg'd to dye,
   Such was God's blessed will:
Who did confess the very truth,
   As here hath been display'd: 150
Their uncle having dyed in gaol,
   Where he for debt was layd.

You that executors be made,
   And overseers eke
Of children that be fatherless,   155
   And infants mild and meek;
Take you example by this thing,
   And yield to each his right,
Lest God with such like miserye
   Your wicked minds requite.

_____

XX.

A Lover of Late.

PRINTED, with a few slight corrections, from the Editor's folio MS.

    A LOVER of late was I,
        For Cupid would have it soe,
    The boy that hath never an eye,
        As every man doth know:
I sighed and sobbed, and cryed, alas!   5
For her that laught, and called me ass.

    Then knew not I what to doe,
        When I saw itt was in vaine
    A lady soe coy to wooe,
        Who gave me the asse soe plaine: 10
Yet would I her asse freelye bee,
Soe shee would helpe, and beare with mee.

    An' I were as faire as shee,
        Or shee were as kind as I,
    What payre cold have made, as wee,   15
        Soe prettye a sympathye:
I was as kind as shee was faire,
But for all this wee cold not paire.

    Paire with her that will for mee,
        With her I will never paire;   20
    That cunningly can be coy,
        For being a little faire.
The asse Ile leave to her disdaine;
And now I am myselfe againe.

Ver. 13, faine. MS.

XXI.

The King and Miller of Mansfield.

IT has been a favourite subject with our English ballad-makers, to represent our kings conversing, either by accident or design, with the meanest of their subjects. Of the former kind, besides the song of the King and the Miller, we have King Henry and the Soldier; King James I. and the Tinker; King William III. and the Forester, &c. Of the latter sort are King Alfred and the Shepherd; King Edwand IV. and the Tanner; King Henry VIII. and the Cobler, &c. — A few of the best of these are admitted into this collection. Both the author of the following ballad, and others who have written on the same plan, seem to have copied a very ancient poem, entitled *John the Reeve*, which is built on an adventure of the same kind, that happened between King Edward Longshanks and one of his reeves or bailiffs. This is a piece of great antiquity, being written before the time of Edward the Fourth, and for its genuine humour, diverting incidents, and faithful picture of rustic manners, is infinitely superior to all that have been since written in imitation of it. The Editor has a copy in his ancient folio MS., but its length rendered it improper for this volume, it consisting of more than 900 lines. It contains also some corruptions, and the Editor chooses to defer its publication, in hopes that some time or other he shall be able to remove them.

The following is printed, with corrections, from the Editor's folio MS. collated with an old black-letter copy in the Pepys collection, entitled, "A pleasant ballad of King Henry II. and the Miller of Mansfield," &c.

PART THE FIRST.

HENRY, our royall king, would ride a hunting
  To the greene forest so pleasant and faire;
To see the harts skipping, and dainty does tripping:
  Unto merry Sherwood his nobles repaire:

12*

Hawke and hound were unbound, all things prepar'd   5
For the game, in the same, with good regard.

All a long summers day rode the king pleasantlye,
  With all his princes and nobles eche one;
Chasing the hart and hind, and the bucke gallantlye,
  Till the dark evening forc'd all to turne home.   10
Then at last, riding fast, he had lost quite
All his lords in the wood, late in the night.

Wandering thus wearilye, all alone, up and downe,
  With a rude miller he mett at the last:
Asking the ready way unto faire Nottingham;   15
  Sir, quoth the miller, I meane not to jest,
Yet I thinke, what I thinke, sooth for to say,
You doe not lightlye ride out of your way.

Why, what dost thou think of me, quoth our king merrily,
  Passing thy judgment upon me so briefe?   20
Good faith, sayd the miller, I meane not to flatter thee;
  I guess thee to bee but some gentleman thiefe;
Stand thee backe, in the darke; light not adowne,
Lest that I presentlye crack thy knaves crowne.

Thou dost abuse me much, quoth the king, saying thus;   25
  I am a gentleman; lodging I lacke.
Thou hast not, quoth th' miller, one groat in thy purse;
  All thy inheritance hanges on thy backe.
[1]I have gold to discharge all that I call;
If it be forty pence, I will pay all.   30

If thou beest a true man, then quoth the miller,
  I sweare by my toll-dish, I'll lodge thee all night.
Here's my hand, quoth the king, that was I ever.
  Nay, soft, quoth the miller, thou may'st be a sprite
Better I'll know thee, ere hands we will shake;   35
With none but honest men hands will I take.

<hr />

[1] The king says this.

Thus they went all along unto the millers house:
  Where they were seething of puddings and souse:
The miller first enter'd in, after him went the king;
  Never came hee in soe smoakye a house.   40
Now, quoth hee, let me see here what you are.
Quoth our king, looke your fill, and doe not spare.

I like well thy countenance, thou hast an honest face;
  With my son Richard this night thou shalt lye.
Quoth his wife, by my troth, it is a handsome youth,   45
  Yet it's best, husband, to deal warilye.
Art thou no run away, prythee, youth, tell?
Shew me thy passport, and all shal be well.

Then our king presentlye, making lowe courtesye,
  With his hatt in his hand, thus he did say;   50
I have no passport, nor never was servitor,
  But a poor courtyer, rode out of my way:
And for your kindness here offered to mee,
I will requite you in everye degree.

Then to the miller his wife whisper'd secretlye,   55
  Saying, It seemeth, this youth's of good kin,
Both by his apparel, and eke by his manners;
  To turne him out, certainlye, were a great sin.
Yea, quoth hee, you may see, he hath some grace
When he doth speake to his betters in place.   60

Well, quo' the millers wife, young man, ye're welcome here;
  And, though I say it, well lodged shall be:
Fresh straw will I have, laid on thy bed so brave,
  And good brown hempen sheets likewise, quoth shee.
Aye, quoth the good man; and when that is done,   65
Thou shalt lye with no worse than our own sonne.

Nay, first, quoth Richard, good-fellowe, tell me true,
  Hast thou noe creepers within thy gay hose?
Or art thou not troubled with the scabbado?
  I pray, quoth the king, what creatures are those?   70

Art thou not lowsy, nor scabby? quoth he:
If thou beest, surely thou lyest not with mee.

This caus'd the king, suddenlye, to laugh most heartilye,
    Till the teares trickled fast downe from his eyes.
Then to their supper were they set orderlye,   75
    With hot bag-puddings, and good apple-pyes;
Nappy ale, good and stale, in a browne bowle,
Which did about the board merrilye trowle.

Here, quoth the miller, good fellowe, I drinke to thee,
    And to all 'cuckholds, wherever they bee.'   80
I pledge thee, quoth our king, and thanke thee heartilye
    For my good welcome in everye degree:
And here, in like manner, I drinke to thy sonne.
Do then, quoth Richard, and quicke let it come.

Wife, quoth the miller, fetch me forth lightfoote,   85
    And of his sweetnesse a little we'll taste.
A fair ven'son pastye brought she out presentlye.
    Eate, quoth the miller, but, sir, make no waste.
Here's dainty lightfoote! In faith, sayd the king,
I never before eat so daintye a thing.   90

I wis, quoth Richard, no daintye at all it is,
    For we doe eate of it everye day.
In what place, sayd our king, may be bought like to this?
    We never pay pennye for itt, by my fay:
From merry Sherwood we fetch it home here;   95
Now and then we make bold with our kings deer.

Then I thinke, sayd our king, that it is venison.
    Eche foole, quoth Richard, full well may know that:
Never are wee without two or three in the roof,
    Very well fleshed, and excellent fat: 100
But, prythee, say nothing wherever thou goe;
We would not, for two pence, the king should it knowe.

Ver. 80, courtnalls, that courteous be. MS. and PC.

Doubt not, then sayd the king, my promist secresy;
  The king shall never know more on't for mee.
A cupp of lambs-wool they dranke unto him then,   105
  And to their bedds they past presentlie.
The nobles, next morning, went all up and down,
For to seeke out the king in everye towne.

At last, at the millers 'cott,' soone they espy'd him out,
  As he was mounting upon his faire steede;   110
To whom they came presently, falling down on their knee;
  Which made the millers heart wofully bleede;
Shaking and quaking, before him he stood,
Thinking he should have been hang'd, by the rood.

The king perceiving him fearfully trembling,   115
  Drew forth his sword, but nothing he sed:
The miller downe did fall, crying before them all,
  Doubting the king would have cut off his head.
But he his kind courtesye for to requite,
Gave him great living, and dubb'd him a knight.   120

PART THE SECONDE.

When as our royall king came home from Nottingham,
  And with his nobles at Westminster lay;
Recounting the sports and pastimes they had taken,
  In this late progress along on the way;
Of them all, great and small, he did protest,   5
The miller of Mansfield's sport liked him best.

And now, my lords, quoth the king, I am determined
  Against St. Georges next sumptuous feast,
That this old miller, our new confirm'd knight,
  With his son Richard, shall here be my guest: 10
For, in this merryment, 'tis my desire
To talke with the jolly knight, and the young squire.

When as the noble lords saw the kinges pleasantness,
  They were right joyfull and glad in their hearts:
A pursuivant there was sent straighte on the business,   15
  The which had often-times been in those parts.
When he came to the place, where they did dwell,
His message orderlye then 'gan he tell.

God save your worshippe, then said the messenger,
  And grant your ladye her own hearts desire;   20
And to your sonne Richard good fortune and happiness;
  That sweet, gentle, and gallant young squire.
Our king greets you well, and thus he doth say,
You must come to the court on St. George's day;

Therfore, in any case, faile not to be in place.   25
  I wis, quoth the miller, this is an odd jest:
What should we doe there? faith, I am halfe afraid.
  I doubt, quoth Richard, to be hang'd at the least.
Nay, quoth the messenger, you doe mistake;
Our king he provides a great feast for your sake.   30

Then sayd the miller, By my troth, messenger,
  Thou hast contented my worshippe full well.
Hold here are three farthings, to quite thy gentleness,
  For these happy tydings, which thou dost tell.
Let me see, hear thou mee; tell to our king,   35
We'll wayt on his mastershipp in everye thing.

The pursuivant smiled at their simplicitye,
  And, making many leggs, tooke their reward;
And his leave taking with great humilitye
  To the kings court againe he repair'd;   40
Shewing unto his grace, merry and free,
The knightes most liberall gift and bountie.

When he was gone away, thus gan the miller say,
  Here come expences and charges indeed;
Now must we needs be brave, tho' we spend all we have; 45
  For of new garments we have great need:

Of horses and serving-men we must have store,
With bridles and saddles, and twentye things more.

Tushe, sir John, quoth his wife, why should you frett, or
      frowne?
  You shall ne'er be att no charges for mee;   50
For I will turne and trim up my old russet gowne,
  With everye thing else as fine as may bee;
And on our mill-horses swift we will ride,
With pillowes and pannells, as we shall provide.

In this most statelye sort, rode they unto the court,   55
  Their jolly sonne Richard rode foremost of all;
Who set up, for good hap, a cocks feather in his cap,
  And so they jetted downe to the kings hall;
The merry old miller with hands on his side;
His wife, like maid Marian, did mince at that tide.   60

The king and his nobles that heard of their coming,
  Meeting this gallant knight with his brave traine;
Welcome, sir knight, quoth he, with your gay lady:
  Good sir John Cockle, once welcome againe:
And so is the squire of courage soe free.   65
Quoth Dicke, A bots on you! do you know mee?

Quoth our king gentlye, how should I forget thee?
  Thou wast my owne bed-fellowe, well it I wot.
Yea, sir, quoth Richard, and by the same token,
  Thou with thy farting didst make the bed hot.   70
Thou whore-son unhappy knave, then quoth the knight,
Speake cleanly to our king, or else go sh***.

The king and his courtiers laugh at this heartily,
  While the king taketh them both by the hand;

V. 57, for good hap: *i. e.* for good luck; they were going on an hazardous expedition.

V. 60. Maid Marian, in the Morris dance, was represented by a man in woman's clothes, who was to take short steps in order to sustain the female character.

With the court-dames, and maids, like to the queen of
      spades   75
  The millers wife did soe orderly stand.
A milk-maids courtesye at every word;
And downe all the folkes were set to the board.

There the king royally, in princelye majestye,
  Sate at his dinner with joy and delight;   80
When they had eaten well, then he to jesting fell,
  And in a bowle of wine dranke to the knight:
Here's to you both, in wine, ale and beer;
Thanking you heartilye for my good cheer.

Quoth sir John Cockle, I'll pledge you a pottle,   85
  Were it the best ale in Nottinghamshire:
But then said our king, now I think of a thing;
  Some of your lightfoote I would we had here.
Ho! ho! quoth Richard, full well I may say it,
'Tis knavery to eate it, and then to betray it.   90

Why art thou angry? quoth our king merrilye;
  In faith, I take it now very unkind:
I thought thou wouldst pledge me in ale and wine heartily.
  Quoth Dicke, You are like to stay till I have din'd:
You feed us with twatling dishes soe small;   95
Zounds, a blacke-pudding is better than all.

Aye, marry, quoth our king, that were a daintye thing,
  Could a man get but one here for to eate.
With that Dicke straite arose, and pluckt one from his hose,
  Which with heat of his breech gan to sweate.   100
The king made a proffer to snatch it away: —
'Tis meat for your master: good sir, you must stay.

Thus in great merriment was the time wholly spent;
  And then the ladyes prepared to dance.
Old sir John Cockle, and Richard, incontinent   105
  Unto their places the king did advance.

Here with the ladyes such sport they did make,
The nobles with laughing did make their sides ake.

Many thankes for their paines did the king give them,   110
 Asking young Richard then, if he would wed;
Among these ladyes free, tell me which liketh thee?
 Quoth he, Jugg Grumball, Sir, with the red head:
She's my love, she's my life, her will I wed;
She hath sworn I shall have her maidenhead.

Then sir John Cockle the king call'd unto him,   115
 And of merry Sherwood made him o'er seer;
And gave him out of hand three hundred pound yearlye;
 Take heed now you steale no more of my deer:
And once a quarter let's here have your view;
And now, sir John Cockle, I bid you adieu.   120

XXII

The Shepherd's Resolution.

This beautiful old song was written by a poet, whose
name would have been utterly forgotten, if it had not been
preserved by Swift, as a term of contempt. "Dryden and
Wither" are coupled by him like the Bavius and Mævius of
Virgil. Dryden, however, has had justice done him by
posterity: and as for Wither, though of subordinate merit,
that he was not altogether devoid of genius will be judged
from the following stanzas. The truth is, Wither was a
very voluminous party-writer: and as his political and satiri-
cal strokes rendered him extremely popular in his life-time;
so afterwards, when these were no longer relished, they to-
tally consigned his writings to oblivion.

George Wither was born June 11, 1588, and in his
younger years distinguished himself by some pastoral pieces,
that were not inelegant; but growing afterwards involved in
the political and religious disputes in the times of James I.

and Charles I., he employed his poetical vein in severe pasquils on the court and clergy, and was occasionally a sufferer for the freedom of his pen. In the civil war that ensued, he exerted himself in the service of the Parliament, and became a considerable sharer in the spoils. He was even one of those provincial tyrants whom Oliver distributed over the kingdom, under the name of Major-Generals, and had the fleecing of the county of Surrey: but, surviving the Restoration, he outlived both his power and his affluence; and giving vent to his chagrin in libels on the court, was long a prisoner in Newgate and the Tower. He died at length on the 2nd of May, 1667.

During the whole course of his life, Wither was a continual publisher; having generally for opponent Taylor the Water-poet. The long list of his productions may be seen in Wood's Athenæ Oxon. vol. ii. His most popular satire is entitled, *Abuses whipt and stript*, 1613. His most poetical pieces were eclogues, entitled, *The Shepherd's Hunting*, 1615, 8vo, and others printed at the end of Browne's *Shepherd's Pipe*, 1614, 8vo. The following sonnet is extracted from a long pastoral piece of his, entitled, *The Mistresse of Philarete*, 1622, 8vo, which is said in the preface to be one of the author's first poems; and may therefore be dated as early as any of the foregoing.

SHALL I, wasting in dispaire,
Dye because a woman's faire?
Or make pale my cheeks with care
'Cause another's rosie are?
Be shee fairer then the day,   5
Or the flowry meads in may;
   If she be not so to me,
   What care I how faire shee be?

Shall my foolish heart be pin'd
'Cause I see a woman kind?   10

Or a well-disposed nature
Joyned with a lovely feature?
Be shee meeker, kinder, than
The turtle-dove or pelican:
   If shee be not so to me, 15
    What care I how kind shee be?

Shall a woman's virtues move
Me to perish for her love?
Or, her well-deservings knowne,
Make me quite forget mine owne? 20
Be shee with that goodnesse blest,
Which may merit name of Best;
   If she be not such to me,
    What care I how good she be?

Cause her fortune seems too high, 25
Shall I play the foole and dye?
Those that beare a noble minde,
Where they want of riches find,
Thinke what with them they would doe,
That without them dare to woe; 30
   And, unlesse that minde I see,
    What care I how great she be?

Great or good, or kind or faire,
I will ne'er the more dispaire:
If she love me, this beleeve; 35
I will die ere she shall grieve.
If she slight me when I wooe,
I can scorne and let her goe:
   If she be not fit for me,
    What care I for whom she be? 40

XXIII.

𝔔ueen 𝔇ido.

SUCH is the title given in the Editor's folio MS. to this ex-
cellent old ballad, which, in the common printed copies, is
inscribed, *Eneas, wandering Prince of Troy.* It is here given
from that MS. collated with two different printed copies,
both in black-letter, in the Pepys collection.

The reader will smile to observe with what natural and
affecting simplicity our ancient ballad-maker has engrafted
a Gothic conclusion on the classic story of Virgil, from
whom, however, it is probable he had it not. Nor can it be
denied, but he has dealt out his poetical justice with a more
impartial hand than that celebrated poet.

———

> WHEN Troy towne had, for ten yeeres 'past,'
>   Withstood the Greekes in manfull wise,
> Then did their foes encrease soe fast,
>   That to resist none could suffice:
> Wast lye those walls, that were soe good,   5
> And corne now growes where Troy towne stoode.
>
> Æneas, wandering prince of Troy,
>   When he for land long time had sought,
> At length arriving with great joy,
>   To mighty Carthage walls was brought;   10
> Where Dido queene, with sumptuous feast,
> Did entertaine that wandering guest.
>
> And, as in hall at meate they sate,
>   The queene, desirous newes to heare,
> 'Says, of thy Troys unhappy fate'   15
>   Declare to me thou Trojan deare:

Ver. 1, 21, war. MS. and P. P. C.

The heavy hap and chance soe bad,
That thou, poore wandering prince, hast had.

And then anon this comelye knight,
  With words demure, as he cold well,   20
Of his unhappy ten yeares 'fight,'
  Soe true a tale began to tell,
With words soe sweete, and sighes soe deepe,
That oft he made them all to weepe.

And then a thousand sighes he fet,   25
  And every sigh brought teares amaine;
That where he sate the place was wett,
  As though he had seene those warrs againe:
Soe that the queene, with ruth therfore,
Said, Worthy prince, enough, no more   30

And then the darksome night drew on,
  And twinkling starres the skye bespred;
When he his dolefull tale had done,
  And every one was layd in bedd:
Where they full sweetly tooke their rest,   35
Save only Dido's boyling brest.

This silly woman never slept,
  But in her chamber, all alone,
As one unhappye, alwayes wept,
  And to the walls shee made her mone;   40
That she shold still desire in vaine
The thing, she never must obtaine.

And thus in grieffe she spent the night,
  Till twinkling starres the skye were fled,
And Phœbus, with his glistering light,   45
  Through misty cloudes appeared red;
Then tidings came to her anon,
That all the Trojan shipps were gone.

And then the queene with bloody knife
    Did arme her hart as hard as stone,   50
Yet, something loth to loose her life,
    In woefull wise she made her mone;
And, rowling on her carefull bed,
With sighes and sobbs, these words shee sayd:

O wretched Dido queene! quoth shee,   55
    I see thy end approacheth neare;
For hee is fled away from thee,
    Whom thou didst love and hold so deare:
What is he gone, and passed by?
O hart, prepare thyselfe to dye.   60

Though reason says, thou shouldst forbeare,
    And stay thy hand from bloudy stroke;
Yet fancy bids thee not to fear,
    Which fetter'd thee in Cupids yoke.
Come death, quoth shee, resolve my smart! —   65
And with those words shee peerced her hart.

When death had pierced the tender hart
    Of Dido, Carthaginian queene;
Whose bloudy knife did end the smart,
    Which shee sustain'd in mournfull teene;   70
Æneas being shipt and gone,
Whose flattery caused all her mone;

Her funerall most costly made,
    And all things finisht mournfullye;
Her body fine in mold was laid,   75
    Where itt consumed speedilye:
Her sisters teares her tombe bestrewde;
Her subjects griefe their kindnesse shewed.

Then was Æneas in an ile
    In Grecya, where he stayd long space,   80

Wheras her sister in short while
  Writt to him to his vile disgrace;
In speeches bitter to his mind
Shee told him plaine he was unkind.

False-harted wretch, quoth shee, thou art; 85
  And traiterouslye thou hast betraid
Unto thy lure a gentle hart,
  Which unto thee much welcome made;
My sister deare, and Carthage' joy,
Whose folly bred her deere annoy. 90

Yett on her death-bed when shee lay,
  Shee prayd for thy prosperitye,
Beseeching god, that every day
  Might breed thy great felicitye:
Thus by thy meanes I lost a friend; 95
Heavens send thee such untimely end.

When he these lines, full fraught with gall,
  Perused had, and wayed them right,
His lofty courage then did fall;
  And straight appeared in his sight 100
Queene Dido's ghost, both grim and pale:
Which made this valliant souldier quaile.

Æneas, quoth this ghastly ghost,
  My whole delight when I did live,
Thee of all men I loved most; 105
  My fancy and my will did give;
For entertainment I thee gave,
Unthankefully thou didst me grave.

Therfore prepare thy flitting soule
  To wander with me in the aire: 110
Where deadlye griefe shall make it howle,
  Because of me thou tookst no care:
Delay not time, thy glasse is run,
Thy date is past, thy life is done.

O stay a while, thou lovely sprite,   115
    Be not soe hasty to convay
My soule into eternall night,
    Where itt shall ne're behold bright day.
O doe not frowne; thy angry looke
Hath 'all my soule with horror shooke.'   120

    But, woe is me! all is in vaine,
      And bootless is my dismall crye;
    Time will not be recalled againe,
      Nor thou surcease before I dye.
O lett me live, and make amends   125
To some of thy most dearest friends.

    But seeing thou obdurate art,
      And wilt no pittye on me show,
    Because from thee I did depart,
      And left unpaid what I did owe: 130
I must content myselfe to take
What lott to me thou wilt partake.

    And thus, as one being in a trance,
      A multitude of uglye feinds
    About this woffull prince did dance;   135
      He had no helpe of any friends:
His body then they tooke away,
And no man knew his dying day.

V. 120, MS. *Hath* made my breath my life forsooke.

XXIV.

The Witches' Song,

FROM Ben Jonson's Masque of Queens, presented at White-
hall, Feb. 2, 1609.

The Editor thought it incumbent on him to insert some
old pieces on the popular superstition concerning witches,

hobgoblins, fairies, and ghosts. The last of these make their appearance in most of the tragical ballads; and in the following songs will be found some description of the former.

It is true, this Song of the Witches, falling from the learned pen of Ben Jonson, is rather an extract from the various incantations of classical antiquity, than a display of the opinions of our own vulgar. But let it be observed, that a parcel of learned wiseacres had just before busied themselves on this subject, in compliment to King James I., whose weakness on this head is well known: and these had so ransacked all writers, ancient and modern, and so blended and kneaded together the several superstitions of different times and nations, that these of genuine English growth could no longer be traced out and distinguished.

By good luck, the whimsical belief of fairies and goblins could furnish no pretences for torturing our fellow-creatures, and therefore we have this handed down to us pure and unsophisticated.

----

1 WITCH.

I HAVE been all day looking after
A raven feeding upon a quarter:
And, soone as she turn'd her beak to the south,
I snatch'd this morsell out of her mouth.

2 WITCH.

I have beene gathering wolves haires,   5
The madd dogges foames, and adders eares;
The spurging of a deadmans eyes:
And all since the evening starre did rise.

3 WITCH.

I last night lay all alone
O' the ground, to heare the mandrake grone;   10
And pluckt him up, though he grew full low:
And, as I had done, the cocke did crow.

13*

4 WITCH.

And I ha' beene chusing out this scull
From charnell houses that were full;
From private grots, and publike pits;   15
And frighted a sexton out of his wits.

5 WITCH.

Under a cradle I did crepe
By day; and, when the childe was a-sleepe
At night, I suck'd the breath; and rose,
And pluck'd the nodding nurse by the nose.   20

6 WITCH.

I had a dagger: what did I with that?
Killed an infant to have his fat.
A piper it got at a church-ale.
I bade him again blow wind i' the taile.

7 WITCH.

A murderer, yonder, was hung in chaines;   25
The sunne and the wind had shrunke his veines:
I bit off a sinew; I clipp'd his haire;
I brought off his ragges, that danc'd i' the ayre.

8 WITCH.

The scrich-owles egges and the feathers blacke,
The bloud of the frogge, and the bone in his backe   30
I have been getting; and made of his skin
A purset, to keepe sir Cranion in.

9 WITCH.

And I ha' beene plucking (plants among)
Hemlock, henbane, adders-tongue,
Night-shade, moone-wort, libbards-bane;   35
And twise by the dogges was like to be tane.

10 WITCH.

I from the jawes of a gardiner's bitch
Did snatch these bones, and then leap'd the ditch:

Yet went I back to the house againe,
Kill'd the blacke cat, and here is the braine.   40

11 WITCH.

I went to the toad, breedes under the wall,
I charmed him out, and he came at my call;
I scratch'd out the eyes of the owle before;
I tore the batts wing: what would you have more?

DAME.

Yes: I have brought, to helpe your vows,   45
Horned poppie, cypresse boughes,
    The fig-tree wild, that growes on tombes,
And juice, that from the larch-tree comes,
    The basiliskes bloud, and the vipers skin:
    And now our orgies let's begin.   50

XXV.

Robin Good-Fellow,

ALIAS *Pucke*, alias *Hobgoblin*, in the creed of ancient
superstition, was a kind of merry sprite, whose character
and achievements are recorded in this ballad, and in those
well-known lines of Milton's *L'Allegro*, which the antiquarian
Peck supposes to be owing to it:

> "Tells how the drudging *Goblin* swet
> To earn his creame-bowle duly set:
> When in one night, ere glimpse of morne,
> His shadowy flail hath thresh'd the corn
> That ten day-labourers could not end;
> Then lies him down the lubber fiend,
> And stretch'd out all the chimneys length,
> Bask at the fire his hairy strength,
> And crop-full out of doors he flings,
> Ere the first cock his matins rings."

The reader will observe, that our simple ancestors had
reduced all these whimsies to a kind of system, as regular,
and perhaps more consistent, than many parts of classic

mythology: a proof of the extensive influence and vast antiquity of these superstitions. Mankind, and especially the common people, could not every where have been so unanimously agreed concerning these arbitrary notions, if they had not prevailed among them for many ages. Indeed, a learned friend in Wales assures the Editor, that the existence of Fairies and Goblins is alluded to by the most ancient British bards, who mention them under various names, one of the most common of which signifies "The spirits of the mountains." See also preface to Song XXVI.

This song, which Peck attributes to Ben Jonson (though it is not found among his works), is chiefly printed from an ancient black-letter copy in the British Museum. It seems to have been originally intended for some Masque.

This ballad is entitled, in the old black-letter copies. "The merry Pranks of Robin Goodfellow. To the tune of *Dulcina*," &c. (See No. xiii. above.)

FROM Oberon, in fairye land,
　　The king of ghosts and shadowes there,
Mad Robin I, at his command,
　　Am sent to viewe the night-sports here.
　　　　What revell rout　　　　　　　　　5
　　　　Is kept about,
　　In every corner where I go,
　　　　I will o'ersee,
　　　　And merry bee,
　　And make good sport, with ho, ho, ho!　　10

More swift than lightening can I flye
　　About this aery welkin soone,
And in a minutes space, descrye
　　Each thing that's done belowe the moone,
　　　　There's not a hag　　　　　　　　15
　　　　Or ghost shall wag,

Or cry, ware Goblins! where I go;
   But Robin I
     Their feates will spy,
And send them home, with ho, ho, ho!   20

Whene'er such wanderers I meete,
  As from their night-sports they trudge home;
With counterfeiting voice I greete
  And call them on, with me to roame
     Thro' woods, thro' lakes,   25
     Thro' bogs, thro' brakes;
  Or else, unseene, with them I go,
     All in the nicke
     To play some tricke
And frolicke it, with ho, ho, ho!   30

Sometimes I meete them like a man;
  Sometimes, an ox, sometimes, a hound;
And to a horse I turn me can;
  To trip and trot about them round.
     But if, to ride,   35
     My backe they stride,
More swift than wind away I go,
     Ore hedge and lands,
     Thro' pools and ponds
I whirry, laughing, ho, ho, ho!   40

When lads and lasses merry be,
  With possets and with juncates fine;
Unseene of all the company,
  I eat their cakes and sip their wine;
     And, to make sport,   45
     I fart and snort;
And out the candles I do blow:
     The maids I kiss;
     They shrieke — Who's this?
I answer nought, but ho, ho, ho!   50

Yet now and then, the maids to please,
  At midnight I card up their wooll;
And while they sleepe, and take their ease,
  With wheel to threads their flax I pull.
      I grind at mill   55
      Their malt up still;
  I dress their hemp, I spin their tow.
      If any 'wake,
      And would me take,
  I wend me, laughing, ho, ho, ho!   60

When house or harth doth sluttish lye,
  I pinch the maidens black and blue;
The bed-clothes from the bedd pull I,
  And lay them naked all to view.
      'Twixt sleepe and wake,   65
      I do them take,
  And on the key-cold floor them throw.
      If out they cry,
      Then forth I fly,
  And loudly laugh out, ho, ho, ho!   70

When any need to borrowe ought,
  We lend them what they do require:
And for the use demand we nought;
  Our owne is all we do desire.
      If to repay,   75
      They do delay,
  Abroad amongst them then I go,
      And night by night,
      I them affright
  With pinchings, dreames, and ho, ho, ho!   80

When lazie queans have nought to do,
  But study how to cog and lye;
To make debate and mischief too,
  'Twixt one another secretlye:

I marke their gloze,   85
  And it disclose,
To them whom they have wronged so;
  When I have done,
  I get me gone,
And leave them scolding, ho, ho, ho!   90

When men do traps and engins set
  In loop holes, where the vermine creepe,
Who from their foldes and houses, get
  Their duckes and geese, and lambes and sheepe:
    I spy the gin,   95
    And enter in,
  And seeme a vermine taken so;
    But when they there
    Approach me neare,
I leap out laughing, ho, ho, ho!   100

By wells and rills, in meadowes greene,
  We nightly dance our hey-day guise;
And to our fairye king and queene
  We chant our moon-light minstrelsies.
    When larks 'gin sing,   105
    Away we fling;
And babes new borne steal as we go,
    And elfe in bed
    We leave instead,
And wend us laughing, ho, ho, ho!   110

From hag-bred Merlin's time have I
  Thus nightly revell'd to and fro:
And for my pranks men call me by
  The name of Robin Good-fellòw.
    Fiends, ghosts, and sprites,   115
    Who haunt the nightes,
The hags and goblins do me know;
    And beldames old
    My feates have told;
So *Vale, Vale;* ho, ho, ho!   120

XXVI.

𝕿𝖍𝖊 𝕱𝖆𝖎𝖗𝖞 𝕼𝖚𝖊𝖊𝖓.

WE have here a short display of the popular belief con-
cerning FAIRIES. It will afford entertainment to a con-
templative mind to trace these whimsical opinions up to their
origin. Whoever considers how early, how extensively, and
how uniformly they have prevailed in these nations, will not
readily assent to the hypothesis of those who fetch them
from the East so late as the time of the Croisades. Whereas
it is well known that our Saxon ancestors, long before they
left their German forests, believed the existence of a kind of
diminutive demons, or middle species between men and spi-
rits, whom they called *Duergar* or *Dwarfs*, and to whom they
attributed many wonderful performances, far exceeding
human art. Vid. Hervarer Saga Olaj Verelj. 1675. Hickes'
Thesaur. &c.

This song is given (with some corrections by another
copy) from a book entitled, "The Mysteries of Love and
Eloquence," &c. Lond. 1648, 8vo.

COME, follow, follow me,
You, fairy elves that be:
Which circle on the greene,
Come follow Mab your queene.
Hand in hand let's dance around,   5
For this place is fairye ground.

When mortals are at rest,
And snoring in their nest;
Unheard, and unespy'd,
Through key-holes we do glide;   10
Over tables, stools, and shelves,
We trip it with our fairy elves.

And, if the house be foul
With platter, dish, or bowl,
Up stairs we nimbly creep,   15
And find the sluts asleep:
There we pinch their armes and thighes;
None escapes, nor none espies.

But if the house be swept,
And from uncleanness kept,   20
We praise the houshold maid,
And duely she is paid:
For we use before we goe
To drop a tester in her shoe.

Upon a mushroomes head   25
Our table-cloth we spread;
A grain of rye, or wheat,
Is manchet, which we eat;
Pearly drops of dew we drink
In acorn cups fill'd to the brink.   30

The brains of nightingales,
With unctuous fat of snailes,
Between two cockles stew'd,
Is meat that's easily chew'd;
Tailes of wormes, and marrow of mice   35
Do make a dish, that's wonderous nice.

The grashopper, gnat, and fly,
Serve for our minstrelsie;
Grace said, we dance a while,
And so the time beguile: 40
And if the moon doth hide her head,
The gloe-worm lights us home to bed.

On tops of dewie grasse
So nimbly do we passe,

The young and tender stalk 45
Ne'er bends when we do walk:
Yet in the morning may be seen
Vhere we the night before have been.

XXVII.

The Fairies' Farewell.

THIS humorous old song fell from the hand of the witty
Dr. Corbet (afterwards bishop of Norwich, &c.), and is
printed from his *Poëtica Stromata*, 1648, 12mo, (compared
with a third edition of his Poems, 1672.) It is there called,
"A proper new Ballad, entitled, The Fairies Farewell, or
God-a-mercy Will, to be sung or whistled to the tune of The
Meddow Brow, by the learned; by the unlearned, to the
tune of Fortune."

The departure of Fairies is here attributed to the aboli-
tion of monkery: Chaucer has, with equal humour, assigned
a cause the very reverse, in his *Wife of Bath's Tale.*

"In olde dayes of the king Artour,
Of which that Bretons speken gret honour,
All was this lond fulfilled of faerie;
The elf-quene, with hirè joly compagnie
Danced ful oft in many a grene mede.
This was the old opinion as I rede;
I speke of many hundred yeres ago;
But now can no man see non elves mo,
For now the grete charitee and prayeres
Of limitoures and other holy freres,
That serchen every land and every streme,
As thikke as motes in the sonne beme,
Blissing halles, chambres, kichenes, and boures,
Citees and burghes, castles high, and toures,
Thropes and bernes, shepenes and dairies,
This maketh that ther ben no faeries:
For ther as wont to walken was an elf,
Ther walketh now the limitour himself,
In undermeles and in morweninges,
And sayth his Matines and his holy thinges,
As he goth in his limitatioun.
Women may now go safely up and doun,

In every bush, and under every tree,
Ther is non other incubus but he,
And he ne will don hem no dishonour."
                    Tyrwhitt's Chaucer, i. p. 255.

Dr. Richard Corbet, having been bishop of Oxford about
three years, and afterwards as long bishop of Norwich, died
in 1635, ætat. 52.

───────

FAREWELL rewards and Fairies!
 Good housewives now may say;
For now foule sluts in dairies,
 Doe fare as well as they:
And though they sweepe their hearths no less 5
 Than mayds were wont to doe,
Yet who of late for cleaneliness
 Finds sixe-pence in her shoe?

Lament, lament old Abbies,
 The fairies lost command; 10
They did but change priests babies,
 But some have chang'd your land:
And all your children stoln from thence
 Are now growne Puritanes,
Who live as changelings ever since, 15
 For love of your demaines.

At morning and at evening both
 You merry were and glad,
So little care of sleepe and sloth,
 These prettie ladies had. 20
When Tom came home from labour,
 Or Ciss to milking rose,
Then merrily went their tabour,
 And nimbly went their toes.

Witness those rings and roundelayes 25
 Of theirs, which yet remaine;

Were footed in queene Maries dayes
   On many a grassy playne.
But since of late Elizabeth
   And later James came in;   30
They never danc'd on any heath,
   As when the time hath bin.

By which wee note the fairies
   Were of the old profession:
Their songs were *Ave Maries*,   35
   Their dances were procession.
But now, alas! they all are dead,
   Or gone beyond the seas,
Or farther for religion fled,
   Or else they take their ease.   40

A tell-tale in their company
   They never could endure;
And whoso kept not secretly
   Their mirth, was punish'd sure:
It was a just and christian deed   45
   To pinch such blacke and blue:
O how the common-welth doth need
   Such justices as you!

Now they have left our quarters;
   A Register they have,   50
Who can preserve their charters;
   A man both wise and grave.
An hundred of their merry pranks
   By one that I could name
Are kept in store; con twenty thanks   55
   To William for the same.

To William Churne of Staffordshire
   Give laud and praises due,
Who every meale can mend your cheare
   With tales both old and true: 60

To William all give audience,
   And pray yee for his noddle:
For all the fairies evidence
   Were lost, if it were addle.

*** After these Songs on the Fairies, the reader may be curious to see the manner in which they were formerly invoked and bound to human service. In Ashmole's collection of MSS. at Oxford [num. 8259. 1406. 2], are the papers of some Alchymist, which contain a variety of Incantations and Forms of Conjuring both Fairies, Witches, and Demons, principally, as it should seem, to assist him in his great work of transmuting metals. Most of them are too impious to be reprinted: but the two following may be very innocently laughed at.

Whoever looks into Ben Jonson's *Alchymist*, will find that these impostors, among their other secrets, affected to have a power over Fairies: and that they were commonly expected to be seen in a crystal glass, appears from that extraordinary book, "The Relation of Dr. John Dee's actions with Spirits, 1659," folio.

"An excellent way to gett a Fayrie. (For myself I call Margarett Barrance; but this will obteine ony one that is not allready bownd.)

"First, gett a broad square christall or Venice glasse, in length and breadth 3 inches. Then lay that glasse or christall in the bloud of a white henne, 3 Wednesdayes, or 3 Fridayes. Then take it out, and wash it with holy aq. and fumigate it. Then take 3 hazle sticks, or wands of an yeare groth: pill them fayre and white; and make 'them' soe longe, as you write the Spiritts name, or Fayries name, which you call, 3 times on every sticke being made flatt on one side. Then bury them under some hill, whereas you suppose Fayries haunt, the Wednesday before you call her: and the Friday followinge take them uppe, and call her at 8 or 3 or 10 of the clocke, which be good planetts and houres for that turne:

but when you call, be in cleane life, and turne thy face towards the east. And when you have her, bind her to that stone or glasse."

"AN UNGUENT to annoynt under the Eyelids, and upon the Eyelids eveninge and morninge: but especially when you call; or find your sight not perfect.

"R. A pint of sallet-oyle, and put it into a viall glasse: but first wash it with rose-water, and marygold-water: the flowers 'to' be gathered towards the east. Wash it till the oyle come white; then put it into the glasse, ut supra: and then put thereto the budds of holyhocke, the flowers of marygold, the flowers or toppes of wild thime, the budds of young hazle: and the thime must be gathered neare the side of a hill where FAYRIES use to be: and 'take' the grasse of a fayrie throne, there. All these put into the oyle, into the glasse: and set it to dissolve 3 dayes in the sunne, and then keep it for thy use; ut supra."

After this receipt for the Unguent follows a form of Incantation, wherein the Alchymist conjures a Fairy, named Elaby Gathon, to appear to him in that crystal glass, meekly and mildly: to resolve him truly in all manner of questions; and to be obedient to all his commands, under pain of damnation, &c.

One of the vulgar opinions about Fairies is, that they cannot be seen by human eyes, without a particular charm exerted in favour of the person who is to see them: and that they strike with blindness such as, having the gift of seeing them, take notice of them mal-a-propos.

As for the hazel sticks mentioned above, they were to be, probably, of that species called the Witch Hazel; which received its name from this manner of applying it in incantations.

END OF THE SECOND BOOK.

RELIQUES

OF

ANCIENT POETRY.

&c.

SERIES THE THIRD.

BOOK III.

I.

𝔗𝔥𝔢 𝔅𝔦𝔯𝔱𝔥 𝔬𝔣 𝔖𝔱. 𝔊𝔢𝔬𝔯𝔤𝔢.

THE incidents in this, and the other ballad of *St. George and the Dragon*, are chiefly taken from the old story-book of the Seven Champions of Christendome; which, though now the plaything of children, was once in high repute. Bishop Hall, in his Satires, published in 1597, ranks

"St. George's sorell, and his cross ofe blood,"

among the most popular stories of his time: and an ingenious critic thinks that Spenser himself did not disdain to borrow hints from it[1]: though I much doubt whether this popular romance were written so early as the Faerie Queen.

The author of this book of the Seven Champions was one Richard Johnson, who lived in the reigns of Elizabeth and James, as we collect from his other publications; viz. — "The nine worthies of London: 1592," 4to. — "The pleasant walks of Moor fields: 1607," 4to. — "A crown garland of Goulden Roses, gathered, &c. 1612," 8vo. — "The life and

---

[1] Mr. Warton. Vide Observations on the Faerie Queen, 2 vol. 1762, 12mo, passim.

death of Rob. Cecill, E. of Salisbury, 1612," 4to. — "The Hist. of Tom of Lincoln," 4to, is also by R. J., who likewise reprinted "Don Flores of Greece," 4to.

The Seven Champions, though written in a wild inflated style, contains some strong Gothic painting; which seems for the most part copied from the metrical romances of former ages. At least the story of St. George and the fair Sabra is taken almost verbatim from the old poetical legend of "Syr Bevis of Hampton."

This very antique poem was in great fame in Chaucer's time [see above, page 112], and so continued till the introduction of printing, when it ran through several editions: two of which are in black-letter, 4to, "imprinted by Wyllyam Copland," without date; containing great variations.

As a specimen of the poetic powers of this very old rhymist, and as a proof how closely the author of the Seven Champions has followed him, take a description of the dragon slain by Sir Bevis.

> "—— Whan the dragon, that foule is,
> Had a syght of syr Bevis,
> He cast up a loude cry,
> As it had thondred in the sky;
> He turned his bely towarde the son;
> It was greater than any tonne:
> His scales was bryghter then the glas,
> And harder they were than any bras:
> Betwene his shulder and his tayle,
> Was forty fote withoute fayle.
> He waltred out of his denne,
> And Bevis pricked his stede then,
> And to hym a spere he thraste
> That all to shyvers he it braste:
> The dragon then gan Bevis assayle,
> And smote syr Bevis with his tayle:
> Then downe went horse and man,
> And two rybbes of Bevis brused than."

After a long fight, at length, as the dragon was preparing to fly, Sir Bevis

> "Hit him under the wynge,
> As he was in his flyenge,
> There he was tender without scale,

And Bevis thought to be his bale.
He smote after, as I you saye,
With his good sword Morglaye.
Up to the hiltes Morglay yode
Through harte, lyver, bone, and bloude:
To the ground fell the dragon,
Great joye syr Bevis begon.
Under the scales al on hight
He smote off his head forth right,
And put it on a spere:" &c.   Sign. K. iv.

Sir Bevis's dragon is evidently the parent of that in the Seven Champions, see chapter iii. viz., "The dragon no sooner had a sight of him [St. George] but he gave such a terrible peal, as though it had thundered in the elements. ... Betwixt his shoulders and his tail were fifty feet in distance, his scales glistering as bright as silver, but far more hard than brass; his belly of the colour of gold, but bigger than a tun. Thus weltered he from his den, &c. ... The champion ... gave the dragon such a thrust with his spear, that it shivered in a thousand pieces: whereat the furious dragon so fiercely smote him with his venomous tail, that down fell man and horse: in which fall two of St. George's ribs were so bruised, &c. — At length ... St. George smote the dragon under the wing where it was tender without scale, whereby his good sword Ascalon with an easie passage went to the very hilt through both the dragon's heart, liver, bone, and blood. — Then St. George cut off the dragon's head, and pitcht it upon the truncheon of a spear, &c."

The History of the Seven Champions, being written just before the decline of books of chivalry, was never, I believe, translated into any foreign language: but "Le Roman de Beuves of Hantonne" was published at Paris in 1502, 4to, Let. Gothique.

The learned Selden tells us, that about the time of the Norman invasion was Bevis famous with the title of Earl of Southampton, whose residence was at Duncton in Wiltshire; but he observes, that the monkish enlargements of his story have made his very existence doubted. See notes on Poly-Olbion, song iii.

14*

This hath also been the case of St. George himself; whose martial history is allowed to be apocryphal. But to prove that there really existed an orthodox Saint of this name (although little or nothing, it seems, is known of his genuine story), is the subject of "An Historical and Critical Inquiry into the Existence and Character of Saint George, &c. By the Rev. J. Milner, F.S.A., 1792, 8vo."

The equestrian figure worn by the Knights of the Garter, has been understood to be an emblem of the Christian warrior, in his spiritual armour, vanquishing the old serpent.

But on this subject the inquisitive reader may consult "A Dissertation on the Original of the Equestrian Figure of the George and of the Garter, ensigns of the most noble order of that name. Illustrated with copper-plates. By John Pettingal, A.M., Fellow of the Society of Antiquaries, London, 1753," 4to. This learned and curious work the author of the Historical and Critical Inquiry would have done well to have seen.

It cannot be denied, but that the following ballad is for the most part modern: for which reason it would have been thrown to the end of the volume, had not its subject procured it a place here.

LISTEN, lords, in bower and hall,
   I sing the wonderous birth
Of brave St. George, whose valorous arm
   Rid monsters from the earth:

Distressed ladies to relieve   5
   He travell'd many a day;
In honour of the Christian faith,
   Which shall endure for aye.

In Coventry sometime did dwell
   A knight of worthy fame,   10
High steward of this noble realme;
   Lord Albret was his name.

He had to wife a princely dame,
  Whose beauty did excell.
This virtuous lady, being with child,   15
  In sudden sadness fell:

For thirty nights no sooner sleep
  Had clos'd her wakeful eyes,
But, lo! a foul and fearful dream
  Her fancy would surprize: 20

She dreamt a dragon fierce and fell
  Conceiv'd within her womb;
Whose mortal fangs her body rent
  Ere he to life could come.

All woe-begone, and sad was she;   25
  She nourisht constant woe:
Yet strove to hide it from her lord,
  Lest he should sorrow know.

In vaine she strove, her tender lord,
  Who watch'd her slightest look,   30
Discover'd soon her secret pain,
  And soon that pain partook.

And when to him the fearful cause
  She weeping did impart,
With kindest speech he strove to heal   35
  The anguish of her heart.

Be comforted, my lady dear,
  Those pearly drops refrain;
Betide me weal, betide me woe,
  I'll try to ease thy pain.   40

And for this foul and fearful dream,
  That causeth all thy woe,
Trust me I'll travel far away,
  But I'll the meaning knowe.

Then giving many a fond embrace, 45
 And shedding many a teare,
To the weïrd lady of the woods,
 He purpos'd to repaire.

To the weïrd lady of the woods,
 Full long and many a day, 50
Thro' lonely shades and thickets rough
 He winds his weary way.

At length he reach'd a dreary dell
 With dismal yews o'erhung;
Where cypress spred its mournful boughs, 55
 And pois'nous nightshade sprung.

No chearful gleams here pierc'd the gloom,
 He hears no chearful sound;
But shrill night-ravens' yelling scream,
 And serpents hissing round. 60

The shriek of fiends and damned ghosts
 Ran howling thro' his ear:
A chilling horror froze his heart,
 Tho' all unus'd to fear.

Three times he strives to win his way, 65
 And pierce those sickly dews:
Three times to bear his trembling corse
 His knocking knees refuse.

At length upon his beating breast
 He signs the holy crosse; 70
And, rouzing up his wonted might,
 He treads th' unhallow'd mosse.

Beneath a pendant craggy cliff,
 All vaulted like a grave,
And opening in the solid rock, 75
 He found the inchanted cave.

An iron gate clos'd up the mouth,
  All hideous and forlorne;
And, fasten'd by a silver chain,
  Near hung a brazed horne.   80

Then offering up a secret prayer,
  Three times he blowes amaine:
Three times a deepe and hollow sound
  Did answer him againe.

"Sir knight, thy lady beares a son,   85
  Who, like a dragon bright,
Shall prove most dreadful to his foes,
  And terrible in fight.

"His name advanc'd in future times
  On banners shall be worn:
But lo! thy lady's life must passe   90
  Before he can be born."

All sore opprest with fear and doubt
  Long time lord Albret stood;
At length he winds his doubtful way   95
  Back thro' the dreary wood.

Eager to clasp his lovely dame
  Then fast he travels back:
But when he reach'd his castle gate,
  His gate was hung with black.   100

In every court and hall he found
  A sullen silence reigne;
Save where, amid the lonely towers,
  He heard her maidens 'plaine;

And bitterly lament and weep,   105
  With many a grievous grone:
Then sore his bleeding heart misgave,
  His lady's life was gone.

With faultering step he enters in,
   Yet half affraid to goe;   110
With trembling voice asks why they grieve,
   Yet fears the cause to knowe.

"Three times the sun hath rose and set;"
   They said, then stopt to weep:
"Since heaven hath laid thy lady deare   115
   In death's eternal sleep.

"For, ah! in travel sore she fell,
   So sore that she must dye;
Unless some shrewd and cunning leech
   Could ease her presentlye.   120

"But when a cunning leech was fet,
   Too soon declared he,
She, or her babe must lose its life;
   Both saved could not be.

"Now take my life, thy lady said,   125
   My little infant save:
And O commend me to my lord,
   When I am laid in grave.

"O tell him how that precious babe
   Cost him a tender wife: 130
And teach my son to lisp her name,
   Who died to save his life.

"Then calling still upon thy name,
   And praying still for thee;
Without repining or complaint,   135
   Her gentle soul did flee."

What tongue can paint lord Albret's woe,
   The bitter tears he shed,
The bitter pangs that wrung his heart,
   To find his lady dead?   140

He beat his breast: he tore his hair;
  And shedding many a tear,
At length he askt to see his son;
  The son that cost so dear.

New sorrowe seiz'd the damsells all;   145
  At length they faultering say;
"Alas! my lord, how shall we tell?
  Thy son is stoln away.

"Fair as the sweetest flower of spring,
  Such was his infant mien: 150
And on his little body stampt
  Three wonderous marks were seen:

"A blood-red cross was on his arm;
  A dragon on his breast:
A little garter all of gold   155
  Was round his leg exprest.

"Three carefull nurses we provide
  Our little lord to keep:
One gave him sucke, one gave him food,
  And one did lull to sleep.   160

"But lo! all in the dead of night,
  We heard a fearful sound:
Loud thunder clapt; the castle shook;
  And lightning flasht around.

"Dead with affright at first we lay;   165
  But rousing up anon,
We ran to see our little lord:
  Our little lord was gone!

"But how or where we could not tell;
  For lying on the ground,   170
In deep and magic slumbers laid,
  The nurses there we found."

O grief on grief! lord Albret said:
　No more his tongue cou'd say,
When falling in a deadly swoone,   175
　Long time he lifeless lay.

At length restor'd to life and sense
　He nourisht endless woe,
No future joy his heart could taste,
　No future comfort know.   180

So withers on the mountain top
　A fair and stately oake,
Whose vigorous arms are torne away
　By some rude thunder-stroke.

At length his castle irksome grew,   185
　He loathes his wonted home;
His native country he forsakes,
　In foreign lands to roame.

There up and downe he wandered far,
　Clad in a palmer's gown: 190
Till his brown locks grew white as wool,
　His beard as thistle down.

At length, all wearied, down in death
　He laid his reverend head.
Meantime amid the lonely wilds   195
　His little son was bred.

There the weïrd lady of the woods
　Had borne him far away,
And train'd him up in feates of armes,
　And every martial play.   200

　　　⁎

II.

St. George and the Dragon.

THE following ballad is given (with some corrections) from two ancient black-letter copies in the Pepys collection: one of which is in 12mo, the other in folio.

OF Hector's deeds did Homer sing;
 And of the sack of stately Troy,
What griefs fair Helena did bring,
 Which was sir Paris' only joy:
And by my pen I will recite   5
St. George's deeds, an English knight.

Against the Sarazens so rude
 Fought he full long and many a day;
Where many gyants he subdu'd,
 In honour of the Christian way: 10
And after many adventures past
To Egypt land he came at last.

Now, as the story plain doth tell,
 Within that countrey there did rest
A dreadful dragon fierce and fell,   15
 Whereby they were full sore opprest:
Who by his poisonous breath each day,
Did many of the city slay.

The grief whereof did grow so great
 Throughout the limits of the land,   20
That they their wise-men did intreat
 To shew their cunning out of hand;
What way they might this fiend destroy,
That did the countrey thus annoy.

The wise-men all before the king   25
   This answer fram'd incontinent;
The dragon none to death might bring
   By any means they could invent:
His skin more hard than brass was found,
That sword nor spear could pierce nor wound.   30

When this the people understood,
   They cryed out most piteouslye,
The dragon's breath infects their blood,
   That every day in heaps they dye:
Among them such a plague it bred,   35
The living scarce could bury the dead.

No means there were, as they could hear,
   For to appease the dragon's rage,
But to present some virgin clear,
   Whose blood his fury might asswage;   40
Each day he would a maiden eat,
For to allay his hunger great.

This thing by art the wise-men found,
   Which truly must observed be;
Wherefore throughout the city round   45
   A virgin pure of good degree
Was by the king's commission still
Taken up to serve the dragon's will

Thus did the dragon every day
   Untimely crop some virgin flowr,   50
Till all the maids were worn away,
   And none were left him to devour:
Saving the king's fair daughter bright,
Her father's only heart's delight.

Then came the officers to the king   55
   That heavy message to declare,

Which did his heart with sorrow sting;
   She is, quoth he, my kingdom's heir:
O let us all be poisoned here,
Ere she should die, that is my dear.   60

Then rose the people presently,
   And to the king in rage they went;
They said his daughter dear should dye,
   The dragon's fury to prevent.
Our daughters all are dead, quoth they,   65
And have been made the dragon's prey:

And by their blood we rescued were,
   And thou hast sav'd thy life thereby;
And now in sooth it is but faire,
   For us thy daughter so should die.   70
O save my daughter, said the king;
And let ME feel the dragon's sting.

Then fell fair Sabra on her knee,
   And to her father dear did say,
O father, strive not thus for me,   75
   But let me be the dragon's prey;
It may be, for my sake alone
This plague upon the land was thrown.

Tis better I should dye, she said,
   Than all your subjects perish quite;   80
Perhaps the dragon here was laid,
   For my offence to work his spite:
And after he hath suckt my gore,
Your land shall feel the grief no more

What hast thou done, my daughter dear,   85
   For to deserve this heavy scourge?
It is my fault, as may appear,
   Which makes the gods our state to purge;
Then ought I die, to stint the strife,
And to preserve thy happy life.   90

Like mad-men, all the people cried,
   Thy death to us can do no good;
Our safety only doth abide
   In making her the dragon's food.
Lo! here I am, I come, quoth she,   95
Therefore do what you will with me.

Nay stay, dear daughter, quoth the queen,
   And as thou art a virgin bright,
That hast for vertue famous been,
   So let me cloath thee all in white;   100
And crown thy head with flowers sweet,
An ornament for virgins meet.

And when she was attired so,
   According to her mother's mind,
Unto the stake then did she go;   105
   To which her tender limbs they bind:
And being bound to stake a thrall,
She bade farewell unto them all.

Farewell, my father dear, quoth she,
   And my sweet mother meek and mild;   110
Take you no thought nor weep for me,
   For you may have another child:
Since for my country's good I dye,
Death I receive most willinglye.

The king and queen and all their train   115
   With weeping eyes went then their way,
And let their daughter there remain,
   To be the hungry dragon's prey:
But as she did there weeping lye,
Behold St. George came riding by.   120

And seeing there a lady bright
   So rudely tyed unto a stake,

As well became a valiant knight,
 He straight to her his way did take:
Tell me, sweet maiden, then quoth he,   125
What caitif thus abuseth thee?

And, lo! by Christ his cross I vow,
 Which here is figured on my breast,
I will revenge it on his brow,
 And break my lance upon his chest: 130
And speaking thus whereas he stood,
The dragon issued from the wood.

The lady that did first espy
 The dreadful dragon coming so,
Unto St. George aloud did cry,   135
 And willed him away to go;
Here comes that cursed fiend, quoth she,
That soon will make an end of me.

St. George then looking round about,
 The fiery dragon soon espy'd,
And like a knight of courage stout,   140
 Against him did most fiercely ride;
And with such blows he did him greet,
 He fell beneath his horse's feet.

For with his launce that was so strong,   145
 As he came gaping in his face,
In at his mouth he thrust along;
 For he could pierce no other place;
And thus within the lady's view
This mighty dragon straight he slew.   150

The savour of his poisoned breath
 Could do this holy knight no harı
Thus he the lady sav'd from death,
 And home he led her by the arm;
Which when king Ptolemy did see,   155
There was great mirth and melody.

When as that valiant champion there
   Had slain the dragon in the field,
To court he brought the lady fair,
   Which to their hearts much joy did yield.   160
He in the court of Egypt staid
Till he most falsely was betray'd.

That lady dearly lov'd the knight,
   He counted her his only joy;
But when their love was brought to light,   165
   It turn'd unto their great annoy:
Th' Morocco king was in the court,
Who to the orchard did resort,

Dayly to take the pleasant air,
   For pleasure sake he us'd to walk,   170
Under a wall he oft did hear
   St. George with lady Sabra talk:
Their love he shew'd unto the king,
Which to St. George great woe did bring.

Those kings together did devise   175
   To make the Christian knight away,
With letters him in curteous wise
   They straightway sent to Persia:
But wrote to the sophy him to kill,
And treacherously his blood to spill.   180

Thus they for good did him reward
   With evil, and most subtilly
By such vile meanes they had regard
   To work his death most cruelly;
Who, as through Persia land he rode,   185
With zeal destroy'd each idol god.

For which offence he straight was thrown
   Into a dungeon dark and deep;

Where, when he thought his wrongs upon,
  He bitterly did wail and weep:
Yet like a knight of courage stout,   190
At length his way he digged out.

Three grooms of the king of Persia
  By night this valiant champion slew,
Though he had fasted many a day;   195
  And then away from thence he flew
On the best steed the sophy had;
Which when he knew he was full mad.

Towards Christendom he made his flight,
  But met a gyant by the way,   200
With whom in combat he did fight
  Most valiantly a summer's day:
Who yet, for all his bats of steel,
Was forc'd the sting of death to feel.

Back o'er the seas with many bands   205
  Of warlike souldiers soon he past,
Vowing upon those heathen lands
  To work revenge; which at the last,
Ere thrice three years were gone and spent,
He wrought unto his heart's content.   210

Save onely Egypt land he spar'd
  For Sabra bright her only sake,
And, ere for her he had regard,
  He meant a tryal kind to make:
Mean while the king, o'ercome in field,   215
Unto saint George did quickly yield.

Then straight Morocco's king he slew,
  And took fair Sabra to his wife,
But meant to try if she were true
  Ere with her he would lead his life: 220
And, tho' he had her in his train,
She did a virgin pure remain.

Percy. III.   15

Toward England then that lovely dame
 The brave St. George conducted strait,
An eunuch also with them came,   225
 Who did upon the lady wait;
These three from Egypt went alone.
Now mark St. George's valour shown.

When as they in a forest were,
 The lady did desire to rest;   230
Mean while St. George to kill a deer,
 For their repast did think it best:
Leaving her with the eunuch there,
Whilst he did go to kill the deer.

But lo! all in his absence came   235
 Two hungry lyons fierce and fell,
And tore the eunuch on the same
 In pieces small, the truth to tell;
Down by the lady then they laid,
Whereby they shew'd, she was a maid.   240

But when he came from hunting back,
 And did behold this heavy chance,
Then for his lovely virgin's sake
 His courage strait he did advance,
And came into the lions sight,   245
Who ran at him with all their might.

Their rage did him no whit dismay,
 Who, like a stout and valiant knight,
Did both the hungry lyons slay
 Within the lady Sabra's sight: 250
Who all this while sad and demure,
There stood most like a virgin pure.

Now when St. George did surely know
 This lady was a virgin true,

His heart was glad, that erst was woe,   255
   And all his love did soon renew:
He set her on a palfrey steed,
And towards England came with speed.

Where being in short space arriv'd
   Unto his native dwelling place;   260
Therein with his dear love he liv'd,
   And fortune did his nuptials grace:
They many years of joy did see,
And led their lives at Coventry.

III.

Love will find out the Way.

THIS excellent song is ancient: but we could only give it from a modern copy.

OVER the mountains,
   And over the waves;
Under the fountains,
   And under the graves;
Under floods that are deepest,   5
   Which Neptune obey;
Over rocks that are steepest,
   Love will find out the way.

Where there is no place
   For the glow-worm to lye;   10
Where there is no space
   For receipt of a fly;
Where the midge dares not venture,
   Lest herself fast she lay;
If love come, he will enter,   15
   And soon find out his way.

15*

You may esteem him
    A child for his might;
Or you may deem him
    A coward from his flight: 20
But if she, whom love doth honour,
    Be conceal'd from the day,
Set a thousand guards upon her,
    Love will find out the way.

Some think to lose him,   25
    By having him confin'd;
And some do suppose him,
    Poor thing, to be blind;
But if ne'er so close ye wall him,
    Do the best that you may,   30
Blind love, if so ye call him,
    Will find out his way.

You may train the eagle
    To stoop to your fist;
Or you may inveigle   35
    The phenix of the east;
The lioness, ye may move her
    To give o'er her prey;
But you'll ne'er stop a lover:
    He will find out his way.   40

**

IV.

Lord Thomas and Fair Annet,

A SCOTTISH BALLAD.

SEEMS to be composed (not without improvements) out of
two ancient English ones, printed in the former part of this
volume. See book i., ballad xv.; and book ii., ballad iv. If
this had been the original, the authors of those two ballads
would hardly have adopted two such different stories: besides,

this contains enlargements not to be found in either of the
others. It is given, with some corrections, from a MS. copy
transmitted from Scotland.

Lord Thomas and fair Annet
   Sate a' day on a hill;
Whan night was cum, and sun was sett,
   They had not talkt their fill.

Lord Thomas said a word in jest,   5
   Fair Annet took it ill:
A'! I will nevir wed a wife
   Against my ain friends will.

Gif ye wull nevir wed a wife,
   A wife wull neir wed yee.   10
Sae he is hame to tell his mither,
   And knelt upon his knee:

O rede, O rede, mither, he says,
   A gude rede gie to mee:
O sall I tak the nut-browne bride,   15
   And let faire Annet bee?

The nut-browne bride haes gowd and gear,
   Fair Annet she has gat nane;
And the little beauty fair Annet has,
   O it wull soon be gane!   20

And he has till his brother gane:
   Now, brother, rede ye mee;
A' sall I marrie the nut-browne bride,
   And let fair Annet bee?

The nut-browne bride has oxen, brother,   25
   The nut-browne bride has kye;
I wad hae ye marrie the nut-browne bride,
   And cast fair Annet bye.

Her oxen may dye i' the house, Billie,
　And her kye into the byre; 30
And I sall hae nothing to my sell,
　Bot a fat fadge by the fyre.

And he has till his sister gane:
　Now, sister, rede ye mee;
O sall I marrie the nut-browne bride, 35
　And set fair Annet free?

Ise rede ye tak fair Annet, Thomas,
　And let the browne bride alane;
Lest ye sould sigh and say, Alace!
　What is this we brought hame? 40

No, I will tak my mithers counsel,
　And marrie me owt o' hand;
And I will tak the nut-browne bride;
　Fair Annet may leive the land.

Up then rose fair Annets father 45
　Twa hours or it wer day,
And he is gane into the bower,
　Wherein fair Annet lay.

Rise up, rise up, fair Annet, he says,
　Put on your silken sheene; 50
Let us gae to St. Maries kirke,
　And see that rich weddeen.

My maides, gae to my dressing-roome,
　And dress to me my hair;
Whair-eir yee laid a plait before, 55
　See yee lay ten times mair.

My maids, gae to my dressing-room,
　And dress to me my smock;
The one half is o' the holland fine,
　The other o' needle-work. 60

The horse fair Annet rade upon,
  He amblit like the wind,
Wi' siller he was shod before,
  Wi' burning gowd behind.

Four and twanty siller bells   65
  Wer a' tyed till his mane,
And yae tift o' the norland wind,
  They tinkled ane by ane.

Four and twanty gay gude knichts
  Rade by fair Annets side,   70
And four and twanty fair ladies,
  As gin she had bin a bride.

And whan she cam to Maries kirk,
  She sat on Maries stean:
The cleading that fair Annet had on   75
  It skinkled in their een.

And whan she cam into the kirk,
  She shimmer'd like the sun;
The belt that was about her waist,
  Was a' wi' pearles bedone.   80

She sat her by the nut-browne bride,
  And her een they wer sae clear,
Lord Thomas he clean forgat the bride,
  When fair Annet she drew near.

He had a rose into his hand,   85
  And he gave it kisses three,
And reaching by the nut-browne bride,
  Laid it on fair Annets knee.

Up than spak the nut-browne bride,
  She spak wi' meikle spite;   90
And whair gat ye that rose-water,
  That does mak yee sae white?

O I did get the rose-water
  Whair ye wull neir get nane,
For I did get that very rose-water   95
  Into my mithers wame.

The bride she drew a long bodkin,
  Frae out her gay head-gear,
And strake fair Annet unto the heart,
  That word she nevir spak mair.   100

Lord Thomas he saw fair Annet wex pale,
  And marvelit what mote bee:
But whan he saw her dear hearts blude,
  A' wood-wroth wexed hee.

He drew his dagger, that was sae sharp,   105
  That was sae sharp and meet,
And drave into the nut-browne bride,
  That fell deid at his feit.

Now stay for me, dear Annet, he sed,
  Now stay, my dear, he cry'd;   110
Then strake the dagger untill his heart,
  And fell deid by her side.

Lord Thomas was buried without kirk-wa',
  Fair Annet within the quiere;
And o' the tane thair grew a birk,   115
  The other a bonny briere.

And ay they grew, and ay they threw,
  As they wad faine be neare;
And by this ye may ken right weil,
  They were twa luvers deare.   120

V.

Unfading Beauty.

THIS little beautiful sonnet is reprinted from a small volume of "Poems by Thomas Carew, Esq., one of the gentlemen of the privie-chamber, and sewer in ordinary to his majesty. (Charles I.) Lond. 1640." This elegant and almost-forgotten writer, whose poems have been deservedly revived, died, in the prime of his age, in 1639.

In the original follows a third stanza; which, not being of general application, nor of equal merit, I have ventured to omit.

HEE, that loves a rosie cheeke,
   Or a corall lip admires,
Or from star-like eyes doth seeke
   Fuell to maintaine his fires,
As old time makes these decay,   5
So his flames must waste away.

But a smooth and stedfast mind,
   Gentle thoughts, and calme desires,
Hearts with equal love combin'd,
   Kindle never-dying fires: 10
Where these are not, I despise
Lovely cheekes, or lips, or eyes.
   *   *   *   *   *

VI.

George Barnwell.

THE subject of this ballad is sufficiently popular from the modern play which is founded upon it. This was written by George Lillo, a jeweller of London, and first acted about 1730. As for the ballad, it was printed at least as early as the middle of the last century.

It is here given from three old printed copies, which exhibit a strange intermixture of Roman and black-letter. It is also collated with another copy in the Ashmole collection at Oxford, which is thus entitled, "An excellent ballad of George Barnwell, an apprentice of London, who . . . thrice robbed his master and murdered his vncle in Ludlow." The tune is *The Merchant*.

This tragical narrative seems to relate a real fact; but when it happened, I have not been able to discover.

────────────

THE FIRST PART.

ALL youths of fair Englànd
　　That dwell both far and near,
Regard my story that I tell,
　　And to my song give ear.

A London lad I was,　　　　　　　　　　　　　5
　　A merchant's prentice bound;
My name George Barnwell; that did spend
　　My master many a pound.

Take heed of harlots then,
　　And their enticing trains;　　　　　　　　　10
For by that means I have been brought
　　To hang alive in chains.

As I, upon a day,
　　Was walking through the street
About my master's business,　　　　　　　　　15
　　A wanton I did meet.

A gallant dainty dame,
　　And sumptuous in attire;
With smiling look she greeted me,
　　And did my name require.　　　　　　　　　20

Which when I had declar'd,
  She gave me then a kiss,
And said, if I would come to her,
  I should have more than this.

Fair mistress, then quoth I,   25
  If I the place may know,
This evening I will be with you,
  For I abroad must go

To gather monies in,
  That are my master's due: 30
And ere that I do home return,
  I'll come and visit you.

Good Barnwell, then quoth she,
  Do thou to Shoreditch come,
And ask for Mrs. Millwood's house,   35
  Next door unto the Gun.

And trust me on my truth,
  If thou keep touch with me,
My dearest friend, as my own heart
  Thou shalt right welcome be.   40

Thus parted we in peace,
  And home I passed right;
Then went abroad, and gathered in,
  By six o'clock at night,

An hundred pound and one: 45
  With bag under my arm
I went to Mrs. Millwood's house,
  And thought on little harm;

And knocking at the door,
  Straightway herself came down;   50
Rustling in most brave attire,
  With hood and silken gown.

Who, through her beauty bright,
  So gloriously did shine,
That she amaz'd my dazzling eyes,   55
  She seemed so divine.

She took me by the hand,
  And with a modest grace,
Welcome, sweet Barnwell, then quoth she,
  Unto this homely place.   60

And since I have thee found
  As good as thy word to be:
A homely supper, ere we part,
  Thou shalt take here with me.

O pardon me, quoth I,   65
  Fair mistress, I you pray;
For why, out of my master's house,
  So long I dare not stay.

Alas, good sir, she said,
  Are you so strictly ty'd,   70
You may not with your dearest friend
  One hour or two abide?

Faith, then the case is hard:
  If it be so, quoth she,
I would I were a prentice bound,   75
  To live along with thee:

Therefore, my dearest George,
  List well what I shall say,
And do not blame a woman much,
  Her fancy to bewray.   80

Let not affection's force
  Be counted lewd desire;
Nor think it not immodesty,
  I should thy love require.

With that she turn'd aside,
  And with a blushing red,
A mournful motion she bewray'd
  By hanging down her head.   85

A handkerchief she had
  All wrought with silk and gold: 90
Which she to stay her trickling tears
  Before her eyes did hold.

This thing unto my sight
  Was wondrous rare and strange;
And in my soul and inward thought
  It wrought a sudden change: 95

That I so hardy grew,
  To take her by the hand:
Saying, Sweet mistress, why do you
  So dull and pensive stand?   100

Call me no mistress now,
  But Sarah, thy true friend,
Thy servant, Millwood, honouring thee,
  Until her life hath end.

If thou wouldst here alledge,   105
  Thou art in years a boy;
So was Adonis, yet was he
  Fair Venus' only joy.

Thus I, who ne'er before
  Of woman found such grace,   110
But seeing now so fair a dame
  Give me a kind embrace,

I supt with her that night,
  With joys that did abound;
And for the same paid presently,   115
  In money twice three pound.

An hundred kisses then,
   For my farewel she gave;
Crying, Sweet Barnwell, when shall I
   Again thy company have?   120

O stay not hence too long,
   Sweet George, have me in mind.
Her words bewicht my childishness,
   She uttered them so kind:

So that I made a vow,   125
   Next Sunday without fail,
With my sweet Sarah once again
   To tell some pleasant tale.

When she heard me say so,
   The tears fell from her eye;   130
O George, quoth she, if thou dost fail,
   Thy Sarah sure will dye.

Though long, yet loe! at last,
   The appointed day was come,
That I must with my Sarah meet;   135
   Having a mighty sum

Of money in my hand[1],
   Unto her house went I,
Whereas my love upon her bed
   In saddest sort did lye.   140

What ails my heart's delight,
   My Sarah dear? quoth I;
Let not my love lament and grieve,
   Nor sighing pine, and die.

---

[1] The having a sum of money with him on Sunday, &c. shows this narrative to have been penned before the civil wars: the strict observance of the Sabbath was owing to the change of manners at that period.

But tell me, dearest friend,   145
 What may thy woes amend,
And thou shalt lack no means of help,
 Though forty pound I spend.

With that she turn'd her head,
 And sickly thus did say,   150
Oh me, sweet George, my grief is great,
 Ten pound I have to pay

Unto a cruel wretch;
 And God he knows, quoth she,
I have it not. Tush, rise, I said, 155
 And take it here of me.

Ten pounds, nor ten times ten,
 Shall make my love decay.
Then from my bag into her lap,
 I cast ten pound straightway. 160

All blithe and pleasant then,
 To banqueting we go;
She proffered me to lye with her,
 And said it should be so.

And after that same time,   165
 I gave her store of coyn,
Yea, sometimes fifty pound at once;
 All which I did purloyn.

And thus I did pass on;
 Until my master then   170
Did call to have his reckoning in
 Cast up among his men.

The which when as I heard,
 I knew not what to say:
For well I knew that I was out 175
 Two hundred pound that day.

Then from my master straight
  I ran in secret sort;
And unto Sarah Millwood there
  My case I did report.　　　　　180

"But how she us'd this youth,
  In this his care and woe,
And all a strumpet's wiley ways,
  The SECOND PART may showe."

THE SECOND PART.

YOUNG Barnwell comes to thee,
  Sweet Sarah, my delight;
I am undone unless thou stand
  My faithful friend this night.

Our master to accompts　　　　　5
  Hath just occasion found;
And I am caught behind the hand
  Above two hundred pound:

And now his wrath to 'scape,
  My love, I fly to thee,　　　　　10
Hoping some time I may remaine
  In safety here with thee.

With that she knit her brows,
  And looking all aquoy,
Quoth she, What should I have to do　　15
  With any prentice boy?

And seeing you have purloyn'd
  Your master's goods away,
The case is bad, and therefore here
  You shall no longer stay.　　　　　20

Why, dear, thou know'st, I said,
  How all which I could get,

I gave it, and did spend it all
   Upon thee every whit.

Quoth she, Thou art a knave,   25
   To charge me in this sort,
Being a woman of credit fair,
   And known of good report:

Therefore I tell thee flat,
   Be packing with good speed;   30
I do defie thee from my heart,
   And scorn thy filthy deed.

Is this the friendship, that
   You did to me protest?
Is this the great affection, which   35
   You so to me exprest?

Now fie on subtle shrews!
   The best is, I may speed
To get a lodging any where
   For money in my need.   40

False woman, now farewell,
   Whilst twenty pound doth last,
My anchor in some other haven
   With freedom I will cast.

When she perceiv'd by this,   45
   I had store of money there:
Stay, George, quoth she, thou art too quick:
   Why, man, I did but jeer:

Dost think for all my speech,
   That I would let thee go?   50
Faith no, said she, my love to thee
   I wiss is more than so.

You scorne a prentice boy,
    I heard you just now swear,
Wherefore I will not trouble you.——   55
        ——Nay, George, hark in thine ear;

Thou shalt not go to-night,
    What chance soe're befall:
But, man, we'll have a bed for thee,
    Or else the devil take all.   60

So I by wiles bewitcht,
    And snar'd with fancy still,
Had then no power to 'get' away,
    Or to withstand her will.

For wine on wine I call'd,   65
    And cheer upon good cheer;
And nothing in the world I thought
    For Sarah's love too dear

Whilst in her company,
    I had such merriment;   70
All, all too little I did think,
    That I upon her spent.

A fig for care and thought!
    When all my gold is gone,
In faith, my girl, we will have more,   75
    Whoever I light upon.

My father's rich, why then
    Should I want store of gold?
Nay with a father sure, quoth she,
    A son may well make bold.   80

I've a sister richly wed,
    I'll rob her ere I'll want.
Nay then, quoth Sarah, they may well
    Consider of your scant.

Nay, I an uncle have;　　　　　　　85
　　At Ludlow he doth dwell:
He is a grazier, which in wealth
　　Doth all the rest excell.

Ere I will live in lack,
　　And have no coyn for thee:　　　90
I'll rob his house, and murder him.
　　Why should you not? quoth she:

Was I a man, ere I
　　Would live in poor estate;
On father, friends, and all my kin,　　95
　　I would my talons grate.

For without money, George,
　　A man is but a beast:
But bringing money, thou shalt be
　　Always my welcome guest.　　　100

For shouldst thou be pursued
　　With twenty hues and cryes,
And with a warrant searched for
　　With Argus' hundred eyes,

Yet here thou shalt be safe;　　　105
　　Such privy ways there be,
That if they sought an hundred years,
　　They could not find out thee.

And so carousing both
　　Their pleasures to content:　　　110
George Barnwell had in little space
　　His money wholly spent.

Which done, to Ludlow straight
　　He did provide to go,
To rob his wealthy uncle there;　　115
　　His minion would it so.

16*

And once he thought to take
    His father by the way,
But that he fear'd his master had
    Took order for his stay [1].   120

Unto his uncle then
    He rode with might and main,
Who with a welcome and good cheer
    Did Barnwell entertain.

One fortnight's space he stayed,   125
    Until it chanced so,
His uncle with his cattle did
    Unto a market go.

His kinsman rode with him,
    Where he did see right plain,   130
Great store of money he had took:
    When coming home again,

Sudden within a wood,
    He struck his uncle down,
And beat his brains out of his head;   135
    So sore he crackt his crown.

Then seizing fourscore pound,
    To London straight he hyed,
And unto Sarah Millwood all
    The cruell fact descryed.   140

Tush, 'tis no matter, George,
    So we the money have.
To have good cheer in jolly sort,
    And deck us fine and brave.

Thus lived in filthy sort,   145
    Until their store was gone:

---

[1] *i. e.* for stopping, and apprehending him at his father's.

When means to get them any more,
  I wis, poor George had none.

Therefore in railing sort,
  She thrust him out of door;   150
Which is the just reward of those,
  Who spend upon a whore.

O! do me not disgrace
  In this my need, quoth he.
She call'd him thief and murderer,   155
  With all the spight might be:

To the constable she sent,
  To have him apprehended;
And shewed how far, in each degree,
  He had the laws offended.   160

When Barnwell saw her drift,
  To sea he got straightway;
Where fear and sting of conscience
  Continually on him lay.

Unto the lord mayor then,   165
  He did a letter write;
In which his own and Sarah's fault
  He did at large recite.

Whereby she seized was
  And then to Ludlow sent:
Where she was judg'd, condemn'd, and hang'd,   170
  For murder incontinent.

There dyed this gallant quean,
  Such was her greatest gains:
For murder in Polonia,   175
  Was Barnwell hang'd in chains.

Lo! here's the end of youth,
  That after harlots haunt;
Who in the spoil of other men,
  About the streets do flaunt.   180

VII.

The Stedfast Shepherd.

THESE beautiful stanzas were written by George Wither,
of whom some account was given in the former part of this
volume: see the song entitled, *The Shepherd's Resolution*,
book ii. song xxii. In the first edition of this work, only a
small fragment of this sonnet was inserted. It was after-
wards rendered more complete and entire by the addition of
five stanzas more, extracted from Wither's pastoral poem,
entitled, *The Mistress of Philarete*, of which this song makes
a part. It is now given still more correct and perfect by
comparing it with another copy, printed by the author in his
improved edition of *The Shepherd's Hunting*, 1620, 8vo.

HENCE away, thou Syren, leave me,
  Pish! unclaspe these wanton armes;
Sugred words can ne'er deceive me,
  (Though they prove a thousand charmes).
    Fie, fie, forbeare;   5
    No common snare
Can ever my affection chaine:
    Thy painted baits,
    And poore deceits,
Are all bestowed on me in vaine.   10

I'me no slave, to such as you be;
  Neither shall that snowy brest,
Rowling eye, and lip of ruby
  Ever robb me of my rest:
    Goe, goe, display   15
    Thy beautie's ray

To some more-soone enamour'd swaine:
   Those common wiles
   Of sighs and smiles
Are all bestowed on me in vaine.   20

I have elsewhere vowed a dutie;
  Turne away thy tempting eye:
Shew not me a painted beautie;
  These impostures I defie:
   My spirit lothes   25
   Where gawdy clothes
And fained othes may love obtaine:
   I love her so,
   Whose looke sweares No;
That all your labours will be vaine.   30

Can he prize the tainted posies,
  Which on every brest are worne;
That may plucke the virgin roses
  From their never-touched thorne?
   I can goe rest   35
   On her sweet brest,
That is the pride of Cynthia's traine:
   Then stay thy tongue;
   Thy mermaid song
Is all bestowed on me in vaine.   40

Hee's a foole, that basely dallies,
  Where each peasant mates with him:
Shall I haunt the thronged vallies,
  Whilst ther's noble hils to climbe?
   No, no, though clownes   45
   Are scar'd with frownes,
I know the best can but disdaine:
   And those Ile prove:
   So will thy love
Be all bestowed on me in vaine.   50

I doe scorne to vow a dutie,
  Where each lustfull lad may wooe:
Give me her, whose sun-like beautie
  Buzzards dare not soare unto:
    Shee, shee it is   55
    Affoords that blisse
For which I would refuse no paine:
    But such as you,
    Fond fooles, adieu;
You seeke to captive me in vaine.   60

Leave me then, you Syrens, leave me;
  Seeke no more to worke my harmes:
Craftie wiles cannot deceive me,
  Who am proofe against your charmes:
    You labour may   65
    To lead astray
The heart, that constant shall remaine:
    And I the while
    Will sit and smile
To see you spend your time in vaine.   70

VIII.

The Spanish Virgin, or Effects of Jealousy.

THE subject of this ballad is taken from a folio collection of tragical stories, entitled, "The theatre of God's judgments, by Dr. Beard and Dr. Taylor, 1642." Pt. ii. p. 89. — The text is given (with corrections) from two copies; one of them in black-letter in the Pepys collection. In this every stanza is accompanied with the following distich by way of burden:

> "Oh jealousie! thou art nurst in holl:
> Depart from hence, and therein dwell."

ALL tender hearts, that ake to hear
   Of those that suffer wrong;
All you, that never shed a tear,
   Give heed unto my song.

Fair Isabella's tragedy   5
   My tale doth far exceed:
Alas, that so much cruelty
   In female hearts should breed!

In Spain a lady liv'd of late,
   Who was of high degree;   10
Whose wayward temper did create
   Much woe and misery.

Strange jealousies so fill'd her head
   With many a vain surmize,
She thought her lord had wrong'd her bed,   15
   And did her love despise.

A gentlewoman passing fair,
   Did on this lady wait;
With bravest dames she might compare;
   Her beauty was compleat.   20

Her lady cast a jealous eye
   Upon this gentle maid;
And taxt her with disloyaltye;
   And did her oft upbraid.

In silence still this maiden meek   25
   Her bitter taunts would bear,
While oft adown her lovely cheek
   Would steal the falling tear.

In vain in humble sort she strove
   Her fury to disarm: 30
As well the meekness of the dove
   The bloody hawke might charm.

Her lord, of humour light and gay,
   And innocent the while,
As oft as she came in his way,   35
   Would on the damsell smile.

And oft before his lady's face,
   As thinking her her friend,
He would the maiden's modest grace
   And comeliness commend.   40

All which incens'd his lady so,
   She burnt with wrath extreame;
At length the fire that long did glow,
   Burst forth into a flame.

For on a day it so befell,   45
   When he was gone from home,
The lady all with rage did swell,
   And to the damsell come.

And charging her with great offence,
   And many a grievous fault;   50
She bade her servants drag her thence,
   Into a dismal vault,

That lay beneath the common-shore:
   A dungeon dark and deep:
Where they were wont, in days of yore,   55
   Offenders great to keep.

There never light of chearful day
   Dispers'd the hideous gloom;
But dank and noisome vapours play
   Around the wretched room: 60

And adders, snakes, and toads therein,
   As afterwards was known,
Long in this loathsome vault had bin,
   And were to monsters grown.

Into this foul and fearful place,   65
 The fair one innocent
Was cast, before her lady's face;
 Her malice to content.

This maid no sooner enter'd is,
 But strait, alas! she hears   70
The toads to croak, and snakes to hiss:
 Then grievously she fears.

Soon from their holes the vipers creep,
 And fiercely her assail:
Which makes the damsel sorely weep, 75
 And her sad fate bewail.

With her fair hands she strives in vain
 Her body to defend:
With shrieks and cries she doth complain,
 But all is to no end.   80

A servant listning near the door,
 Struck with her doleful noise,
Strait ran his lady to implore;
 But she'll not hear his voice.

With bleeding heart he goes agen 85
 To mark the maiden's groans;
And plainly hears, within the den,
 How she herself bemoans.

Again he to his lady hies
 With all the haste he may: 90
She into furious passion flies,
 And orders him away.

Still back again does he return
 To hear her tender cries;
The virgin now had ceas'd to mourn; 95
 Which fill'd him with surprize.

In grief, and horror, and affright,
　　He listens at the walls;
But finding all was silent quite,
　　He to his lady calls.　　　　　　　　　　　100

Too sure, O lady, now quoth he,
　　Your cruelty hath sped;
Make hast, for shame, and come and see;
　　I fear the virgin's dead.

She starts to hear her sudden fate,　　　　　105
　　And does with torches run:
But all her haste was now too late,
　　For death his worst had done.

The door being open'd, strait they found
　　The virgin stretch'd along:　　　　　　　110
Two dreadful snakes had wrapt her round,
　　Which her to death had stung.

One round her legs, her thighs, her wast,
　　Had twined his fatal wreath:
The other close her neck embrac'd,　　　　　115
　　And stopt her gentle breath.

The snakes, being from her body thrust,
　　Their bellies were so fill'd,
That with excess of blood they burst,
　　Thus with their prey were kill'd.　　　　　120

The wicked lady, at this sight,
　　With horror strait ran mad;
So raving dy'd, as was most right,
　　'Cause she no pity had.

Let me advise you, ladies all,　　　　　　　125
　　Of jealousy beware:
It causeth many a one to fall,
　　And is the devil's snare.

　　　　　　　　　　　　　　　　　　　⁎

IX.

Jealousy, Tyrant of the Wind.

THIS song is by Dryden, being inserted in his Tragi-Comedy of *Love Triumphant*, &c.   On account of the subject, it is inserted here.

WHAT state of life can be so blest,
As love that warms the gentle brest;
Two souls in one: the same desire
To grant the bliss, and to require?
   If in this heaven a hell we find,   5
     Tis all from thee,
     O Jealousie!
   Thou tyrant, tyrant of the mind.

All other ills, though sharp they prove,
Serve to rèfine and perfect love: 10
In absence, or unkind disdaine,
Sweet hope relieves the lovers paine:
   But, oh, no cure but death we find
     To sett us free
     From jealousie,   15
   Thou tyrant, tyrant of the mind.

False in thy glass all objects are,
Some sett too near, and some too far;
Thou art the fire of endless night,
The fire that burns, and gives no light.   20
   All torments of the damn'd we find
     In only thee,
     O Jealousie!
   Thou tyrant, tyrant of the mind.

X.

Constant Penelope.

THE ladies are indebted for the following notable documents to the Pepys collection, where the original is preserved in black-letter, and is entitled, "A Looking-Glass for Ladies, or a Mirrour for Married Women. Tune, Queen Dido, or Troy town."

———

WHEN Greeks and Trojans fell at strife,
    And lords in armour bright were seen,
When many a gallant lost his life
    About fair Hellen, beauty's queen;
Ulysses, general so free,   5
Did leave his dear Penelope.

When she this wofull news did hear,
    That he would to the warrs of Troy;
For grief she shed full many a tear,
    At parting from her only joy: 10
Her ladies all about her came,
To comfort up this Grecian dame.

Ulysses, with a heavy heart,
    Unto her then did mildly say,
The time is come that we must part: 15
    My honour calls me hence away;
Yet in my absence, dearest, be
My constant wife, Penelope

Let me no longer live, she sayd,
    Then to my lord I true remain;   20
My honour shall not be betray'd
    Until I see my love again;
For I will ever constant prove,
As is the loyal turtle-dove.

Thus did they part with heavy chear,   25
  And to the ships his way he took;
Her tender eyes dropt many a tear;
  Still casting many a longing look:
She saw him on the surges glide,
And unto Neptune thus she cry'd: 30

Thou god, whose power is in the deep,
  And rulest in the ocean main,
My loving lord in safety keep
  Till he return to me again:
That I his person may behold,   35
To me more precious far than gold.

Then straight the ships with nimble sails
  Were all convey'd out of her sight:
Her cruel fate she then bewails,
  Since she had lost her hearts delight.   40
Now shall my practice be, quoth she,
True vertue and humility

My patience I will put in ure,
  My charity I will extend;
Since for my woe there is no cure,   45
  The helpless now I will befriend:
The widow and the fatherless
I will relieve, when in distress.

Thus she continued year by year
  In doing good to every one;   50
Her fame was noised every where,
  To young and old the same was known,
That she no company would mind,
Who were to vanity inclin'd.

Mean while Ulysses fought for fame,   55
  'Mongst Trojans hazarding his life:

Young gallants, hearing of her name,
  Came flocking for to tempt his wife:
For she was lovely, young, and fair,
No lady might with her compare,   60

With costly gifts and jewels fine,
  They did endeavour her to win;
With banquets and the choicest wine,
  For to allure her unto sin:
Most persons were of high degree,   65
Who courted fair Penelope.

With modesty and comely grace
  Their wanton suits she did denye:
No tempting charms could e'er deface
  Her dearest husband's memorye;   70
But constant she would still remain,
Hopeing to see him once again.

Her book her dayly comfort was,
  And that she often did peruse;
She seldom looked in her glass;   75
  Powder and paint she ne'er would use.
I wish all ladies were as free
From pride, as was Penelope.

She in her needle took delight,
  And likewise in her spinning-wheel; 80
Her maids about her every night
  Did use the distaff and the reel:
The spiders, that on rafters twine,
Scarce spin a thread more soft and fine.

Sometimes she would bewail the loss   85
  And absence of her dearest love:
Sometimes she thought the seas to cross,
  Her fortune on the waves to prove.
I fear my lord is slain, quoth she,
He stays so from Penelope.

At length the ten years siege of Troy
 Did end; in flames the city burn'd;
And to the Grecians was great joy,
 To see the towers to ashes turn'd:
Then came Ulysses home to see   95
His constant, dear, Penelope.

O blame her not if she was glad,
 When she her lord again had seen.
Thrice-welcome home, my dear, she said,
 A long time absent thou hast been: 100
The wars shall never more deprive
Me of my lord whilst I'm alive.

Fair ladies all, example take;
 And hence a worthy lesson learn,
All youthful follies to forsake,   105
 And vice from virtue to discern:
And let all women strive to be
As constant as Penelope.

XI.

To Lucasta, on going to the Wars.

By Colonel Richard Lovelace: from the volume of his
poems, entitled, *Lucasta*, Lond. 1649, 12mo. The elegance
of this writer's manner would be more admired if it had
somewhat more of simplicity.

Tell me not, sweet, I am unkinde,
 That from the nunnerie
Of thy chaste breast and quiet minde,
 To warre and armes I flie.

True, a new mistresse now I chase,　　　　5
　　The first foe in the field;
And with a stronger faith imbrace
　　A sword, a horse, a shield.

Yet this inconstancy is such,
　　As you too shall adore;　　　　　　10
I could not love thee, deare, so much,
　　Lov'd I not honour more.

XII.

Valentine and Ursine.

THE old story-book of Valentine and Orson (which sug-
gested the plan of this tale, but it is not strictly followed in
it) was originally a translation from the French, being one
of their earliest attempts at romance.　See "Le Bibliothéque
de Romans, &c."

The circumstance of the bridge of bells is taken from the
old metrical legend of *Sir Bevis*, and has also been copied in
the *Seven Champions*.　The original lines are,

> "Over the dyke a bridge there lay,
> 　That man and beest might passe away:
> 　Under the brydge were sixty belles;
> 　Right as the Romans telles;
> 　That there might no man passe in,
> 　But all they rang with a gyn."
> 　　　　　　　　　Sign. E. iv.

In the Editor's folio MS. was an old poem on this subject,
in a wretched corrupt state, unworthy the press: from which
were taken such particulars as could be adopted.

PART THE FIRST.

WHEN Flora 'gins to decke the fields
　　With colours fresh and fine,
Then holy clerkes their mattins sing
　　To good Saint Valentine!

The king of France that morning fair   5
  He would a hunting ride:
To Artois forest prancing forth
  In all his princelye pride.

To grace his sports a courtly train
  Of gallant peers attend;   10
And with their loud and cheerful cryes
  The hills and valleys rend.

Through the deep forest swift they pass,
  Through woods and thickets wild;
When down within a lonely dell   15
  They found a new-born child;

All in a scarlet kercher lay'd
  Of silk so fine and thin:
A golden mantle wrapt him round,
  Pinn'd with a silver pin.   20

The sudden sight surpriz'd them all;
  The courtiers gather'd round;
They look, they call, the mother seek;
  No mother could be found.

At length the king himself drew near,   25
  And as he gazing stands,
The pretty babe look'd up and smil'd,
  And stretch'd his little hands.

Now, by the rood, king Pepin says,
  This child is passing fair: 30
I wot he is of gentle blood;
  Perhaps some prince's heir.

Goe bear him home unto my court
  With all the care ye may:
Let him be christen'd Valentine,   35
  In honour of this day:

And look me out some cunning nurse;
 Well nurtur'd let him bee;
Nor ought be wanting that becomes
 A bairn of high degree.   40

They look'd him out a cunning nurse;
 And nurtur'd well was hee;
Nor ought was wanting that became
 A bairn of high degree.

Thus grewe the little Valentine, 45
 Belov'd of king and peers;
And shew'd in all he spake or did
 A wit beyond his years.

But chief in gallant feates of arms
 He did himself advance,   50
That ere he grewe to man's estate
 He had no peere in France.

And now the early downe began
 To shade his youthful chin;
When Valentine was dubb'd a knight, 55
 That he might glory win.

A boon, a boon, my gracious liege,
 I beg a boon of thee!
The first adventure that befalls,
 May be reserv'd for mee.   60

The first adventure shall be thine;
 The king did smiling say.
Nor many days, when lo! there came
 Three palmers clad in graye.

Help, gracious lord, they weeping say'd; 65
 And knelt, as it was meet:
From Artoys forest we be come,
 With weak and wearye feet.

Within those deep and drearye woods
  There wends a savage boy;   70
Whose fierce and mortal rage doth yield
  Thy subjects dire annoy.

'Mong ruthless beares he sure was bred;
  He lurks within their den:
With beares he lives; with beares he feeds,   75
  And drinks the blood of men.

To more than savage strength he joins
  A more than human skill:
For arms, ne cunning may suffice
  His cruel rage to still: 80

Up then rose sir Valentine,
  And claim'd that arduous deed.
Go forth and conquer, say'd the king,
  And great shall be thy meed.

Well mounted on a milk-white steed,   85
  His armour white as snow;
As well beseem'd a virgin knight,
  Who ne'er had fought a foe:

To Artoys forest he repairs
  With all the haste he may;   90
And soon he spies the savage youth
  A rending of his prey.

His unkempt hair all matted hung
  His shaggy shoulders round:
His eager eye all fiery glow'd: 95
  His face with fury frown'd.

Like eagles' talons grew his nails:
  His limbs were thick and strong;
And dreadful was the knotted oak
  He bare with him along.   100

Soon as sir Valentine approach'd,
 He starts with sudden spring;
And yelling forth a hideous howl,
 He made the forests ring.

As when a tyger fierce and fell   105
 Hath spyed a passing roe,
And leaps at once upon his throat;
 So sprung the savage foe;

So lightly leap'd with furious force
 The gentle knight to seize: 110
But met his tall uplifted spear,
 Which sunk him on his knees.

A second stroke so stiff and stern
 Had laid the savage low;
But springing up, he rais'd his club,   115
 And aim'd a dreadful blow.

The watchful warrior bent his head,
 And shun'd the coming stroke;
Upon his taper spear it fell,
 And all to shivers broke.   120

Then lighting nimbly from his steed,
 He drew his burnisht brand:
The savage quick as lightning flew
 To wrest it from his hand.

Three times he grasp'd the silver hilt; 125
 Three times he felt the blade;
Three times it fell with furious force;
 Three ghastly wounds it made.

Now with redoubled rage he roar'd;
 His eye-ball flash'd with fire;   130
Each hairy limb with fury shook;
 And all his heart was ire.

Then closing fast with furious gripe
   He clasp'd the champion round,
And with a strong and sudden twist   135
   He laid him on the ground.

But soon the knight, with active spring,
   O'erturn'd his hairy foe:
And now between their sturdy fists
   Past many a bruising blow.   140

They roll'd and grappled on the ground,
   And there they struggled long:
Skilful and active was the knight;
   The savage he was strong.

But brutal force and savage strength   145
   To art and skill must yield:
Sir Valentine at length prevail'd,
   And won the well-fought field.

Then binding strait his conquer'd foe
   Fast with an iron chain,   150
He tyes him to his horse's tail,
   And leads him o'er the plain.

To court his hairy captive soon
   Sir Valentine doth bring;
And kneeling downe upon his knee,   155
   Presents him to the king.

With loss of blood and loss of strength
   The savage tamer grew;
And to sir Valentine became
   A servant try'd and true.   160

And 'cause with beares he erst was bred,
   Ursine they call his name;
A name which unto future times
   The Muses shall proclame.

PART THE SECOND.

In high renown with prince and peere
   Now liv'd sir Valentine:
His high renown with prince and peere
   Made envious hearts repine.

It chanc'd the king upon a day   5
   Prepar'd a sumptuous feast:
And there came lords, and dainty dames,
   And many a noble guest.

Amid their cups, that freely flow'd,
   Their revelry, and mirth,   10
A youthful knight tax'd Valentine
   Of base and doubtful birth.

The foul reproach, so grossly urg'd,
   His generous heart did wound:
And strait he vow'd he ne'er would rest   15
   Till he his parents found.

Then bidding king and peers adieu,
   Early one summer's day,
With faithful Ursine by his side,
   From court he took his way.   20

O'er hill and valley, moss and moor,
   For many a day they pass;
At length, upon a moated lake,
   They found a bridge of brass.

Beyond it rose a castle fair,   25
   Y-built of marble stone:
The battlements were gilt with gold,
   And glittred in the sun.

Ver. 23, *i. e.* a lake that served for a moat to a castle.

Beneath the bridge, with strange device,
　　A hundred bells were hung;　　　　　　　30
That man, nor beast, might pass thereon,
　　But strait their larum rung.

This quickly found the youthful pair,
　　Who boldly crossing o'er,
The jangling sound bedeaft their ears,　　35
　　And rung from shore to shore.

Quick at the sound the castle gates
　　Unlock'd and opened wide,
And strait a gyant huge and grim
　　Stalk'd forth with stately pride.　　　　40

Now yield you, caytiffs, to my will;
　　He cried with hideous roar;
Or else the wolves shall eat your flesh,
　　And ravens drink your gore.

Vain boaster, said the youthful knight,　　45
　　I scorn thy threats and thee:
I trust to force thy brazen gates,
　　And set thy captives free.

Then putting spurs unto his steed,
　　He aim'd a dreadful thrust;　　　　　　50
The spear against the gyant glanc'd,
　　And caus'd the blood to burst.

Mad and outrageous with the pain,
　　He whirl'd his mace of steel:
The very wind of such a blow　　　　　　55
　　Had made the champion reel.

It haply mist; and now the knight
　　His glittering sword display'd,
And riding round with whirlwind speed
　　Oft made him feel the blade.　　　　　60

As when a large and monstrous oak
  Unceasing axes hew:
So fast around the gyant's limbs
  The blows quick-darting flew.

As when the boughs with hideous fall   65
  Some hapless woodman crush:
With such a force the enormous foe
  Did on the champion rush.

A fearful blow, alas! there came,
  Both horse and knight it took,   70
And laid them senseless in the dust;
  So fatal was the stroke.

Then smiling forth a hideous grin,
  The gyant strides in haste,
And, stooping, aims a second stroke: 75
  "Now caytiff breathe thy last!"

But ere it fell, two thundering blows
  Upon his scull descend:
From Ursine's knotty club they came,
  Who ran to save his friend.   80

Down sunk the gyant gaping wide,
  And rolling his grim eyes:
The hairy youth repeats his blows:
  He gasps, he groans, he dies.

Quickly sir Valentine reviv'd   85
  With Ursine's timely care:
And now to search the castle walls
  The venturous youths repair.

The blood and bones of murder'd knights
  They found where'er they came: 90
At length within a lonely cell
  They saw a mournful dame.

Her gentle eyes were dim'd with tears;
   Her cheeks were pale with woe:
And long sir Valentine besought   95
   Her doleful tale to know.

"Alas! young knight," she weeping said,
   "Condole my wretched fate;
A childless mother here you see;
   A wife without a mate   100

"These twenty winters here forlorn
   I've drawn my hated breath;
Sole witness of a monster's crimes,
   And wishing aye for death.

"Know, I am sister of a king,   105
   And in my early years
Was married to a mighty prince,
   The fairest of his peers.

"With him I sweetly liv'd in love
   A twelvemonth and a day:
When, lo! a foul and treacherous priest   110
   Y-wrought our loves' decay.

"His seeming goodness wan him pow'r;
   He had his master's ear:
And long to me and all the world   115
   He did a saint appear.

"One day, when we were all alone,
   He proffer'd odious love:
The wretch with horrour I repuls'd,
   And from my presence drove.   120

"He feign'd remorse, and piteous beg'd
   His crime I'd not reveal:
Which, for his seeming penitence
   I promis'd to conceal.

"With treason, villainy, and wrong,   125
  My goodness he repay'd:
With jealous doubts he fill'd my lord,
  And me to woe betray'd.

"He hid a slave within my bed,
  Then rais'd a bitter cry.   130
My lord, possest with rage, condemn'd
  Me, all unheard, to dye.

"But, 'cause I then was great with child,
  At length my life he spar'd:
But bade me instant quit the realme,   135
  One trusty knight my guard.

"Forth on my journey I depart,
  Opprest with grief and woe;
And tow'rds my brother's distant court,
  With breaking heart, I goe.   140

"Long time thro' sundry foreign lands
  We slowly pace along:
At length, within a forest wild,
  I fell in labour strong:

"And while the knight for succour sought,   145
  And left me there forlorn,
My childbed pains so fast increast.
  Two lovely boys were born.

"The eldest fair, and smooth, as snow
  That tips the mountain hoar: 150
The younger's little body rough
  With hairs was cover'd o'er.

"But here afresh begin my woes:
  While tender care I took
To shield my eldest from the cold,   155
  And wrap him in my cloak;

"A prowling bear burst from the wood,
  And seiz'd my younger son:
Affection lent my weakness wings,
  And after them I run. 160

"But all forewearied, weak and spent,
  I quickly swoon'd away;
And there beneath the greenwood shade
  Long time I lifeless lay.

"At length the knight brought me relief, 165
  And rais'd me from the ground:
But neither of my pretty babes
  Could ever more be found.

"And, while in search we wander'd far,
  We met that gyant grim;
Who ruthless slew my trusty knight, 170
  And bare me off with him.

"But charm'd by heav'n, or else my griefs,
  He offer'd me no wrong;
Save that within these lonely walls 175
  I've been immur'd so long."

Now, surely, said the youthful knight,
  You are lady Bellisance,
Wife to the Grecian emperor:
  Your brother's king of France. 180

For in your royal brother's court
  Myself my breeding had;
Where oft the story of your woes
  Hath made my bosom sad.

If so, know your accuser's dead, 185
  And dying own'd his crime;
And long your lord hath sought you out
  Thro' every foreign clime.

And when no tidings he could learn
   Of his much-wronged wife,   190
He vow'd thenceforth within his court
   To lead a hermit's life.

Now heaven is kind! the lady said;
   And dropt a joyful tear:
Shall I once more behold my lord?   195
   That lord I love so dear?

But, madam, said sir Valentine,
   And knelt upon his knee;
Know you the cloak that wrapt your babe,
   If you the same should see?   200

And pulling forth the cloth of gold,
   In which himself was found;
The lady gave a sudden shriek,
   And fainted on the ground.

But by his pious care reviv'd,   205
   His tale she heard anon;
And soon by other tokens found,
   He was indeed her son.

But who's this hairy youth? she said;
   He much resembles thee: 210
The bear devour'd my younger son,
   Or sure that son were he.

Madam, this youth, with bears was bred,
   And rear'd within their den.
But recollect ye any mark   215
   To know your son agen?

Upon his little side, quoth she,
   Was stampt a bloody rose.
Here, lady, see the crimson mark
   Upon his body grows!   220

Then clasping both her new-found sons
  She bath'd their cheeks with tears;
And soon towards her brother's court
  Her joyful course she steers.

What pen can paint king Pepin's joy,   225
  His sister thus restor'd!
And soon a messenger was sent
  To chear her drooping lord:

Who came in haste with all his peers,
  To fetch her home to Greece;   230
Where many happy years they reign'd
  In perfect love and peace.

To them sir Ursine did succeed,
  And long the scepter bare.
Sir Valentine he stay'd in France,   235
  And was his uncle's heir.

                                     ***

XIII.

The Dragon of Wantley.

THIS humorous song (as a former Editor[1] has well observed) is to old metrical romances and ballads of chivalry, what *Don Quixote* is to prose narratives of that kind, — a lively satire on their extravagant fictions. But although the satire is thus general, the subject of this ballad is local and peculiar; so that many of the finest strokes of humour are lost for want of our knowing the minute circumstances to which they allude. Many of them can hardly now be recovered, although we have been fortunate enough to learn the general subject to which the satire referred, and shall detail the information with which we have been favoured in a separate memoir at the end of the poem

[1] Collection of Historical Ballads, in 3 vols. 1727.

In handling his subject, the author has brought in most of the common incidents which occur in romance. The description of the dragon[2] — his outrages — the people flying to the knight for succour — his care in choosing his armour — his being drest for fight by a young damsel — and most of the circumstances of the battle and victory (allowing for the burlesque turn given to them), are what occur in every book of chivalry, whether in prose or verse.

If any one piece more than another is more particularly levelled at, it seems to be the old rhyming legend of Sir Bevis. There a dragon is attacked from a well in a manner not very remote from this of the ballad:

> "There was a well, so have I wynne,
> And Bevis stumbled ryght therein.
>   *   *   *   *
> Than was he glad without fayle,
> And rested a whyle for his avayle;
> And dranke of that water his fyll;
> And than he lepte out, with good wyll,
> And with Morglay his brande
> He assayled the dragon, I underſtande:
> On the dragon he smote so faste,
> Where that he hit the scales braste:
> The dragon then faynted sore,
> And cast a galon and more
> Out of his mouthe of venim strong,
> And on sir Bevis he it flong:
> It was venymous y-wis."

This seems to be meant by the Dragon of Wantley's stink, ver. 110. As the politic knight's creeping out, and attacking the dragon, &c., seems evidently to allude to the following:

> "Bevis blessed himselfe, and forth yode,
> And lepte out with haste full good;
> And Bevis unto the dragon gone is;
> And the dragon also to Bevis.
> Longe and harde was that fyght
> Betwene the dragon and that knyght:
> But ever whan syr Bevis was hurt sore,
> He went to the well, and washed him thore;
> He was as hole as any man,
> Ever freshe as whan he began.

---

[2] See above, pp. 113 and 210.

The dragon sawe it might not avayle
Besyde the well to hold batayle;
He thought he would, wyth some wyle,
Out of that place Bevis begyle;
He woulde have flowen then awaye,
But Bevis lepte after with good Morglaye,
And hyt him under the wynge,
As he was in his flyenge," &c.

Sign. M. jv. L. j. &c.

After all, perhaps the writer of this ballad was acquainted
with the above incidents only through the medium of Spenser,
who has assumed most of them in his *Faerie Queen*. At least
some particulars in the description of the dragon, &c. seem
evidently borrowed from the latter. See book i. canto ii.
where the dragon's "two wynges like sayls—huge long tayl
—with stings—his cruel rending clawes—and yron teeth—
his breath of smothering smoke and sulphur"—and the dura-
tion of the fight for upwards of two days, bear a great re-
semblance to passages in the following ballad; though it
must be confessed that these particulars are common to all
old writers of romance.

Although this ballad must have been written early in the
last century, we have met with none but such as were com-
paratively modern copies. It is here printed from one in
Roman letter, in the Pepys collection, collated with such
others as could be procured.

OLD stories tell, how Hercules
  A dragon slew at Lerna,
With seven heads, and fourteen eyes,
  To see and well discerne-a:
But he had a club, this dragon to drub,   5
  Or he had ne'er done it, I warrant ye:
But More of More-Hall, with nothing at all,
  He slew the dragon of Wantley.

This dragon had two furious wings,
  Each one upon each shoulder;   10

Percy. III.   18

With a sting in his tayl, as long as a flayl,
    Which made him bolder and bolder.
He had long claws, and in his jaws
    Four and forty teeth of iron;
With a hide as tough as any buff,   15
    Which did him round environ.

Have you not heard how the Trojan horse
    Held seventy men in his belly?
This dragon was not quite so big,
    But very near, I'll tell ye.   20
Devoured he poor children three,
    That could not with him grapple;
And at one sup he eat them up,
    As one would eat an apple.

All sorts of cattle this dragon did eat,   25
    Some say he ate up trees,
And that the forests sure he would
    Devour up by degrees:
For houses and churches were to him geese and turkies;
    He ate all, and left none behind,   30
But some stones, dear Jack, that he could not crack,
    Which on the hills you will find.

In Yorkshire, near fair Rotherham,
    The place I know it well;
Some two or three miles, or thereabouts,   35
    I vow I cannot tell;
But there is a hedge, just on the hill edge,
    And Matthew's house hard by it;
O there and then was this dragon's den,
    You could not chuse but spy it.   40

Some say, this dragon was a witch;
    Some say he was a devil,

Ver. 29, were to him gorse and birches. Other copies.

For from his nose a smoke arose,
   And with it burning snivel;
Which he cast off, when he did cough,   45
   In a well that he did stand by;
Which made it look, just like a brook
   Running with burning brandy.

Hard by a furious knight there dwelt,
   Of whom all towns did ring,   50
For he could wrestle, play at quarter-staff, kick, cuff
     and huff,
   Call son of a whore, do any kind of thing:
By the tail and the main, with his hands twain
   He swung a horse till he was dead;
And that which is stranger, he for very anger   55
   Eat him all up but his head.

These children, as I told, being eat;
   Men, women, girls, and boys,
Sighing and sobbing, came to his lodging,
   And made a hideous noise: 60
O save us all, More of More-hall,
   Thou peerless knight of these woods;
Do but slay this dragon, who won't leave us a rag on,
   We'll give thee all our goods.

Tut, tut, quoth he, no goods I want: 65
   But I want, I want, in sooth,
A fair maid of sixteen, that's brisk, and keen,
   With smiles about the mouth;
Hair black as sloe, skin white as snow,
   With blushes her cheeks adorning;   70
To anoynt me o'er night, ere I go to fight,
   And to dress me in the morning.

This being done, he did engage
   To hew the dragon down;

18*

But first he went, new armour to   75
   Bespeak at Sheffield town;
With spikes all about, not within but without,
   Of steel so sharp and strong;
Both behind and before, arms, legs, and all o'er,
   Some five or six inches long.   80

Had you but seen him in this dress,
   How fierce he look'd and how big,
You would have thought him for to be
   Some Egyptian porcupig:
He frighted all, cats, dogs, and all,   85
   Each cow, each horse, and each hog:
For fear they did flee, for they took him to be
   Some strange outlandish hedge-hog.

To see this fight, all people then
   Got up on trees and houses,   90
On churches some, and chimneys too;
   But these put on their trowses,
Not to spoil their hose.   As soon as he rose,
   To make him strong and mighty,
He drank by the tale, six pots of ale,   95
   And a quart of aqua-vitæ.

It is not strength that always wins,
   For wit doth strength excell;
Which made our cunning champion
   Creep down into a well;   100
Where he did think, this dragon would drink;
   And so he did in truth;
And as he stoop'd low, he rose up and cry'd, boh!
   And hit him in the mouth.

Oh, quoth the dragon, pox take thee, come out,   105
   Thou disturb'st me in my drink:
And then he turn'd, and s ... at him;
   Good lack how he did stink;

Beshrew thy soul, thy body's foul,
　Thy dung smells not like balsam;   110
Thou son of a whore, thou stink'st so sore,
　Sure thy diet is unwholesome.

　Our politick knight, on the other side,
　　Crept out upon the brink,
　And gave the dragon such a douse,   115
　　He knew not what to think:
By cock, quoth he, say you so, do you see?
　And then at him he let fly
With hand and with foot, and so they went to't;
　And the word it was, Hey boys, hey!   120

　Your words, quoth the dragon, I don't understand;
　　Then to it they fell at all,
　Like two wild boars so fierce, if I may
　　Compare great things with small.
Two days and a night, with this dragon did fight   125
　Our champion on the ground;
Tho' their strength it was great, their skill it was neat,
　They never had one wound.

　At length the hard earth began to quake,
　　The dragon gave him a knock,   130
　Which made him to reel, and straitway he thought,
　　To lift him as high as a rock,
And thence let him fall. But More of More-hall,
　Like a valiant son of Mars,
As he came like a lout, so he turn'd him about,   135
　And hit him a kick on the a . . .

　Oh, quoth the dragon, with a deep sigh,
　　And turn'd six times together,
　Sobbing and tearing, cursing and swearing
　　Out of his throat of leather;
More of More-hall! O thou rascal!   140
　Would I had seen thee never;

With the thing at thy foot, thou hast prick'd my a ... gut,
And I'm quite undone for ever.

Murder, murder, the dragon cry'd,   145
    Alack, alack, for grief;
Had you but mist that place, you could
    Have done me no mischief.
Then his head he shaked, trembled and quaked,
    And down he laid and cry'd;   150
First on one knee, then on back tumbled he,
    So groan'd, kickt, s ..., and dy'd.

*** A description of the supposed scene of the foregoing
ballad, which was communicated to the Editor in 1767, is
here given in the words of the relater:

"In Yorkshire, six miles from Rotherham, is a village
called Wortley, the seat of the late Wortley Montague, Esq.
About a mile from this village is a lodge, named Warncliff
Lodge, but vulgarly called Wantley: here lies the scene of
the song. I was there above forty years ago: and it being a
woody rocky place, my friend made me clamber over rocks
and stones, not telling me to what end, till I came to a sort
of cave; then asked my opinion of the place, and pointing
to one end, says, Here lay the dragon killed by Moor, of
Moor-hall: here lay his head; here lay his tail: and the
stones we came over on the hill, are those he could not crack;
and yon white house you see half a mile off, is Moor-hall. I
had dined at the lodge, and knew the man's name was Mat-
thew, who was a keeper to Mr. Wortley, and, as he
endeavoured to persuade me, was the same Matthew men-
tioned in the song: in the house is the picture of the dragon
and Moor of Moor-hall, and near it a well, which, says he, is
the well described in the ballad."

*** Since the former editions of this humorous old song
were printed, the following key to the satire hath been com-
municated by Godfrey Bosville, Esq., of Thorp, near Malton,

in Yorkshire; who, in the most obliging manner, gave full permission to subjoin it to the poem.

Warncliffe Lodge, and Warncliffe Wood (vulgarly pronounced Wantley), are in the parish of Penniston, in Yorkshire. The rectory of Penniston was part of the dissolved monastery of St. Stephen's, Westminster; and was granted to the Duke of Norfolk's family: who therewith endowed an hospital, which he built at Sheffield, for women. The trustees let the impropriation of the great tithes of Penniston to the Wortley family, who got a great deal by it, and wanted to get still more: for Mr. Nicholas Wortley attempted to take the tithes in kind; but Mr. Francis Bosville opposed him, and there was a decree in favour of the modus in 37th Eliz. The vicarage of Penniston did not go along with the rectory, but with the copyhold rents, and was part of a large purchase made by Ralph Bosville, Esq., from Queen Elizabeth, in the second year of her reign: and that part he sold in 12th Eliz. to his elder brother Godfrey, the father of Francis; who left it, with the rest of his estate, to his wife for her life, and then to Ralph third son of his uncle Ralph. The widow married Lyonel Rowlestone, lived eighteen years, and survived Ralph.

This premised, the ballad apparently relates to the lawsuit carried on concerning this claim of tithes made by the Wortley family. "Houses and churches were to him geese and turkeys;" which are titheable things, the dragon chose to live on. Sir Francis Wortley, the son of Nicholas, attempted again to take the tithes in kind: but the parishioners subscribed an agreement to defend their modus. And at the head of the agreement was Lyonel Rowlestone, who is supposed to be one of "the stones, dear Jack, which the dragon could not crack." The agreement is still preserved in a large sheet of parchment, dated 1st of James I., and is full of names and seals, which might be meant by the coat of armour "with spikes all about, both within and without." More of More-hall was either the attorney, or counsellor, who conducted the suit He is not distinctly remembered,

but More-hall is still extant at the very bottom of Wantley
[Warncliff] Wood, and lies so low, that it might be said to
be in a well: as the dragon's den [Warncliff Lodge] was at
the top of the wood, "with Matthew's house hard by it." The
keepers belonging to the Wortley family were named, for
many generations, Matthew Northall; the last of them left
this lodge, within memory, to be keeper to the Duke of Nor-
folk. The present owner of More-hall still attends Mr.
Bosville's manor-court at Ox-spring, and pays a Rose a year.
"More of More-hall, with nothing at all, slew the Dragon of
Wantley." He gave him, instead of tithes, so small a modus,
that it was in effect nothing at all, and was slaying him with
a vengeance. "The poor children three," &c., cannot surely
mean the three sisters of Francis Bosville, who would have
been co-heiresses had he made no will? The late Mr. Bosville
had a contest with the descendants of two of them, the late
Sir George Saville's father, and Mr. Copley, about the pre-
sentation to Penniston, they supposing Francis had not the
power to give this part of the estate from the heirs at law;
but it was decided against them. The dragon (Sir Francis
Wortley) succeeded better with his cousin Wordesworth, the
freehold lord of the manor (for it is the copyhold manor that
belongs to Mr. Bosville), having persuaded him not to join
the refractory parishioners, under a promise that he would
let him his tithes cheap: and now the estates of Wortley
and Wordesworth are the only lands that pay tithes in the
parish.

N.B. The "two days and a night," mentioned in verse
125, as the duration of the combat, was probably that of the
trial at law.

XIV.

St. George for England.

THE FIRST PART.

As the former song is in ridicule of the extravagant inci-
dents in old ballads and metrical romances; so this is a bur-

lesque of their style; particularly of the rambling transitions and wild accumulation of unconnected parts, so frequent in many of them.

This ballad is given from an old black-letter copy in the Pepys collection, "imprinted at London, 1612." It is more ancient than many of the preceding; but we place it here for the sake of connecting it with the SECOND PART.

WHY doe you boast of Arthur and his knightes,
Knowing 'well' how many men have endured fightes?
For besides king Arthur, and Lancelot du lake,
Or sir Tristram de Lionel, that fought for ladies sake;
Read in old histories, and there you shall see
How St. George, St. George the dragon made to flee.
St. George he was for England; St. Dennis was for France;
    Sing, *Honi soit qui mal y pense.*

Mark our father Abraham, when first he resckued Lot
Onely with his household, what conquest there he got:
David was elected a prophet and a king,
He slew the great Goliah, with a stone within a sling:
Yet these were not knightes of the table round;
Nor St. George, St. George, who the dragon did confound.
St. George he was for England; St. Dennis was for France;
    Sing, *Honi soit qui mal y pense.*

Jephthah and Gideon did lead their men to fight,
They conquered the Amorites, and put them all to flight:
Hercules his labours 'were' on the plaines of Basse;
And Sampson slew a thousand with the jawbone of an asse,
And eke he threw a temple downe, and did a mighty spoyle:
But St. George, St. George he did the dragon foyle.
St. George he was for England; St. Dennis was for France;
    Sing, *Honi soit qui mal y pense.*

The warres of ancient monarchs it were too long to tell,
And likewise of the Romans, how farre they did excell;

Hannyball and Scipio in many a fielde did fighte:
Orlando Furioso he was a worthy knighte:
Remus and Romulus, were they that Rome did builde:
But St. George, St. George the dragon made to yielde.
St. George he was for England; St. Dennis was for France;
   Sing, *Honi soit qui mal y pense.*

The noble Alphonso, that was the Spanish king,
The order of the red scarffes and bandrolles in did bring[1]:
He had a troope of mighty knightes, when first he did
     begin,
Which sought adventures farre and neare, that conquest
     they might win;
The ranks of the Pagans he often put to flight:
But St. George, St. George did with the dragon fight.
St. George he was for England; St. Dennis was for France;
   Sing, *Honi soit qui mal y pense.*

Many 'knights' have fought with proud Tamberlaine:
Cutlax the Dane, great warres he did maintaine:
Rowland of Beame, and good 'sir' Olivere
In the forest of Acon slew both woolfe and beare:
Besides that noble Hollander, 'sir' Goward with the bill:
But St. George, St. George the dragon's blood did spill.
St. George he was for England; St. Dennis was for France;
   Sing, *Honi soit qui mal y pense.*

Valentine and Orson were of king Pepin's blood:
Alfride and Henry they were brave knightes and good:
The four sons of Aymon, that follow'd Charlemaine:
Sir Hughon of Burdeaux, and Godfrey of Bullaine:
These were all French knightes that lived in that age:
But St. George, St. George the dragon did assuage:
St. George he was for England; St. Dennis was for France;
   Sing, *Honi soit qui mal y pense.*

---

[1] This probably alludes to "An ancient Order of Knighthood, called the
Order of the Band, instituted by Don Alphonsus, king of Spain, ... to wear
a red riband of three fingers breadth," &c. See Ames, Typog. p. 327.

Bevis conquered Ascapart, and after slew the boare,
And then he crost beyond the seas to combat with the
      moore:
Sir Isenbras and Eglamore, they were knightes most bold;
And good Sir John Mandeville of travel much hath told:
There were many English knights that Pagans did convert:
But St. George, St. George pluckt out the dragon's heart.
St. George he was for England; St. Dennis was for France;
  Sing, *Honi soit qui mal y pense.*

The noble earl of Warwick, that was call'd sir Guy,
The infidels and pagans stoutlie did defie;
He slew the giant Brandimore, and after was the death
Of that most ghastly dun cowe, the divell of Dunsmore
      heath;
Besides his noble deeds all done beyond the seas:
But St. George, St. George the dragon did appease.
St. George he was for England; St. Dennis was for France;
  Sing, *Honi soit qui mal y pense.*

Richard Cœur-de-lion, erst king of this land,
He the lion gored with his naked hand[2]:
The false duke of Austria nothing did he feare;
But his son he killed with a boxe on the eare;
Besides his famous actes done in the holy lande:
But St. George, St. George the dragon did withstande.
St. George he was for England; St. Dennis was for France;
  Sing, *Honi soit qui mal y pense.*

Henry the fifth he conquered all France,
And quartered their arms, his honour to advance:
He their cities razed, and threw their castles downe,
And his head he honoured with a double crowne:
He thumped the French-men, and after home he came:
But St. George, St. George he did the dragon tame.

---

[2] Alluding to the fabulous exploits attributed to this king in the old Romances. See the Dissertation prefixed to this volume.

St. George he was for England; St. Dennis was for France;
  Sing, *Honi soit qui mal y pense.*

St. David of Wales the Welsh-men much advance:
St. Jaques of Spaine, that never yet broke lance:
St. Patricke of Ireland, which was St. Georges boy,
Seven yeares he kept his horse, and then stole him away:
For which knavish act, as slaves they doe remaine:
But St. George, St. George the dragon he hath slaine.
St. George he was for England; St. Dennis was for France;
  Sing, *Honi soit qui mal y pense.*

XV.

St. George for England.

THE SECOND PART.

WAS written by John Grubb, M.A., of Christ Church,
Oxford. The occasion of its being composed is said to have
been as follows. A set of gentlemen of the university had
formed themselves into a club, all the members of which
were to be of the name of George: their anniversary feast
was to be held on St. George's day. Our author solicited
strongly to be admitted; but his name being unfortunately
John, this disqualification was dispensed with only upon this
condition,—that he would compose a song in honour of their
patron saint, and would every year produce one or more new
stanzas, to be sung on their annual festival. This gave birth
to the following humorous performance, the several stanzas
of which were the produce of many successive anniversaries [1].

This diverting poem was long handed about in manu-
script; at length a friend of Grubb's undertook to get it
printed, who, not keeping pace with the impatience of his

---

[1] To this circumstance it is owing that the Editor has never met with
two copies in which the stanzas are arranged alike: he has therefore thrown
them into what appeared the most natural order. The verses are properly
long Alexandrines, but the narrowness of the page made it necessary to
subdivide them: they are here printed with many improvements.

friends, was addressed in the following whimsical macaronic lines, which, in such a collection as this, may not improperly accompany the poem itself.

EXPOSTULATIUNCULA, sive QUERIMONIUNCULA ad ANTONIUM [ATHERTON] ob Poema JOHANNIS GRUBB, Viri τον πανυ ingeniosissimi in lucem nondum editi.

TONI! Tune sines divina poemata Grubbi
Intomb'd in secret thus still to remain any longer,
Τουνομα σου shall last, Ω Γρυββε διαμπερες αει
Grubbe tuum nomen vivet dum nobilis ale-a
Efficit heroas, dignamque heroe puellam.
Est genus heroum, quos nobilis efficit ale-a
Qui pro niperkin clamant, quaternque liquoris
Quem vocitant Homines Brandy, Superi Cherry-brandy.
Sæpe illi long-cut, vel small-cut flare Tobacco
Sunt soliti pipos. Ast si generosior herba
(Per varios casus, per tot discrimina rerum)
Mundungus desit, tum non funcare recusant
Brown-paper tostâ, vel quod fit arundine bed-mat.
Hic labor, hoc opus est heroum ascendere sedes!
Ast ego quo rapiar? quo me feret entheus ardor,
Grubbe, tui memorem? Divinum expande poema.
Quæ mora? quæ ratio est, quin Grubbi protinus anser
Virgilii, Flaccique simul canat inter olores?

At length the importunity of his friends prevailed, and Mr. Grubb's song was published at Oxford, under the following title:

THE BRITISH HEROES,
A New Poem in honour of St. George
By Mr. JOHN GRUBB
School-master of Christ-Church
OXON. 1688.
Favete linguis: carmina non prius
Audita, musarum sacerdos
Canto.—— HOR.
Sold by Henry Clements. Oxon.

THE story of king Arthur old
    Is very memorable,
The number of his valiant knights,
    And roundness of his table:
The knights around his table in
    A circle sate, d'ye see:

5

And altogether made up one
　　Large hoop of chivalry.
He had a sword, both broad and sharp,
　　Y-cleped Caliburn,   10
Would cut a flint more easily
　　Than pen-knife cuts a corn;
As case-knife does a capon carve,
　　So would it carve a rock,
And split a man at single slash,   15
　　From noddle down to nock.
As Roman Augur's steel of yore
　　Dissected Tarquin's riddle,
So this would cut both conjurer
　　And whetstone thro' the middle.   20
He was the cream of Brecknock,
　　And flower of all the Welsh:
But George he did the dragon fell,
　　And gave him a plaguy squelsh.
St. George he was for England; St. Dennis was for France; 25
　　Sing, *Honi soit qui mal y pense.*

Pendragon, like his father Jove,
　　Was fed with milk of goat;
And like him made a noble shield
　　Of she-goat's shaggy coat: 30
On top of burnisht helmet he
　　Did wear a crest of leeks
And onions' heads, whose dreadful nod
　　Drew tears down hostile cheeks.
Itch and Welsh blood did make him hot,   35
　　And very prone to ire;
H' was ting'd with brimstone, like a match,
　　And would as soon take fire.
As brimstone he took inwardly
　　When scurf gave him occasion,   40
His postern puff of wind was a
　　Sulphureous exhalation.

The Briton never tergivers'd,
　　But was for adverse drubbing,
And never turn'd his back to aught,　　　　45
　　But to a post for scrubbing.
His sword would serve for battle, or
　　For dinner, if you please;
When it had slain a Cheshire man,
　　'Twould toast a Cheshire cheese.　　　　50
He wounded, and, in their own blood,
　　Did anabaptize Pagans:
But George he made the dragon an
　　Example to all dragons.
St. George he was for England; St. Dennis was for France; 55
Sing, *Honi soit qui mal y pense.*

Brave Warwick Guy, at dinner time,
　　Challeng'd a gyant savage;
And streight came out the unwieldy lout
　　Brim-full of wrath and cabbage:　　　　60
He had a phiz of latitude,
　　And was full thick i' th' middle;
The cheeks of puffed Trumpeter,
　　And paunch of squire Beadle[2].
But the knight fell'd him like an oak,　　　　65
　　And did upon his back tread;
The valiant knight his weazon cut,
　　And Atropos his packthread.
Besides he fought with a dun cow,
　　As say the poets witty,　　　　70
A dreadful dun, and horned too,
　　Like dun of Oxford city:
The fervent dog-days made her mad,
　　By causing heat of weather,
Syrius and Procyon baited her,　　　　75
　　As bull-dogs did her father:

[2] Men of bulk answerable to their places, as is well known at Oxford.

Grasiers, nor butchers this fell beast,
   E'er of her frolick hindred;
John Dosset[3] she'd knock down as flat,
   As John knocks down her kindred: 80
Her heels would lay ye all along,
   And kick into a swoon;
Frewin's[4] cow-heels keep up your corpse,
   But hers would beat you down.
She vanquisht many a sturdy wight,   85
   And proud was of the honour;
Was pufft by mauling butchers so,
   As if themselves had blown her.
At once she kickt, and pusht at Guy,
   But all that would not fright him;   90
Who wav'd his winyard o'er sir-loyn,
   As if he'd gone to knight him.
He let her blood, frenzy to cure,
   And eke he did her gall rip;
His trenchant blade, like cook's long spit,   95
   Ran thro' the monster's bald-rib:
He rear'd up the vast crooked rib,
   Instead of arch triumphal:
But George hit th' dragon such a pelt,
   As made him on his bum fall.   100
St. George he was for England; St. Dennis was for France;
   Sing, *Honi soit qui mal y pense.*

Tamerlain, with Tartarian bow,
   The Turkish squadrons slew;
And fetch'd the pagan crescent down,   105
   With half-moon made of yew:
His trusty bow proud Turks did gall
   With showers of arrows thick,
And bow-strings, without strangling, sent
   Grand-Visiers to old Nick: 110

---

[3] A butcher that then served the college.
[4] A cook, who on fast-nights was famous for selling cow-heel and tripe.

Much turbants, and much Pagan pates
   He made to humble in dust;
And heads of Saracens he fixt
   On spear, as on a sign-post:
He coop'd in cage Bajazet the prop   115
   Of Mahomet's religion,
As if't had been the whispering bird,
   That prompted him, the pigeon.
In Turkey-leather scabbard, he
   Did sheath his blade so trenchant: 120
But George he swing'd the dragon's tail,
   And cut off every inch on't.
St. George he was for England; St. Dennis was for France;
   Sing, *Honi soit qui mal y pense.*

The amazon Thalestris was   125
   Both beautiful and bold;
She sear'd her breasts with iron hot,
   And bang'd her foes with cold.
Her hand was like the tool, wherewith
   Jove keeps proud mortals under: 130
It shone just like his lightning,
   And batter'd like his thunder.
Her eye darts lightning, that would blast
   The proudest he that swagger'd,
And melt the rapier of his soul,   135
   In its corporeal scabbard.
Her beauty, and her drum, to foes
   Did cause amazement double;
As timorous larks amazed are
   With light, and with a low-bell: 140
With beauty, and that Lapland-charm[5],
   Poor men she did bewitch all;
Still a blind whining lover had,
   As Pallas had her scrich-owl.

[5] The drum.

She kept the chastness of a nun   145
    In armour, as in cloyster:
But George undid the dragon just
    As you'd undo an oister.
St. George he was for England; St. Dennis was for France;
    Sing, *Honi soit qui mal y pense.*   150

Stout Hercules was offspring of
    Great Jove and fair Alcmene:
One part of him celestial was,
    One part of him terrene.
To scale the hero's cradle walls   155
    Two fiery snakes combin'd,
And, curling into a swaddling cloaths,
    About the infant twin'd:
But he put out these dragons' fires,
    And did their hissing stop;   160
As red-hot iron with hissing noise
    Is quencht in blacksmith's shop.
He cleans'd a stable, and rubb'd down
    The horses of new-comers;
And out of horse-dung he rais'd fame,   165
    As Tom Wrench[6] does cucumbers.
He made a river help him through;
    Alpheus was under-groom;
The stream, disgust at office mean,
    Ran murmuring thro' the room: 170
This liquid ostler to prevent
    Being tired with that long work,
His father Neptune's trident took,
    Instead of three-tooth'd dung-fork.
This Hercules, as soldier, and   175
    As spinster, could take pains;
His club would sometimes spin ye flax,
    And sometimes knock out brains:

---

[6] Who kept Paradise gardens at Oxford.

H' was forc'd to spin his miss a shift
   By Juno's wrath and her-spite;   180
Fair Omphale whipt him to his wheel,
   As cook whips barking turn-spit.
From man, or churn, he well knew how
   To get him lasting fame:
He'd pound a giant, till the blood,   185
   And milk till butter came.
Often he fought with huge battoon,
   And oftentimes he boxed;
Tapt a fresh monster once a month,
   As Hervey [7] doth fresh hogshead.   190
He gave Anteus such a hug,
   As wrestlers give in Cornwall:
But George he did the dragon kill,
   As dead as any door-nail.
St. George he was for England; St. Dennis was for France; 195
   Sing, *Honi soit qui mal y pense.*

The Gemini, sprung from an egg,
   Were put into a cradle:
Their brains with knocks and bottled-ale,
   Were often-times full addle: 200
And, scarcely hatch'd, these sons of him,
   That hurls the bolt trisulcate,
With helmet-shell on tender head,
   Did tustle with red-ey'd pole-cat.
Castor a horseman, Pollux tho'   205
   A boxer was, I wist:
The one was fam'd for iron heel;
   Th' other for leaden fist.
Pollux to shew he was a god,
   When he was in a passion   210
With fist made noses fall down flat
   By way of adoration:

---

[7] A noted drawer at the Mermaid Tavern in Oxford.

This fist, as sure as French disease,
   Demolish'd noses' ridges:
He like a certain lord[8] was fam'd   215
   For breaking down of bridges.
Castor the flame of fiery steed,
   With well-spurr'd boots took down;
As men, with leathern buckets, quench
   A fire in country town.   220
His famous horse, that liv'd on oats,
   Is sung on oaten quill;
By bards' immortal provender
   The nag surviveth still.
This shelly brood on none but knaves   225
   Employ'd their brisk artillery:
And flew as naturally at rogues,
   As eggs at thief in pillory[9].
Much sweat they spent in furious fight,
   Much blood they did effund: 230
Their whites they vented thro' the pores;
   Their yolks thro' gaping wound:
Then both were cleans'd from blood and dust
   To make a heavenly sign;
The lads were, like their armour, scowr'd,   235
   And then hung up to shine;
Such were the heavenly double-Dicks,
   The sons of Jove and Tyndar:
But George he cut the dragon up,
   As he had bin duck or windar.   240
St. George he was for England; St. Dennis was for France;
   Sing, *Honi soit qui mal y pense.*

[8] Lord Lovelace broke down the bridges about Oxford, at the beginning of the Revolution. See on this subject a ballad in Smith's Poems, p. 102. Lond. 1713.

[9] It has been suggested by an ingenious correspondent, that this was a popular subject at that time:

        Not carted Bawd, or Dan de Foe,
        In wooden Ruff ere bluster'd so.
                Smith's Poems, p. 117.

Gorgon a twisted adder wore
  For knot upon her shoulder:
She kemb'd her hissing periwig,   245
  And curling snakes did powder.
These snakes they made stiff changelings
  Of all the folks they hist on;
They turned barbers into hones,
  And masons into free-stone: 250
Sworded magnetic Amazon
  Her shield to load-stone changes;
Then amorous sword by magic belt
  Clung fast unto her haunches.
This shield long village did protect,   255
  And kept the army from-town,
And chang'd the bullies into rocks,
  That came t' invade Long-Compton[10].
She post-diluvian stores unmans,
  And Pyrrha's work unravels;   260
And stares Deucalion's hardy boys
  Into their primitive pebbles.
Red noses she to rubies turns,
  And noddles into bricks:
But George made dragon laxative;   265
  And gave him a bloody flix.
St. George he was for England; St. Dennis was for France;
Sing, *Honi soit qui mal y pense.*

By boar-spear Meleager got
  An everlasting name,   270
And out of haunch of basted swine,
  He hew'd eternal fame.
This beast each hero's trouzers ript,
  And rudely shew'd his bare-breech,
Prickt but the wem, and out there came   275
  Heroic guts and garbadge.

[10] See the account of Rolricht Stones, in Dr. Plott's Hist. of Oxfordshire.

Legs were secured by iron boots
　　No more than peas by peascods:
Brass helmets, with inclosed sculls,
　　Wou'd crackle in's mouth like chesnuts.   280
His tawny hairs erected were
　　By rage, that was resistless;
And wrath, instead of cobler's wax,
　　Did stiffen his rising bristles.
His tusk lay'd dogs so dead asleep,   285
　　Nor horn, nor whip cou'd wake um:
It made them vent both their last blood,
　　And their last album-grecum.
But the knight gor'd him with his spear,
　　To make of him a tame one,   290
And arrows thick, instead of cloves,
　　He stuck in monster's gammon.
For monumental pillar, that
　　His victory might be known,
He rais'd up, in cylindric form,   295
　　A collar of the brawn.
He sent his shade to shades below,
　　In Stygian mud to wallow;
And eke the stout St. George eftsoon,
　　He made the dragon follow.   300
St. George he was for England; St. Dennis was for France;
　　Sing, *Honi soit qui mal y pense.*

Achilles of old Chiron learnt
　　The great horse for to ride;
H' was taught by th' Centaur's rational part,   305
　　The hinnible to bestride.
Bright silver feet, and shining face
　　Had that stout hero's mother;
As rapier 's silver'd at one end,
　　And wounds you at the other   310
Her feet were bright, his feet were swift,
　　As hawk pursuing sparrow:

Her's had the metal, his the speed
   Of Braburn's[1] silver arrow.
Thetis to double pedagogue   315
   Commits her dearest boy;
Who bred him from a slender twig
   To be the scourge of Troy:
But ere he lasht the Trojans, h' was
   In Stygian waters steept;   320
As birch is soaked first in piss,
   When boys are to be whipt.
With skin exceeding hard, he rose
   From lake, so black and muddy,
As lobsters from the ocean rise,   325
   With shell about their body:
And, as from lobster's broken claw,
   Pick out the fish you might:
So might you from one unshell'd heel
   Dig pieces of the knight.   330
His myrmidons robb'd Priam's barns
   And hen-roosts, says the song;
Carried away both corn and eggs,
   Like ants from whence they sprung.
Himself tore Hector's pantaloons,   335
   And sent him down bare-breech'd
To pedant Radamanthus, in
   A posture to be switch'd.
But George he made the dragon look,
   As if he had been bewitch'd.   340
St. George he was for England; St. Dennis was for France;
   Sing, *Honi soit qui mal y pense.*

Full fatal to the Romans was
   The Carthaginian Hanni-
bal; him I mean, who gave them such   345
   A devilish thump at Cannæ:

---

[1] Braburn, a gentleman commoner of Lincoln College, gave a silver
arrow to be shot for by the archers of the University of Oxford.

Moors thick, as goats on Penmenmure,
 Stood on the Alpes's front:
Their one-eyed guide[2], like blinking mole,
 Bor'd thro' the hind'ring mount: 350
Who, baffled by the massy rock,
 Took vinegar for relief;
Like plowmen, when they hew their way
 Thro' stubborn rump of beef.
As dancing louts from humid toes   355
 Cast atoms of ill savour
To blinking Hyatt[3], when on vile crowd
 He merriment does endeavour,
And saws from suffering timber out
 Some wretched tune to quiver: 360
So Romans stunk and squeak'd at sight
 Of Affrican carnivor.
The tawny surface of his phiz
 Did serve instead of vizzard:
But George he made the dragon have   365
 'A grumbling in his gizzard.
St. George he was for England; St. Dennis was for France;
 Sing, *Honi soit qui mal y pense.*

The valour of Domitian,
 It must not be forgotten;   370
Who from the jaws of worm-blowing flies,
 Protected veal and mutton.
A squadron of flies errant,
 Against the foe appears;
With regiments of buzzing knights,   375
 And swarms of volunteers:
The warlike wasp encourag'd 'em
 With animating hum;

[2] Hannibal had but one eye.
[3] A one-eyed fellow, who pretended to make fiddles, as well as play on them; well known at that time in Oxford.

And the loud brazen hornet next,
   He was their kettle-drum: 380
The Spanish don Cantharido
   Did him most sorely pester,
And rais'd on skin of vent'rous knight
   Full many a plaguy blister.
A bee whipt thro' his button-hole, 385
   As thro' key-hole a witch,
And stabb'd him with her little tuck
   Drawn out of scabbard breech:
But the undaunted knight lifts up
   An arm both big and brawny, 390
And slasht her so, that here lay head,
   And there lay bag and honey:
Then 'mongst the rout he flew as swift,
   As weapon made by Cyclops,
And bravely quell'd seditious buz, 395
   By dint of massive fly-flops.
Surviving flies do curses breathe,
   And maggots too at Cæsar:
But George he shav'd the dragon's beard,
   And Askelon[4] was his razor. 400
St. George he was for England; St. Dennis was for France;
   Sing, *Honi soit qui mal y pense.*

John Grubb, the facetious writer of the foregoing song,
makes a distinguished figure among the Oxford wits so
humorously enumerated in the following distich.

Alma novem genuit celebres Rhedycina poetas:
Bub, Stubb, Grubb, Crabb, Trap, Young, Carey, Tickel, Evans.

These were Bub Dodington (the late Lord Melcombe),
Dr. Stubbes, our poet Grubb, Mr. Crabb, Dr. Trapp, the
poetry-professor, Dr. Edward Young, the author of *Night
Thoughts*, Walter Carey, Thomas Tickel, Esq., and Dr. Evans,
the epigrammatist.

[4] The name of St. George's sword.

As for our poet Grubb, all that we can learn further of him, is contained in a few extracts from the University Register, and from his epitaph. It appears from the former that he was matriculated in 1667, being the son of John Grubb, "de Acton Burnel in comitatu Salop. pauperis." He took his degree of Bachelor of Arts, June 28, 1671: and became Master of Arts, June 28, 1675. He was appointed Head Master of the Grammar School at Christ Church; and afterwards chosen into the same employment at Gloucester, where he died in 1697, as appears from his monument in the church of St. Mary de Crypt in Gloucester, which is inscribed with the following epitaph: —

H. S. E.
JOHANNES GRUBB, A.M.
Natus apud Acton Burnel in agro Salopiensi
Anno Dom. 1645.
Cujus variam in linguis notitiam,
et felicem erudiendis pueris industriam,
gratâ adhuc memoriâ testatur Oxonium.
Ibi enim Æde Christi initiatus,
artes excoluit;
Pueros ad easdem mox excolendas
accuratè formavit:
Huc demum
unanimi omnium consensu accitus,
eandem suscepit provinciam,
quam feliciter adeo absolvit,
ut nihil optandum sit
nisi ut diutius nobis interfuisset.
Fuit enim
propter festivam ingenii suavitatem,
simplicem morum candorem, et
præcipuam erga cognatos benevolentiam,
omnibus desideratissimus.
Obiit 2do die Aprilis, Anno D'ni, 1697,
Ætatis suæ 51.

XVI.

Margaret's Ghost.

This ballad, which appeared in some of the public newspapers in or before the year 1724, came from the pen of David Mallet, Esq., who, in the edition of his poems, 3 vols. 1759, informs us that the plan was suggested by the four verses quoted above in page 128, which he supposed to be the beginning of some ballad now lost.

"These lines," says he, "naked of ornament and simple as they are, struck my fancy; and bringing fresh into my mind an unhappy adventure much talked of formerly, gave birth to the following poem, which was written many years ago."

The two introductory lines (and one or two others elsewhere) had originally more of the ballad simplicity, viz.

> "When all was wrapt in dark midnight,
> And all were fast asleep," &c.

'Twas at the silent solemn hour,
 When night and morning meet;
In glided Margaret's grimly ghost,
 And stood at William's feet.

Her face was like an April morn,   5
 Clad in a wintry cloud:
And clay-cold was her lily hand,
 That held her sable shrowd.

So shall the fairest face appear,
 When youth and years are flown: 10
Such is the robe that kings must wear,
 When death has reft their crown.

Her bloom was like the springing flower,
 That sips the silver dew;
The rose was budded in her cheek,   15
 Just opening to the view.

But love had, like the canker-worm,
   Consum'd her early prime:
The rose grew pale, and left her cheek;
   She dy'd before her time.   20

"Awake!" she cry'd, "thy true love calls,
   Come from her midnight grave;
Now let thy pity hear the maid
   Thy love refus'd to save.

"This is the dark and dreary hour   25
   When injur'd ghosts complain;
Now yawning graves give up their dead,
   To haunt the faithless swain.

"Bethink thee, William, of thy fault,
   Thy pledge and broken oath: 30
And give me back my maiden vow,
   And give me back my troth.

"Why did you promise love to me,
   And not that promise keep?
Why did you swear mine eyes were bright,   35
   Yet leave those eyes to weep?

"How could you say my face was fair,
   And yet that face forsake?
How could you win my virgin heart,
   Yet leave that heart to break?   40

"Why did you say my lip was sweet,
   And made the scarlet pale?
And why did I, young witless maid,
   Believe the flattering tale?

"That face, alas! no more is fair: 45
   These lips no longer red:
Dark are my eyes, now clos'd in death,
   And every charm is fled.

"The hungry worm my sister is;
　　This winding-sheet I wear:　　　　　　　　50
And cold and weary lasts our night,
　　Till that last morn appear.

"But hark! the cock has warn'd me hence!
　　A long and last adieu!
Come see, false man, how low she lies,　　　55
　　Who dy'd for love of you."

The lark sung loud; the morning smil'd
　　With beams of rosy red:
Pale William shook in ev'ry limb,
　　And raving left his bed.　　　　　　　　60

He hyed him to the fatal place
　　Where Margaret's body lay:
And stretch'd him on the grass-green turf,
　　That wrapt her breathless clay:

And thrice he call'd on Margaret's name,　　65
　　And thrice he wept full sore:
Then laid his cheek to her cold grave,
　　And word spake never more.

———

₊ In a late publication, entitled, *The Friends*, &c.
Lond. 1773, 2 vols. 12mo, (in the first volume,) is inserted a
copy of the foregoing ballad, with very great variations,
which the editor of that work contends was the original; and
that Mallet adopted it for his own, and altered it, as here
given. But the superior beauty and simplicity of the present
copy gives it so much more the air of an original, that it will
rather be believed that some transcriber altered it from Mal-
let's, and adapted the lines to his own taste; than which
nothing is more common in popular songs and ballads.

———

XVII.

Lucy and Colin,

Was written by Thomas Tickell, Esq., the celebrated friend of Mr. Addison, and editor of his works. He was son of a clergyman in the North of England; had his education at Queen's College, Oxon.; was under-secretary to Mr. Addison and Mr. Craggs, when successively secretaries of state; and was lastly (in June, 1724) appointed secretary to the Lords Justices in Ireland, which place he held till his death in 1740. He acquired Mr. Addison's patronage by a poem in praise of the opera of *Rosamond*, written while he was at the University.

It is a tradition in Ireland, that this song was written at Castletown, in the county of Kildare, at the request of the then Mrs. Conolly,—probably on some event recent in that neighbourhood.

———

Of Leinster, fam'd for maidens fair,
    Bright Lucy was the grace;
Nor e'er did Liffy's limpid stream
    Reflect so fair a face,

Till luckless love and pining care   5
    Impair'd her rosy hue,
Her coral lip, and damask cheek,
    And eyes of glossy blue.

Oh! have you seen a lily pale,
    When beating rains descend?   10
So droop'd the slow-consuming maid;
    Her life now near its end.

By Lucy warn'd, of flattering swains
    Take heed, ye easy fair:
Of vengeance due to broken vows,   15
    Ye perjured swains, beware.

Three times, all in the dead of night,
   A bell was heard to ring;
And at her window, shrieking thrice,
   The raven flap'd his wing.   20

Too well the love-lorn maiden knew
   That solemn boding sound;
And thus, in dying words, bespoke
   The virgins weeping round.

"I hear a voice you cannot hear,   25
   Which says, I must not stay:
I see a hand you cannot see,
   Which beckons me away.

"By a false heart, and broken vows,
   In early youth I die.
Am I to blame, because his bride   30
   Is thrice as rich as I?

"Ah, Colin! give not her thy vows,
   Vows due to me alone:
Nor thou, fond maid, receive his kiss,   35
   Nor think him all thy own.

"To-morrow in the church to wed,
   Impatient, both prepare;
But know, fond maid, and know, false man,
   That Lucy will be there.   40

"Then, bear my corse, ye comrades, bear,
   The bridegroom blithe to meet;
He in his wedding-trim so gay,
   I in my winding-sheet."

She spoke, she died; — her corse was borne,   45
   The bridegroom blithe to meet;
He in his wedding-trim so gay,
   She in her winding-sheet.

Then what were perjur'd Colin's thoughts?
  How were those nuptials kept?   50
The bride-men flock'd round Lucy dead,
  And all the village wept.

Confusion, shame, remorse, despair,
  At once his bosom swell:
The damps of death bedew'd his brow,   55
  He shook, he groan'd, he fell.

From the vain bride (ah, bride no more!)
  The varying crimson fled,
When, stretch'd before her rival's corse,
  She saw her husband dead.   60

Then to his Lucy's new-made grave,
  Convey'd by trembling swains,
One mould with her, beneath one sod,
  For ever now remains.

Oft at their grave the constant hind   65
  And plighted maid are seen;
With garlands gay, and true-love knots,
  They deck the sacred green.

But, swain forsworn, whoe'er thou art,
  This hallow'd spot forbear;   70
Remember Colin's dreadful fate,
  And fear to meet him there.

XVIII.

𝕿𝖍𝖊 𝕭𝖔𝖞 𝖆𝖓𝖉 𝖙𝖍𝖊 𝕸𝖆𝖓𝖙𝖑𝖊.

AS REVISED AND ALTERED BY A MODERN HAND.

MR. WARTON, in his ingenious observations on Spenser,
has given his opinion, that the fiction of the *Boy and the
Mantle* is taken from an old French piece entitled, *Le Court
Mantel*, quoted by M. de St. Palaye, in his curious "Mémoires

sur l'ancienne Chevalerie," Paris, 1759, 2 tom. 12mo; who
tells us the story resembles that of Ariosto's enchanted cup.
'Tis possible our English poet may have taken the hint of
this subject from that old French romance; but he does not
appear to have copied it in the manner of execution: to
which (if one may judge from the specimen given in the
Mémoires) that of the ballad does not bear the least re-
semblance. After all, 'tis most likely that all the old stories
concerning King Arthur are originally of British growth;
and that what the French and other southern nations have of
this kind, were at first exported from this island. See
Mémoires de l'Acad. des Inscrip. tom. xx. p. 352.

In the *Fabliaux ou Contes*, 1781, 5 tom. 12mo, of M. Le
Grand (tom. i. p. 54), is printed a modern version of the old
tale *Le Court Mantel*, under a new title, *Le Manteau maltaillé*,
which contains the story of this ballad much enlarged, so far
as regards the *mantle*, but without any mention of the *knife*
or the *horn*.

In Carleile dwelt king Arthur,
    A prince of passing might;
And there maintain'd his table round,
    Beset with many a knight.

And there he kept his Christmas   5
    With mirth and princely cheare,
When, lo! a straunge and cunning boy
    Before him did appeare.

A kirtle and a mantle
    This boy had him upon,   10
With brooches, rings, and owches,
    Full daintily bedone.

He had a sarke of silk
    About his middle meet;
And thus, with seemely curtesy,   15
    He did king Arthur greet.

"God speed thee, brave king Arthur,
    Thus feasting in thy bowre;
And Guenever thy goodly queen,
    That fair and peerlesse flowre.   20

"Ye gallant lords and lordings,
    I wish you all take heed,
Lest, what ye deem a blooming rose
    Should prove a cankred weed."

Then straitway from his bosome   25
    A little wand he drew;
And with it eke a mantle
    Of wondrous shape and hew.

"Now have thou here, king Arthur,
    Have this here of mee,   30
And give unto thy comely queen,
    All-shapen as you see.

"No wife it shall become,
    That once hath been to blame."
Then every knight in Arthur's court   35
    Slye glaunced at his dame.

And first came lady Guenever,
    The mantle she must trye.
This dame, she was new-fangled,
    And of a roving eye.   40

When she had tane the mantle,
    And all was with it cladde,
From top to toe it shiver'd down,
    As tho' with sheers beshradde.

One while it was too long,   45
    Another while too short,
And wrinkled on her shoulders
    In most unseemly sort.

Now green, now red it seemed,
  Then all of sable hue.
"Beshrew me, quoth king Arthur,   50
  I think thou beest not true."

Down she threw the mantle,
  Ne longer would not stay;
But, storming like a fury,   55
  To her chamber flung away.

She curst the whoreson weaver,
  That had the mantle wrought:
And doubly curst the froward impe,
  Who thither had it brought.   60

"I had rather live in desarts
  Beneath the green-wood tree:
Than here, base king, among thy groomes,
  The sport of them and thee."

Sir Kay call'd forth his lady,   65
  And bade her to come near:
"Yet dame, if thou be guilty,
  I pray thee now forbear."

This lady, pertly gigling,
  With forward step came on,   70
And boldly to the little boy
  With fearless face is gone.

When she had tane the mantle,
  With purpose for to wear:
It shrunk up to her shoulder,   75
  And left her b**side bare.

Then every merry knight,
  That was in Arthur's court,
Gib'd, and laught, and flouted,
  To see that pleasant sport.   80

20*

Downe she threw the mantle,
　No longer bold or gay,
But with a face all pale and wan,
　To her chamber slunk away.

Then forth came an old knight,   85
　A pattering o'er his creed;
And proffer'd to the little boy
　Five nobles to his meed;

"And all the time of Christmass
　Plumb-porridge shall be thine,   90
If thou wilt let my lady fair
　Within the mantle shine."

A saint his lady seemed,
　With step demure and slow,
And gravely to the mantle   95
　With mincing pace doth goe.

When she the same had taken,
　That was so fine and thin,
It shrivell'd all about her,
　And show'd her dainty skin.   100

Ah! little did HER mincing,
　Or HIS long prayers bestead;
She had no more hung on her,
　Than a tassel and a thread.

Down she threwe the mantle,   105
　With terror and dismay,
And with a face of scarlet,
　To her chamber hyed away.

Sir Cradock call'd his lady,
　And bade her to come neare: 110
"Come win this mantle, lady,
　And do me credit here.

"Come win this mantle, lady,
  For now it shall be thine,
If thou hast never done amiss,   115
  Sith first I made thee mine."

The lady gently blushing,
  With modest grace came on,
And now to trye the wondrous charm
  Courageously is gone.   120

When she had tane the mantle,
  And put it on her backe,
About the hem it seemed
  To wrinkle and to cracke.

"Lye still," shee cryed, "O mantle!   125
  And shame me not for nought,
I'll freely own whate'er amiss,
  Or blameful I have wrought.

"Once I kist Sir Cradocke
  Beneathe the green-wood tree: 130
Once I kist Sir Cradocke's mouth
  Before he married mee."

When thus she had her shriven,
  And her worst fault had told,
The mantle soon became her   135
  Right comely as it shold.

Most rich and fair of colour,
  Like gold it glittering shone:
And much the knights in Arthur's court
  Admir'd her every one.   140

Then towards king Arthur's table
  The boy he turn'd his eye:
Where stood a boar's head garnished
  With bayes and rosemarye.

When thrice he o'er the boar's head 145
   His little wand had drawne,
Quoth he, "There's never a cuckold's knife
   Can carve this head of brawne."

Then some their whittles rubbed
   On whetstone, and on hone: 150
Some threwe them under the table,
   And swore that they had none.

Sir Cradock had a little knife,
   Of steel and iron made;
And in an instant thro' the skull 155
   He thrust the shining blade

He thrust the shining blade
   Full easily and fast;
And every knight in Arthur's court
   A morsel had to taste. 160

The boy brought forth a horne,
   All golden was the rim:
Said he, "No cuckolde ever can
   Set mouth unto the brim.

"No cuckold can this little horne 165
   Lift fairly to his head;
But or on this, or that side,
   He shall the liquor shed."

Some shed it on their shoulder,
   Some shed it on their thigh; 170
And hee that could not hit his mouth.
   Was sure to hit his eye.

Thus he, that was a cuckold,
   Was known of every man:
But Cradock lifted easily, 175
   And wan the golden can.

Thus boar's head, horn and mantle,
  Were this fair couple's meed:
And all such constant lovers,
  God send them well to speed.   180

Then down in rage came Guenever,
  And thus could spightful say,
"Sir Cradock's wife most wrongfully
  Hath borne the prize away.

"See yonder shameless woman,   185
  That makes herselfe so clean:
Yet from her pillow taken
  Thrice five gallants have been.

"Priests, clarkes, and wedded men,
  Have her lewd pillow prest: 190
Yet she the wonderous prize forsooth
  Must beare from all the rest."

Then bespake the little boy,
  Who had the same in hold:
"Chastize thy wife, king Arthur,   195
  Of speech she is too bold:

"Of speech she is too bold,
  Of carriage all too free;
Sir king, she hath within thy hall
  A cuckold made of thee.   200

"All frolick light and wanton
  She hath her carriage borne:
And given thee for a kingly crown
  To wear a cuckold's horne."

₊

———

₊ The Rev. Evan Evans, editor of the Specimens of
Welsh poetry, 4to, affirmed that the story of the *Boy and the*

Mantle is taken from what is related in some of the old Welsh MSS. of Tegan Earfron, one of King Arthur's mistresses. She is said to have possessed a mantle that would not fit any immodest or incontinent woman; this (which, the old writers say, was reckoned among the curiosities of Britain) is frequently alluded to by the old Welsh bards.

Carleile, so often mentioned in the ballads of King Arthur, the Editor once thought might probably be a corruption of Caer-leon, an ancient British city on the river Uske, in Monmouthshire, which was one of the places of King Arthur's chief residence: but he is now convinced that it is no other than Carlisle, in Cumberland; the old English Minstrels, being most of them northern men, naturally represented the hero of romance as residing in the north: and many of the places mentioned in the old ballads are still to be found there; as *Tearne-Wadling*, &c.

Near Penrith is still seen a large circle, surrounded by a mound of earth, which retains the name of Arthur's Round Table.

XIX.

THE ANCIENT FRAGMENT OF

The Marriage of Sir Gawaine.

THE second poem in this volume, entitled, *The Marriage of Sir Gawaine*, having been offered to the reader with large conjectural supplements and corrections, the old fragment itself is here literally and exactly printed from the Editor's folio MS. with all its defects, inaccuracies, and errata: that such austere antiquaries as complain that the ancient copies have not been always rigidly adhered to, may see how unfit for publication many of the pieces would have been if all the blunders, corruptions, and nonsense of illiterate reciters and transcribers had been superstitiously retained, without some attempt to correct and amend them.

This ballad has most unfortunately suffered by having

half of every leaf in this part of the MS. torn away; and, as
about nine stanzas generally occur in the half-page now re-
maining, it is concluded that the other half contained nearly
the same number of stanzas.

———

KINGE ARTHUR liues in merry Carleile
and seemely is to see
and there he hath wth him Queene Genev^r
y^t bride so bright of blee

———

And there he hath wth him Queene Genever
y^t bride soe bright in bower
& all his barons about him stoode
y^t were both stiffe and stowre

———

The K. kept a royall Christmasse
of mirth & great honor
.. when ...

[*About nine Stanzas wanting.*]

———

And bring me word what thing it is
ye a woman most desire
this shalbe thy ransome Arthur he sayes
for Ile haue noe other hier

———

K. Arthur then held vp his hand
according thene as was the law
he tooke his leaue of the baron there
and homword can he draw

———

And when he came to Merry Carlile
to his chamber he is gone
and ther came to him his Cozen Sr Gawaine
as he did make his mone

———

And there came to him his Cozen Sr Gawaine[1]
y^t was a curteous knight

¹ Sic.

why sigh yo^u soe sore vnckle Arthur he said
or who hath done thee vnright

—————

O peace o peace thou gentle Gawaine
y^t faire may thee be ffall
for if thou knew my sighing soe deepe
thou would not meruaile att all

—————

Ffor when I came to tearne wadling
a bold barron theré I fand
wth a great club vpon his backe
standing stiffe & strong

—————

And he asked me wether I wold fight
or from him I shold be gone
o^2 else I must him a ransome pay
& soe dep't him from

—————

To fight wth him I saw noe cause
me thought it was not meet
for he was stiffe & strong wth all
his strokes were nothing sweete

—————

Therfor this is my ransome Gawaine
I ought to him to pay
I must come againe as I am sworne
vpon the Newyeers day

—————

And I must bring him word what thing it is
                    [*About nine Stanzas wanting.*]

—————

Then king Arthur drest him for to ryde
in one soe rich array
toward the foresaid Tearne wadling
y^t he might keepe his day

—————

And as he rode over a more
hee see a lady where shee sate

                    ^{2} Sic.

betwixt an oke and a greene hollen
she was clad in red scarlett

Then there as shold have stood her mouth
then there was sett her eye
the other was in her forhead fast
the way that she might see

Her nose was crooked and turnd outward
her mouth stood foule a wry
a worse formed lady then shee was
neuerman saw wth his eye

To halch vpon him k. Arthur
this lady was full faine
but k. Arthur had forgott his lesson
what he shold say againe

What knight art thou the lady sayd
that wilt not speak tome
of me thou nothing dismayd
tho I be vgly to see

for I haue halched yo^u curteouslye
& yo^u will not me againe
yett I may happen S^r knight shee said
to ease thee of thy paine

Giue thou ease me lady he said
or helpe me any thing
thou shalt haue gentle Gawaine my cozen
& marry him wth a ring

Why if I helpe thee not thou noble k. Arthur
of thy owne hearts desiringe
of gentle Gawaine . . . . .

[About nine Stanzas wanting.]

And when he came to the tearne wadling
the baron there cold he srinde[3]
wth a great weapon on his backe
standing stiffe & stronge

And then he tooke k. Arthurs letters in his hands
& away he cold them fling
& then he puld out a good browne sword
& cryd himselfe a k.

And he sayd I haue thee & thy land Arthur
to doe as it pleaseth me
for this is not thy ransome sure
therefore yeeld thee to me

And then bespoke him noble Arthur
& bade him hold his hands
& give me leave to speake my mind
in defence of all my land

the[4] said as I came over a More
I see a lady where shee sate
betweene an oke & a green hollen
shee was clad in redd scarlette

And she says a woman will haue her will
& this is all her cheef desire
doe me right as thou art a baron of sckill
this is thy ransome & all thy hyer

He sayes an early vengeance light on her
she walkes on yonder more
it was my sister that told thee this
she is a misshappen hore

But heer Ile make mine avow to god
to do her an euill turne

3 Sic MS.   4 Sic MS.

for an euer I may thate fowle theefe get
in a fyer I will her burne

[*About nine Stanzas wanting.*]

THE SECOND PART.

Sᴉʀ Lᴀɴᴄᴇʟᴏᴛᴛ & sʳ Steven bold
they rode wᵗʰ them that day
and the formost of the company
there rode the steward Kay

Soe did Sʳ Banier & Sʳ Bore
Sʳ Garrett wᵗʰ them soe gay
soe did Sʳ Tristeram yᵗ gentle k
to the forrest fresh & gay

And when he came to the greene forrest
vnderneath a greene holly tree
their sate that lady in red scarlet
yᵗ vnseemly was to see

Sʳ Kay beheld this Ladys face
& looked vppon her suire
whosoeuer kisses this lady he sayes
of his kisse he stands in feare

Sʳ Kay beheld the lady againe
& looked vpon her snout
whosoeuer kisses this lady he saies
of his kisse he stands in doubt

Peace coz. Kay then said Sʳ Gawaine
amend thee of thy life
for there is a knight amongst us all
yᵗ must marry her to his wife

What wedd her to wiffe then said Sʳ Kay
in the diuells name anon

gett me a wiffe whereere I may
for I had rather be slaine

Then soome tooke vp their hawkes in hast
& some tooke vp their hounds
& some sware they wold not marry her
For Citty nor for towne.

And then be spake him noble k. Arthur
& sware there by this day
for a litle foule sight and misliking

                   [*About nine Stanzas wanting.*]

Then shee said choose thee gentle Gawaine
truth as I doe say
wether thou wilt haue me in this liknesse
in the night or else in the day

And then bespake him Gentle Gawaine
wth one soe mild of moode
sayes well I know what I wold say
god grant it may be good

To haue thee fowle in the night
when I wth thee shold play
yet I had rather if I might
haue thee fowle in the day

What when Lords goe wth ther seires[5] shee said
both to the Ale and wine
alas then I must hyde my selfe
I must not goe withinne

And then bespake him gentle gawaine
said Lady thats but a skill
And because thou art my owne lady
Thou shalt haue all thy will

        [5] Sic in MS. pro *feires*, *i. e.* mates.

Then she said blesed be thou gentle Gawaine
this day y^t I thee see
for as thou see me att this time
from hencforth I wilbe

My father was an old knight
& yett it chanced soe
that he marryed a younge Lady
y^t brought me to this woe

Shee witched me being a faire young Lady
to the greene forrest to dwell
& there I must walke in womans liknesse
most like a feeind of hell

She witched my brother to a Carlist B . . . .

> [*About nine Stanzas wanting.*]

that looked soe foule & that was wont
on the wild more to goe

Come kisse her brother Kay then said Sr Gawaine
& amend the of thy liffe
I sweare this is the same lady
y^t I marryed to my wiffe.

Sr Kay kissed that lady bright
standing vpon his ffeete
he swore as he was trew knight
the spice was neuer soe sweete

Well Coz. Gawaine sayes Sr Kay
thy chance is fallen arright
for thou hast gotten one of the fairest maids
I euer saw wth my sight

It is my fortune said Sr Gawaine
for my Vnckle Arthurs sake

I am glad as grasse wold be of raine
great Joy that I may take

Sr Gawaine tooke the lady by the one arme
Sr Kay tooke her by the tother
they led her straight to k. Arthur
as they were brother & brother

K. Arthur welcomed them there all
& soe did lady Geneuer his queene
wth all the knights of the round table
most seemly to be seene

K. Arthur beheld that lady faire
that was soe faire & bright
he thanked christ in trinity
for S Gawaine that gentle knight

Soe did the knights both more and lesse
reioyced all that day
for the good chance y^t hapened was
to Sr Gawaine & his lady gay.　Ffinis.

In the fac-simile copies, after all the care which has been
taken, it is very possible that a redundant *e*, &c. may have
been added or omitted.

XX.

The Hermit of Warkworth.

This Ballad, together with that already printed, intitled
"The Friar of Orders Gray," forming what may be considered
the whole of Bishop Percy's original compositions, is here
appended as a necessary addition to the foregoing collection.

FIT I.

Dark was the night, and wild the storm,
    And loud the torrent's roar;
And loud the sea was heard to dash
    Against the distant shore.

Musing on man's weak hapless state,
    The lonely Hermit lay;
When, lo! he heard a female voice
    Lament in sore dismay.

With hospitable haste he rose,
    And wak'd his sleeping fire;
And snatching up a lighted brand,
    Forth hied the rev'rend sire.

All sad beneath a neighbouring tree
    A beauteous maid he found,
Who beat her breast, and with her tears
    Bedew'd the mossy ground.

"O weep not, lady, weep not so;
    Nor let vain fears alarm;
My little cell shall shelter thee,
    And keep thee safe from harm."

"It is not for myself I weep,
    Nor for myself I fear;
But for my dear and only friend,
    Who lately left me here:

"And while some sheltering bower he sought
    Within this lonely wood,
Ah! sore I fear his wandering feet
    Have slipt in yonder flood."

"Oh, trust in Heaven," the Hermit said,
    "And to my cell repair!
Doubt not but I shall find thy friend,
    And ease thee of thy care."

Then climbing up his rocky stairs,
    He scales the cliff so high;
And calls aloud, and waves his light
    To guide the stranger's eye.

Among the thickets long he winds,
    With careful steps and slow:
At length a voice return'd his call,
    Quick answering from below:

"O tell me, father, tell me true,
    If you have chanc'd to see
A gentle maid, I lately left
    Beneath some neighbouring tree:

"But either I have lost the place,
    Or she hath gone astray:
And much I fear this fatal stream
    Hath snatch'd her hence away."

"Praise Heaven, my son," the Hermit said;
    "The lady's safe and well:"
And soon he join'd the wandering youth,
    And brought him to his cell.

Then well was seen, these gentle friends,
    They lov'd each other dear:
The youth he press'd her to his heart;
    The maid let fall a tear.

Ah! seldom had their host, I ween,
    Beheld so sweet a pair:
The youth was tall, with manly bloom;
    She, slender, soft, and fair.

The youth was clad in forest green,
    With bugle-horn so bright:
She in a silken robe and scarf,
    Snatch'd up in hasty flight.

"Sit down, my children," says the sage;
  "Sweet rest your limbs require
Then heaps fresh fuel on the hearth,
  And mends his little fire.

"Partake," he said, "my simple store,
  Dried fruits, and milk, and curds;"
And spreading all upon the board,
  Invites with kindly words.

"Thanks, father, for thy bounteous fare;"
  The youthful couple say:
Then freely ate, and made good cheer,
  And talk'd their cares away.

"Now say, my children, (for perchance
  My counsel may avail),
What strange adventure brought you here
  Within this lonely dale?"

"First tell me, father," said the youth,
  "(Nor blame mine eager tongue),
What town is near? What lands are these?
  And to what lord belong?"

"Alas! my son," the Hermit said,
  "Why do I live to say,
The rightful lord of these domains
  Is banish'd far away?

"Ten winters now have shed their snows
  On this my lowly hall,
Since valiant Hotspur (so the North
  Our youthful lord did call)

"Against Fourth Henry Bolingbroke
  Led up his northern powers,
And, stoutly fighting, lost his life
  Near proud Salopia's towers.

21 *

"One son he left, a lovely boy,
 His country's hope and heir;
And, oh! to save him from his foes
 It was his grandsire's care.

"In Scotland safe he plac'd the child
 Beyond the reach of strife,
Nor long before the brave old Earl
 At Braham lost his life.

"And now the Percy name, so long
 Our northern pride and boast,
Lies hid, alas! beneath a cloud;
 Their honours reft and lost.

" No chieftain of that noble house
 Now leads our youth to arms;
The bordering Scots despoil our fields,
 And ravage all our farms.

"Their halls and castles, once so fair,
 Now moulder in decay;
Proud strangers now usurp their lands,
 And bear their wealth away.

"Nor far from hence, where yon full stream
 Runs winding down the lea,
Fair Warkworth lifts her lofty towers,
 And overlooks the sea.

"Those towers, alas! now lie forlorn,
 With noisome weeds o'erspread,
Where feasted lords and courtly dames,
 And where the poor were fed.

"Meantime far off, 'mid Scottish hills,
 The Percy lives unknown:
On strangers' bounty he depends,
 And may not claim his own.

"O might I with these aged eyes
    But live to see him here,
Then should my soul depart in bliss!"—
    He said, and dropt a tear.

"And is the Percy still so lov'd
    Of all his friends and thee?
Then, bless me, father," said the youth,
    "For I, thy guest, am he."

Silent he gaz'd, then turn'd aside
    To wipe the tears he shed;
And lifting up his hands and eyes,
    Pour'd blessings on his head:

"Welcome, our dear and much-lov'd lord,
    Thy country's hope and care:
But who may this young lady be,
    That is so wondrous fair?"

"Now, father! listen to my tale,
    And thou shalt know the truth:
And let thy sage advice direct
    My inexperienc'd youth.

"In Scotland I've been nobly bred
    Beneath the Regent's[1] hand,
In feats of arms, and every lore
    To fit me for command.

"With fond impatience long I burn'd
    My native land to see:
At length I won my guardian friend
    To yield that boon to me.

"Then up and down in hunter's garb
    I wander'd as in chase,

---

[1] Robert Stuart, Duke of Albany. See the continuation of Fordun's Scoti-Chronicon, cap. 18, cap. 23, &c.

Till in the noble Neville's[2] house
    I gain'd a hunter's place.

"Some time with him I liv'd unknown,
    Till I'd the hap so rare
To please this young and gentle dame,
    That Baron's daughter fair."

"Now, Percy," said the blushing maid,
    "The truth I must reveal;
Souls great and generous, like to thine,
    Their noble deeds conceal.

"It happen'd on a summer's day,
    Led by the fragant breeze,
I wander'd forth to take the air
    Among the green-wood trees.

"Sudden a band of rugged Scots,
    That near in ambush lay,
Moss-troopers from the border-side,
    There seiz'd me for their prey.

"My shrieks had all been spent in vain;
    But Heaven, that saw my grief,
Brought this brave youth within my call,
    Who flew to my relief.

"With nothing but his hunting spear,
    And dagger in his hand,
He sprung like lightning on my foes,
    And caus'd them soon to stand.

"He fought till more assistance came:
    The Scots were overthrown;
Thus freed me, captive, from their bands,
    To make me more his own."

2 Ralph Neville, first Earl of Westmoreland, who chiefly resided at his
two castles of Brancepeth, and Raby, both in the Bishoprick of Durham.

"O happy day!" the youth replied:
  "Blest were the wounds I bear!
From that fond hour she deign'd to smile,
  And listen to my prayer.

"And when she knew my name and birth,
  She vow'd to be my bride;
But oh! we fear'd (alas, the while!)
  Her princely mother's pride:

"Sister of haughty Bolingbroke[3],
  Our house's ancient foe,
To me, I thought, a banish'd wight,
  Could ne'er such favour shew.

"Despairing then to gain consent,
  At length to fly with me
I won this lovely timorous maid;
  To Scotland bound are we.

"This evening, as the night drew on,
  Fearing we were pursued,
We turn'd adown the right-hand path,
  And gain'd this lonely wood:

"Then lighting from our weary steeds
  To shun the pelting shower,
We met thy kind conducting hand,
  And reach'd this friendly bower."

"Now rest ye both," the Hermit said;
  "Awhile your cares forego:
Nor, Lady, scorn my humble bed:
  —We'll pass the night below[4]."

[3] Joan, Countess of Westmoreland, mother of the young lady, was daughter of John of Gaunt, and half sister of King Henry IV.

[4] Adjoining to the cliff which contains the Chapel of the Hermitage, are the remains of a small building, in which the Hermit dwelt. This consisted of one lower apartment, with a little bedchamber over it, and is now in ruins; whereas the Chapel, cut in the solid rock, is still very intire and perfect.

LOVELY smil'd the blushing morn,
　And every storm was fled:
But lovelier far, with sweeter smile,
　Fair Eleanor left her bed.

She found her Henry all alone,
　And cheer'd him with her sight;
The youth consulting with his friend
　Had watch'd the livelong night.

What sweet surprise o'erpower'd her breast!
　Her cheek what blushes dyed,
When fondly he besought her there
　To yield to be his bride! —

"Within this lonely hermitage
　There is a chapel meet:
Then grant, dear maid, my fond request,
　And make my bliss complete."

"O Henry, when thou deign'st to sue,
　Can I thy suit withstand?
When thou, lov'd youth, hast won my heart,
　Can I refuse my hand?

"For thee I left a father's smiles,
　And mother's tender care;
And whether weal or woe betide,
　Thy lot I mean to share."

"And wilt thou then, O generous maid!
　Such matchless favour show,
To share with me, a banish'd wight,
　My peril, pain, or woe?

"Now Heaven, I trust, hath joys in store
　To crown thy constant breast:
For know, fond hope assures my heart
　That we shall soon be blest.

"Not far from hence stands Coquet Isle[5]
  Surrounded by the sea;
There dwells a holy friar, well known
  To all thy friends and thee;

"'Tis Father Bernard, so rever'd
  For every worthy deed;
To Raby Castle he shall go,
  And for us kindly plead.

"To fetch this good and holy man
  Our reverend host is gone;
And soon, I trust, his pious hands
  Will join us both in one."

Thus they in sweet and tender talk
  The lingering hours beguile:
At length they see the hoary sage
  Come from the neighbouring isle.

With pious joy and wonder mix'd
  He greets the noble pair,
And glad consents to join their hands
  With many a fervent prayer.

Then strait to Raby's distant walls
  He kindly wends his way:
Meantime in love and dalliance sweet
  They spend the livelong day.

And now, attended by their host,
  The Hermitage they view'd,
Deep-hewn within a craggy cliff,
  And overhung with wood.

And near a flight of shapely steps,
  All cut with nicest skill,

[5] In the little island of Coquet, near Warkworth, are still seen the ruins
of a cell, which belonged to the Benedictine monks of Tinemouth-Abbey.

And piercing through a stony arch,
   Ran winding up the hill:

There deck'd with many a flower and herb
   His little garden stands;
With fruitful trees in shady rows,
   All planted by his hands.

Then, scoop'd within the solid rock,
   Three sacred vaults he shows:
The chief, a chapel, neatly arch'd,
   On branching columns rose.

Each proper ornament was there,
   That should a chapel grace;
The lattice for confession fram'd,
   And holy-water vase.

O'er either door a sacred text
   Invites to godly fear;
And in a little scutcheon hung
   The cross, and crown, and spear.

Up to the altar's ample breadth
   Two easy steps ascend;
And near, a glimmering solemn light
   Two well-wrought windows lend.

Beside the altar rose a tomb
   All in the living stone;
On which a young and beauteous maid
   In goodly sculpture shone.

A kneeling angel, fairly carv'd,
   Lean'd hovering o'er her breast;
A weeping warrior at her feet;
   And near to these her crest[6].

6 This is a Bull's Head, the crest of the Widdrington family. All the
figures, &c. here described are still visible, only somewhat effaced with
length of time.

The clift, the vault, but chief the tomb
  Attract the wondering pair:
Eager they ask, "What hapless dame
  Lies sculptur'd here so fair?"

The Hermit sigh'd, the Hermit wept,
  For sorrow scarce could speak:
At length he wip'd the trickling tears
  That all bedew'd his cheek.

"Alas! my children, human life
  Is but a vale of woe;
And very mournful is the tale
  Which ye so fain would know!"

THE HERMIT'S TALE.

Young lord, thy grandsire had a friend
  In days of youthful fame;
Yon distant hills were his domains,
  Sir Bertram was his name.

Where'er the noble Percy fought,
  His friend was at his side;
And many a skirmish with the Scots
  Their early valour tried.

Young Bertram lov'd a beauteous maid,
  As fair as fair might be;
The dew-drop on the lily's cheek
  Was not so fair as she.

Fair Widdrington the maiden's name,
  Yon towers her dwelling-place[7];
Her sire an old Northumbrian chief,
  Devoted to thy race.

[7] Widdrington Castle is about five miles south of Warkworth.

Many a lord, and many a knight,
　To this fair damsel came;
But Bertram was her only choice;
　For him she felt a flame.

Lord Percy pleaded for his friend,
　Her father soon consents;
None but the beauteous maid herself
　His wishes now prevents.

But she, with studied fond delays,
　Defers the blissful hour;
And loves to try his constancy,
　And prove her maiden power.

"That heart," she said, "is lightly priz'd,
　Which is too lightly won;
And long shall rue that easy maid
　Who yields her love too soon."

Lord Percy made a solemn feast
　In Alnwick's princely hall;
And there came lords, and there came knights,
　His chiefs and barons all.

With wassail, mirth, and revelry,
　The castle rang around:
Lord Percy call'd for song and harp,
　And pipes of martial sound.

The minstrels of thy noble house,
　All clad in robes of blue,
With silver crescents on their arms,
　Attend in order due.

The great achievements of thy race
　They sung: their high command:
How valiant Mainfred o'er the seas
　First led his northern band[8].

[8] See Dugdale's Baronetage, p. 269, &c.

Brave Galfred next to Normandy
　　With venturous Rollo came;
And, from his Norman castles won,
　　Assum'd the Percy name[9].

They sung how in the Conqueror's fleet
　　Lord William shipp'd his powers,
And gain'd a fair young Saxon bride
　　With all her lands and towers[10].

Then journeying to the Holy Land,
　　There bravely fought and died;
But first the silver crescent won,
　　Some paynim Soldan's pride.

They sung how Agnes, beauteous heir,
　　The Queen's own brother wed,
Lord Josceline, sprung from Charlemagne,
　　In princely Brabant bred[1];

How he the Percy name reviv'd,
　　And how his noble line,
Still foremost in their country's cause,
　　With godlike ardour shine.

[9] In Lower Normandy are three places of the name of Percy: whence the family took the surname of De Percy.

[10] William de Percy fifth in descent from Galfred or Geffery de Percy, son of Mainfred) assisted in the conquest of England, and had given him the large possessions, in Yorkshire, of Emma de Porte (so the Norman writers name her), whose father, a great Saxon lord, had been slain fighting along with Harold. This young lady, William from a principle of honour and generosity, married: for having had all her lands bestowed upon him by the Conqueror, "he (to use the words of the old Whitby Chronicle) wedded hyr that was very heire to them, in discharging of his conscience." See Harl. MSS. 692 (26). He died at Mountjoy, near Jerusalem, in the first crusade.

[1] Agnes de Percy, sole heiress of her house, married Josceline de Louvaine, youngest son of Godfrey Barbatus, Duke of Brabant, and brother of Queen Adeliza, second wife of King Henry I. He took the name of Percy, and was ancestor of the earls of Northumberland. His son, lord Richard de Percy, was one of the twenty-six barons chosen to see the Magna Charta duly observed.

With loud acclaims the list'ning crowd
  Applaud the master's song,
And deeds of arms and war became
  The theme of every tongue.

Now high heroic acts they tell,
  Their perils past recall:
When, lo! a damsel young and fair
  Stepp'd forward through the hall.

She Bertram courteously address'd;
  And, kneeling on her knee, —
"Sir knight, the lady of thy love
  Hath sent this gift to thee."

Then forth she drew a glittering helm,
  Well plaited many a fold;
The casque was wrought of temper'd steel,
  The crest of burnish'd gold.

"Sir knight, thy lady sends thee this,
  And yields to be thy bride,
When thou hast prov'd this maiden gift
  Where sharpest blows are tried."

Young Bertram took the shining helm,
  And thrice he kiss'd the same:
"Trust me, I'll prove this precious casque
  With deeds of noblest fame."

Lord Percy, and his Barons bold,
  Then fix upon a day
To scour the marches, late opprest,
  And Scottish wrongs repay.

The knights assembled on the hills
  A thousand horse or more:
Brave Widdrington, though sunk in years,
  The Percy standard bore.

Tweed's limpid current soon they pass,
  And range the borders round:
Down the green slopes of Tiviotdale
  Their bugle-horns resound.

As when a lion in his den
  Hath heard the hunters' cries,
And rushes forth to meet his foes;
  So did the Douglas rise.

Attendant on their chief's command
  A thousand warriors wait:
And now the fatal hour drew on
  Of cruel keen debate.

A chosen troop of Scottish youths
  Advance before the rest;
Lord Percy mark'd their gallant mien,
  And thus his friend address'd:

"Now, Bertram, prove thy lady's helm,
  Attack yon forward band;
Dead or alive I'll rescue thee,
  Or perish by their hand."

Young Bertram bow'd, with glad assent,
  And spurr'd his eager steed,
And calling on his lady's name,
  Rush'd forth with whirlwind speed.

As when a grove of sapling oaks
  The livid lightning rends;
So fiercely 'mid the opposing ranks
  Sir Bertram's sword descends.

This way and that he drives the steel,
  And keenly pierces through;
And many a tall and comely knight
  With furious force he slew.

Now closing fast on every side,
    They hem Sir Bertram round:
But dauntless he repels their rage,
    And deals forth many a wound.

The vigour of his single arm
    Had well nigh won the field;
When ponderous fell a Scottish axe,
    And clave his lifted shield.

Another blow his temples took,
    And reft his helm in twain;
That beauteous helm, his lady's gift!
    ——His blood bedew'd the plain.

Lord Percy saw his champion fall
    Amid th' unequal fight;
"And now, my noble friends," he said,
    "Let's save this gallant knight."

Then rushing in, with stretch'd-out shield,
    He o'er the warrior hung,
As some fierce eagle spreads her wing
    To guard her callow young.

Three times they strove to seize their prey,
    Three times they quick retire:
What force could stand his furious strokes,
    Or meet his martial fire?

Now gathering round on every part
    The battle rag'd amain;
And many a lady wept her lord,
    That hour untimely slain.

Percy and Douglas, great in arms,
    There all their courage show'd;
And all the field was strew'd with dead,
    And all with crimson flow'd.

At length the glory of the day
  The Scots reluctant yield,
And, after wondrous valour show
  They slowly quit the field.

All pale, extended on their shields,
  And weltering in his gore,
Lord Percy's knights their bleeding friend
  To Wark's fair castle bore[2].

"Well hast thou earn'd my daughter's love,"
  Her father kindly said;
"And she herself shall dress thy wounds,
  And tend thee in thy bed."

A message went; no daughter came,
  Fair Isabel ne'er appears;
"Beshrew me," said the aged chief,
  "Young maidens have their fears.

"Cheer up, my son, thou shalt her see,
  So soon as thou canst ride;
And she shall nurse thee in her bower,
  And she shall be thy bride."

Sir Bertram at her name reviv'd,
  He bless'd the soothing sound;
Fond hope supplied the nurse's care,
  And heal'd his ghastly wound.

FIT III.

One early morn, while dewy drops
  Hung trembling on the tree,
Sir Bertram from his sick-bed rose;
  His bride he would go see.

------

[2] Wark Castle, a fortress belonging to the English, and of great note in ancient times, stood on the southern banks of the River Tweed, a little to the east of Tiviotdale, and not far from Kelso. It is now entirely destroyed.

A brother he had in prime of youth,
    Of courage firm and keen;
And he would 'tend him on the way,
    Because his wounds were green.

All day o'er moss and moor they rode,
    By many a lonely tower;
And 'twas the dew-fall of the night
    Ere they drew near her bower.

Most drear and dark the castle seem'd,
    That wont to shine so bright;
And long and loud Sir Bertram call'd
    Ere he beheld a light.

At length her aged nurse arose,
    With voice so shrill and clear,—
"What wight is this, that calls so loud,
    And knocks so boldly here?"

"'Tis Bertram calls, thy lady's love,
    Come from his bed of care:
All day I've ridden o'er moor and moss
    To see thy lady fair."

"Now out, alas!" she loudly shriek'd;
    "Alas! how may this be!
For six long days are gone and past
    Since she set out to thee."

Sad terror seiz'd Sir Bertram's heart,
    And ready was he to fall;
When now the drawbridge was let down,
    And gates were opened all.

"Six days, young knight, are past and gone,
    Since she set out to thee;
And sure, if no sad harm had happ'd,
    Long since thou wouldst her see."

"For when she heard thy grievous chance,
  She tore her hair, and cried,
'Alas! I've slain the comeliest knight,
  All through my folly and pride!

"'And now to atone for my sad fault
  And his dear health regain,
I'll go myself, and nurse my love,
  And soothe his bed of pain.'

"Then mounted she her milk-white steed
  One morn at break of day;
And two tall yeomen went with her,
  To guard her on the way."

Sad terror smote Sir Bertram's heart,
  And grief o'erwhelm'd his mind:
"Trust me," said he, "I ne'er will rest
  Till I thy lady find."

That night he spent in sorrow and care;
  And with sad-boding heart
Or ever the dawning of the day
  His brother and he depart.

"Now, brother, we'll our ways divide,
  O'er Scottish hills to range;
Do thou go north, and I'll go west;
  And all our dress we'll change.

"Some Scottish carle hath seiz'd my love,
  And borne her to his den;
And ne'er will I tread English ground
  Till she's restor'd again."

"The brothers straight their paths divide,
  O'er Scottish hills to range;
And hide themselves in quaint disguise,
  And oft their dress they change.

22*

Sir Bertram, clad in gown of grey,
　　Most like a palmer poor,
To halls and castles wanders round,
　　And begs from door to door.

Sometimes a minstrel's garb he wears,
　　With pipe so sweet and shrill;
And wends to every tower and town,
　　O'er every dale and hill.

One day as he sat under a thorn,
　　All sunk in deep despair,
An aged pilgrim pass'd him by,
　　Who mark'd his face of care.

"All minstrels yet that e'er I saw
　　Are full of game and glee;
But thou art sad and woe-begone!
　　I marvel whence it be!"

"Father, I serve an aged lord,
　　Whose grief afflicts my mind;
His only child is stolen away,
　　And fain I would her find."

"Cheer up, my son; perchance," he said,
　　"Some tidings I may bear:
For oft when human hopes have fail'd,
　　Then heavenly comfort's near.

"Behind yon hills so steep and high,
　　Down in a lowly glen,
There stands a castle fair and strong,
　　Far from the abode of men.

"As late I chanc'd to crave an alms,
　　About this evening hour,
Methought I heard a lady's voice
　　Lamenting in the tower.

"And when I ask'd what harm had happ'd,
   What lady sick there lay?
They rudely drove me from the gate,
   And bade me wend away."

These tidings caught Sir Bertram's ear,
   He thank'd him for his tale;
And soon he hasted o'er the hills,
   And soon he reach'd the vale.

Then drawing near those lonely towers,
   Which stood in dale so low,
And sitting down beside the gate,
   His pipes he 'gan to blow.

"Sir Porter, is thy lord at home,
   To hear a minstrel's song;
Or may I crave a lodging here,
   Without offence or wrong?"

"My lord," he said, "is not at home,
   To hear a minstrel's song;
And, should I lend thee lodging here,
   My life would not be long."

He play'd again so soft a strain,
   Such power sweet sounds impart,
He won the churlish porter's ear,
   And mov'd his stubborn heart.

"Minstrel," he said, "thou play'st so sweet,
   Fair entrance thou should'st win;
But, alas! I'm sworn upon the rood
   To let no stranger in.

"Yet, minstrel, in yon rising cliff
   Thou'lt find a sheltering cave;
And here thou shalt my supper share,
   And there thy lodging have."

All day he sits beside the gate,
  And pipes both loud and clear:
All night he watches round the walls,
  In hopes his love to hear.

The first night, as he silent watch'd
  All at the midnight hour,
He plainly heard his lady's voice
  Lamenting in the tower.

The second night, the moon shone clear,
  And gilt the spangled dew;
He saw his lady through the grate,
  But 'twas a transient view.

The third night, wearied out, he slept
  'Till near the morning tide;
When, starting up, he seiz'd his sword,
  And to the castle hied.

When, lo! he saw a ladder of ropes
  Depending from the wall:
And o'er the moat was newly laid
  A poplar strong and tall.

And soon he saw his love descend
  Wrapt in a tartan plaid,
Assisted by a sturdy youth
  In Highland garb y-clad.

Amaz'd, confounded at the sight,
  He lay unseen and still;
And soon he saw them cross the stream,
  And mount the neighbouring hill.

Unheard, unknown of all within,
  The youthful couple fly;
But what can 'scape the lover's ken,
  Or shun his piercing eye?

With silent step he follows close
  Behind the flying pair,
And saw her hang upon his arm
  With fond familiar air.

"Thanks, gentle youth," she often said;
  "My thanks thou well hast won:
For me what wiles hast thou contriv'd!
  For me what dangers run!

"And ever shall my grateful heart
  Thy services repay:"—
Sir Bertram would no further hear,
  But cried, "Vile traitor, stay!

"Vile traitor! yield that lady up!"
  And quick his sword he drew;
The stranger turn'd in sudden rage,
  And at Sir Bertram flew.

With mortal hate their vigorous arms
  Gave many a vengeful blow;
But Bertram's stronger hand prevail'd,
  And laid the stranger low.

"Die, traitor, die!"—A deadly thrust
  Attends each furious word.
Ah! then fair Isabel knew his voice,
  And rush'd beneath his sword.

"O stop," she cried, "O stop thy arm!
  Thou dost thy brother slay!"—
And here the Hermit paus'd, and wept
  His tongue no more could say.

At length he cried, "Ye lovely pair,
  How shall I tell the rest?
Ere I could stop my piercing sword,
  It fell, and stabb'd her breast."

"Wert thou thyself that hapless youth?
　　Ah! cruel fate!" they said.
The Hermit wept, and so did they:
　　They sigh'd; he hung his head.

"O blind and jealous rage," he cried,
　　"What evils from thee flow?"
The Hermit paus'd; they silent mourn'd:
　　He wept, and they were woe.

Ah! when I heard my brother's name,
　　And saw my lady bleed,
I rav'd, I wept, I curst my arm
　　That wrought the fatal deed.

In vain I clasp'd her to my breast,
　　And clos'd the ghastly wound;
In vain I press'd his bleeding corpse,
　　And rais'd it from the ground.

My brother, alas! spake never more,
　　His precious life was flown:
She kindly strove to soothe my pain,
　　Regardless of her own.

"Bertram," she said, "be comforted,
　　And live to think on me:
May we in heaven that union prove,
　　Which here was not to be!

"Bertram," she said, "I still was true;
　　Thou only hadst my heart:
May we hereafter meet in bliss!
　　We now, alas! must part.

"For thee I left my father's hall,
　　And flew to thy relief,
When, lo! near Cheviot's fatal hills
　　I met a Scottish chief,

"Lord Malcolm's son, whose proffer'd love
  I had refus'd with scorn;
He slew my guards, and seiz'd on me
  Upon that fatal morn;

"And in these dreary hated walls
  He kept me close confin'd;
And fondly sued, and warmly press'd,
  To win me to his mind.

"Each rising morn increas'd my pain,
  Each night increas'd my fear!
When, wandering in this northern garb,
  Thy brother found me here.

"He quickly form'd the brave design
  To set me, captive, free;
And on the moor his horses wait,
  Tied to a neighbouring tree.

"Then haste, my love, escape away,
  And for thyself provide;
And sometimes fondly think on her
  Who should have been thy bride."

Thus, pouring comfort on my soul,
  Even with her latest breath,
She gave one parting, fond embrace,
  And clos'd her eyes in death.

In wild amaze, in speechless woe,
  Devoid of sense, I lay:
Then sudden, all in frantic mood,
  I meant myself to slay.

And, rising up in furious haste,
  I seiz'd the bloody brand[3]:
A sturdy arm here interpos'd,
  And wrench'd it from my hand.

[3] i. e. sword.

A crowd, that from the castle came,
　　Had miss'd their lovely ward;
And seizing me, to prison bare,
　　And deep in dungeon barr'd.

It chanc'd that on that very morn
　　Their chief was prisoner ta'en;
Lord Percy had us soon exchang'd,
　　And strove to soothe my pain.

And soon those honour'd dear remains
　　To England were convey'd;
And there within their silent tombs,
　　With holy rites, were laid.

For me, I loath'd my wretched life,
　　And long to end it thought;
Till time, and books, and holy men,
　　Had better counsels taught.

They rais'd my heart to that pure source
　　Whence heavenly comfort flows:
They taught me to despise the world,
　　And calmly bear its woes.

No more the slave of human pride,
　　Vain hope, and sordid care,
I meekly vow'd to spend my life
　　In penitence and prayer.

The bold Sir Bertram, now no more
　　Impetuous, haughty, wild;
But poor and humble Benedict,
　　Now lowly, patient, mild.

My lands I gave to feed the poor,
　　And sacred altars raise;
And here, a lonely anchorite,
　　I came to end my days.

This sweet sequester'd vale I chose,
    These rocks, and hanging grove;
For oft beside that murmuring stream
    My love was wont to rove.

My noble friend approv'd my choice;
    This blest retreat he gave:
And here I carv'd her beauteous form,
    And scoop'd this holy cave.

Full fifty winters, all forlorn,
    My life I've linger'd here;
And daily o'er this sculptur'd saint
    I drop the pensive tear.

And thou, dear brother of my heart!
    So faithful and so true,
The sad remembrance of thy fate
    Still makes my bosom rue!

Yet not unpitied pass'd my life,
    Forsaken or forgot,
The Percy and his noble sons
    Would grace my lowly cot;

Oft the great Earl, from toils of state
    And cumbrous pomp of power,
Would gladly seek my little cell,
    To spend the tranquil hour.

But length of life is length of woe!
    I liv'd to mourn his fall:
I liv'd to mourn his godlike sons
    And friends and followers all.

But thou the honours of thy race,
    Lov'd youth, shalt now restore;
And raise again the Percy name
    More glorious than before.

He ceas'd; and on the lovely pair
   His choicest blessings laid:
While they, with thanks and pitying tears,
   His mournful tale repaid.

And now what present course to take
   They ask the good old sire;
And, guided by his sage advice,
   To Scotland they retire.

Meantime their suit such favour found
   At Raby's stately hall,
Earl Neville and his princely spouse
   Now gladly pardon all.

She, suppliant, at her nephew's[4] throne
   The royal grace implor'd:
To all the honours of his race
   The Percy was restor'd.

The youthful Earl still more and more
   Admir'd his beauteous dame:
Nine noble sons to him she bore,
   All worthy of their name.

[4] King Henry V. Anno 1414.

END OF THE THIRD BOOK.

A GLOSSARY

OF

THE OBSOLETE AND SCOTTISH WORDS IN THE THIRD VOLUME.

Such words as the reader cannot find here, he is desired to look for in the Glossaries to the other volumes.

A' Au, s. *all.*
Abye, *suffer, to pay for.*
Aff, s. *off.*
Afore, *before.*
Aik, s. *oak.*
Aith, s. *oath.*
Ane, s. *one; an, a.*
Ann, *if.*
Aquoy, p. 240, *coy, shy.*
Astonied, *astonished, stunned.*
Auld, s. *old.*
Avowe, *vow.*
Awa', s. *away.*
Aye, *ever;* also, *ah! alas!*
Azont, s. *beyond.*

B.

Ban, *curse.*
Banderolles, *streamers, little flags.*
Baud, s. *bold.*
Bedeene, *immediately.*
Bedone, *wrought, made up.*
Beere, s. *bier.*
Ben [1], s. *within doors.*
Bent, s. *long grass;* also, *wild fields, where bents, &c. grow.*
Bereth, (Introd.) *beareth.*
Bernes, *barns.*
Beseeme, *become.*
Beshradde, *cut into shreds.*

Beshrew me! *a lesser form of imprecation.*
Besmirche, *to soil, discolour.*
Blee, *complexion.*
Blent, *blended.*
Blinkan, blinkand, s. *twinkling.*
Blinking, p. 296, *squinting.*
Blinks, s. *twinkles, sparkles.*
Blinne, *cease, give over.*
Blyth, blithe, *sprightly, joyous.*
Blyth, p. 89, *joy, sprightliness.*
Bookesman, *clerk, secretary.*
Boon, *favour, request, petition.*
Bore, *born.*
Bower, bowre, *any bowed or arched room; a parlour, chamber;* also, *a dwelling in general.*
Bowre woman, s. *chamber-maid.*
Brae, s. *the brow or side of a hill, a declivity.*
Brakes, *tufts of fern.*
Brand, *sword.*
Brast, *burst.*
Braw, s. *brave.*
Brayde, *drew out, unsheathed.*
Brenn, s. *burn.*
Bridal, (properly bride-ale,) *the nuptial feast.*
Brigue, brigg, *bridge.*
Britled, *carved. Vide* Bryttlynge. Gloss. Vol. i.

---

[1] *Ben* is from the Dutch *Binnen*, Lat. *intra, intus*, which is compounded of the preposition *By*, or *Be*, the same as *By* in English, and of *in* (compare *But*).

Brocht, s. *brought.*

Brooche, brouche, 1st, *a spit;* 2ndly, *a bodkin;* 3rdly, *any ornamental trinket.* Stonebuckles of silver or gold, with which gentlemen and ladies clasp their shirt-bosoms and handkerchiefs, are called in the north *brooches,* from the f. broche, *a spit.*

Bugle, bugle-horn, *a hunting-horn: being the horn of a bugle, or wild bull.*

Burn, bourne, *brook.*

Busk, *dress, deck.*

But if, *unless.*

Butt[2], s. *without, out of doors.*

Byre, s. *cow-house.*

C.

Caitiff, *a slave.*

Can, *'gan, began.*

Canna, s. *cannot.*

Carle, *a churl, clown.*

Carlish, *churlish, discourteous.*

Cau, s. *call.*

Cauld, s. *cold.*

Certes, *certainly.*

Chap, p. 106, *knock.*

Chevaliers, f. *knights.*

Chield, s. is a slight or familiar way of speaking of a person, like our English word *fellow.* The chield, i. e. *the fellow.*

Child, p. 75, *a knight. See* Vol. i. Gloss. &c.

Christentie, *Christendome.*

Church-ale, *a wake; a feast in commemoration of the dedication of a church.*

Churl, *clown; a person of low birth; a villain.*

Claiths, s. *clothes.*

Clead, s. *clothed.*

Cleading, s. *clothing.*

Cled, s. *clad, clothed.*

Clerks, *clergymen, literati, scholars.*

Cliding, s. *clothing.*

Cold, could, p. 35, *knew.*

Coleyne, *Cologne steel.*

Con thanks, *give thanks.*

Courtnalls, note, p. 182.

Cramasie, s. *crimson.*

Cranion, *skull.*

Crinkle, *run in and out, run into flexures, wrinkle.*

Crook, *twist, wrinkle, distort.*

Crowt, *to pucker up.*

Cum, s. *come.*

D.

Dank, *moist, damp.*

Dawes (Introd.) *days.*

Dealan, deland, s. *dealing.*

Deas, deis, *the high table in a hall: from* f. dais, *a canopy.*

Dee, s. *die.*

Deed, (Introd.) *dead.*

Deemed, p. 72, *doomed, judged, &c.:* thus, in the Isle of Man, Judges are called *deemsters.*

Deerely, p. 54, *preciously, richly.*

Deid, s. *dead.*

Deid bell, s. *passing bell.*

Dell, *narrow valley.*

Delt, *dealt.*

Demains, *demesnes; estate in lands.*

Descrye, p. 170, descrive, *describe.*

Dight, *decked.*

Din, dinne, *noise, bustle.*

Ding, *knock, beat.*

Disna, s. *doest not.*

Distrere, *the horse rode by a knight in the tournament.*

Dosend, s. *dosing, drowsy, torpid, benumbed, &c.*

Doublet, *a man's inner garment; waistcoat.*

Doubt, *fear.*

Doubteous, *doubtful.*

Douzty, *doughty.*

Drapping, s. *dropping.*

Dreiry, s. *dreary.*

Dule, s. *dole, sorrow.*

Dwellan, dwelland, s. *dwelling.*

Dyan, dyand, s. *dying.*

E.

Eather, s. *either.*

Ee; een, eyne, s. *eye; eyes.*

---

2 *But,* or *Butt,* is from the Dutch *Buyten,* Latin *extra, prater, præterquam,* which is compounded of the preposition *By* or *Be* (compare *Ben*), and of *uyt,* the same as *out* in English.

Een, *even, evening.*
Effund, *pour forth.*
Eftsoon, *in a short time.*
Eir, s. *e'er, ever.*
Eke, *also.*
Enouch, s. *enough.*
Evanished, s. *vanished.*
Everiche, *every, each.*
Everychone, *every one.*
Ew-boughts, p. 89, or Ewe-boughts, s. are small enclosures, or pens, into which the farmers drive (Scoticè *weir*) their milch ewes, morning and evening, in order to milk them. They are commonly made with *fale-dykes,* i. e. *earthen dykes.*
Ezar, note, p. 107, *azure.*

F.

Fadge, s. *a thick loaf of bread;* figuratively, *any coarse heap of stuff.*
Fain, *glad, fond, well-pleased.*
Falds, s. *thou foldest.*
Fallan', falland, s. *falling.*
Falser, *a deceiver, hypocrite.*
Fa's, s. *thou fallest.*
Faw'n, s. *fallen.*
Faye, *faith.*
Feare, fere, feire, *mate.*
Fee, *reward, recompense;* it also signifies land, when it is connected with the tenure by which it is held; as *knight's fee, &c.*
Fet, *fetched.*
Fillan', filland, s. *filling.*
Find frost, *find mischance,* or *disaster.* A phrase still in use.
Fit, s. *feet.*
Five teen, *fifteen.*
Flayne, *flayed.*
Flindars, s. *pieces, splinters.*
Fonde, *found.*
Foregoe, *quit, give up, resign.*
Forewearied, *much wearied.*
Forthy, *therefore.*
Fou', fow, s. *full.* Item, *drunk.*
Frae, s. fro, *from.*
Furth, *forth.*
Fyers, (Introd.) *fierce.*
Fyled, fyling, *defiled, defiling.*

G.

Gae, s. *gave.*
Gae, gaes, s. *go, goes.*
Gaed, gade, s. *went.*
Gan, *began.*
Gane, s. *gone.*
Gang, s. *go.*
Gar, s. *make.*
Gart, garred, s. *made.*
Gear, geir, s. *geer, goods, furniture.*
Geid, s. *gave.*
Gerte, (Introd.) *pierced.*
Gibed, *jeered.*
Gie, s. *give.*
Giff, *if.*
Gin, s. *if.*
Gin, gyn, *engine, contrivance.*
Gins, *begins.*
Gip, *an interjection of contempt.*
Glee, *merriment, joy.*
Glen, s. *a narrow valley.*
Glente, *glanced, slipt.*
Glowr, s. *stare* or *frown.*
Gloze, *canting dissimulation, fair outside.*
Gode, (Introd.) *good.*
Gone, (Introd.) *go.*
Gowd, s. *gold.*
Greet, s. *weep.*
Groomes, *attendants, servants.*
Gude, guid, s. *good.*
Guerdon, *reward.*
Gule, *red.*
Gyle, *guile.*

H.

Ha' s. *hall.*
Hame, *home.*
Hauss-bane, s. p. 89, *the neck-bone,* (halse-bone,) *a phrase for the neck.*
Heathenness, *the heathen part of the world.*
Hee's, s. *he shall;* also, *he has.*
Hem, *'em, them.*
Hente, (Introd.) *held, pulled.*
Heo, (Introd.) *they.*
Her, hare, *their.*
Hett, hight, *bid, call, command.*
Hewkes, *heralds' coats.*
Hey-day guise, p. 201, *frolick; sportive frolicksome manner* [3].

[3] This word is perhaps, in p. 201, corruptly given; being apparently the same with HEYDEGUIES, or HEYDEGUIVES, which occurs in Spenser, and means a "wild frolick dance." — Johnson's Dictionary.

Hind, s. *behind.*

Hings, s. *hangs.*

Hip, hep, *the berry which contains the stones or seeds of the dog-rose.*

Hir; hir lain, s. *her; herself alone.*

Hole, *whole.*

Hollen, p. 315, probably a corruption for *holly.*

Honde, *hand.*

Hooly, s. *slowly.*

Hose, *stockings.*

Huggle, *hug, clasp.*

Hyt, (Introd.) *it.*

I.

Ilfardly, s. *ill-favouredly, uglily.*

Ilka, s. *each, every one.*

Impe, *a little demon.*

Ingle, s. *fire.*

Jow, s. *joll or jowl.*

Ireful, *angry, furious.*

Ise, s. *I shall.*

K.

Kame, s. *comb.*

Kameing, s. *combing.*

Kantle, *piece, corner*, p. 54.

Kauk, s. *chalk.*

Keel, s. *raddle.*

Kempt, *combed.*

Ken, s. *know.*

Kever-cheves, *handkerchiefs.* (Vid. Introd.)

Kilted, s. *tucked up.*

Kirk, s. *church.*

Kirk-wa', s. p. 232, *church-wall*; or perhaps *church-yard-wall.*

Kirn, s. *churn.*

Kirtle, *a petticoat, woman's gown.*

Kith, *acquaintance.*

Knellan, knelland, s. *knelling, ringing the knell.*

Kyrtell, *vid.* Kirtle. In the Introd. it signifies *a man's under garment* [4].

L.

Lacke, *want.*

Laith, s. *loth.*

Lambs-wool, *a cant phrase for ale and roasted apples*, p. 183.

Lang, s. *long.*

Lap, s. *leaped.*

Largesse, f. *gift, liberality.*

Lee, lea, *field, pasture.*

Lee, s. *lie.*

Leech, *physician.*

Leese, s. *lose.*

Leffe, (Introd.) leefe, *dear.*

Leid, s. *lyed.*

Lemman, *lover.*

Leugh, s. *laughed.*

Lewd, *ignorant, scandalous.*

Libbard, *leopard.*

Libbard's bane, *a herb so called.*

Lichtly, s. *lightly, easily, nimbly.*

Lig, s. *lie.*

Limitacioune, *a certain precinct allowed to a limitour.*

Limitours, *friars licensed to beg within certain limits.*

Lither, *naughty, wicked*, p. 70.

Lo'e, loed, s. *love, loved.*

Lothly, p. 47, (vid. Lodlye, Gloss. vol. ii.) *loathsome* [5].

Lounge, (Introd.) *lung.*

Lourd, lour, s. *lever, had rather.*

Lues, luve, s. *loves, love.*

Lyan, lyand, s. *lying.*

Lystenyth, (Introd.) *listen.*

M.

Mair, *more.*

Mait, s. *might.*

Mark, *a coin, in value* 13s. 4d.

[4] Bale, in his Actes of English Votaries, (2nd Part, fol. 53,) uses the word KYRTLE to signify a Monk's Frock. He says, Roger Earl of Shrewsbury, when he was dying, sent "to Clunyake, in France, for the KYRTLE of holy Hugh, the Abbot there," &c.

[5] The adverbial terminations -SOME and -LY were applied indifferently by our old writers: thus, as we have *lothly* for *loathsome* above; so we have *ugsome* in a sense not very remote from *ugly* in Lord SURREY's Version of Æneid II. viz.

"In every place the UGSOME sightes I saw." Page 29.

Maugre, *in spite of.*
Mavis, s. *a thrush.*
Maun, s. *must.*
Mawt, s. *malt.*
Meed, *reward.*
Micht, *might.*
Mickle, *much, great.*
Midge, *a small insect, a kind of gnat.*
Minstral, s. minstrel, *musician, &c.*
Minstrelsie, *music.*
Mirkie, *dark, black.*
Mishap, *misfortune.*
Mither, s. *mother.*
Moe, *more.*
Mold, *mould, ground.*
Monand, *moaning, bemoaning.*
More, originally and properly signi-
fied *a hill,* (from A. S. mop, *mons,*)
but the hills of the north being
generally full of bogs, a *moor* came
to signify boggy marshy ground in
general.
Morrownynges, *mornings.*
Mosses, *swampy grounds, covered with
peat-moss.*
Mote, mought, *might.*
Mou, s. *mouth.*

N.

Na, nae, s. *no.*
Naithing, s. *nothing.*
Nane, s. *none.*
Newfangle, newfangled, *fond of no-
velty; of new fashions, &c.*
Nicht, s. *night.*
Noble, *a coin, in value 6s. 8d.*
Norland, s. *northern.*
North-gales, *North Wales.*
Nurtured, *educated, bred up.*

O.

Obraid, s. *upbraid.*
Ony, s. *any.*
Or, *ere, before.* — In p. 72, v. 41, *or*
seems to have the force of the
Latin *vel,* and to signify *even.*
Ou, (Introd.) *you.*
Out-brayde, *drew out, unsheathed.*
Owches, *bosses, or buttons of gold.*
Owre, s. *over.*
Owre-word, s. *the last word; the
burden of a song.*

Percy. III.

P.

Pall, *a cloak,* or *mantle of state.*
Palmer, *a pilgrim, who, having been
at the Holy Land, carried a palm-
branch in his hand.*
Paramour, *gallant, lover, mistress.*
Partake, p. 194, *participate, assign to.*
Pattering, *murmuring, mumbling,* from
the manner in which the *Pater-
noster* was anciently hurried over,
in a low inarticulate voice.
Paynim, *pagan.*
Pearlins, s. p. 90, *a coarse sort of
bone-lace.*
Peer, peerless, *equal, without equal.*
Peering, *peeping, looking narrowly.*
Perfight, *perfect.*
Perill, *danger.*
Philomene, *Philomel, the nightingale.*
Piece, s. p. 135, *a little.*
Plaine, *complain.*
Plein, *complain.*
Porcupig, *porcupine,* f. *porcpic.*
Poterner, p. 35, *perhaps pocket,* or
pouch. Pautoniere in Fr. *is a
shepherd's scrip. (Vid. Cotgrave.)*
Preas, prese, *press.*
Pricked, *spurred forward, travelled a
good round pace.*
Prowess, *bravery, valour, military gal-
lantry.*
Puissant, *strong, powerful.*
Purfel, *an ornament of embroidery.*
Purfelled, *embroidered.*

Q.

Quail, *shrink, flinch, yield.*
Quay, quhey, s. *a young heifer, called
a whie in Yorkshire.*
Quean, *sorry, base woman.*
Quelch, *a blow or bang.*
Quell, *subdue;* also, *kill.*
Quha, s. *who.*
Quhair, s. *where.*
Quhan, whan, s. *when.*
Quhaneer, s. *whene'er.*
Quhen, s. *when.*
Quick, *alive, living.*
Quitt, *requite.*
Quo, *quoth.*

R.

Rade, s. *rode.*
Raise, s. *rose.*

23

Reade, rede, s. *advise.*
Reave, *bereave.*
Reeve, *bailiff,*
Reft, *bereft.*
Register, *the officer who keeps the public register.*
Renneth, renning, *runneth, running.*
Riall, (Introd.) *royal.*
Riddle, p. 96, seems to be a vulgar idiom for *unriddle;* or is perhaps a corruption of *reade,* i. e. *advise.*
Rin, s. *run. Rin my errand,* p. 104, a contracted way of speaking, for *run on my errand.* The pronoun is omitted. So the French say, *faire message.*
Rood, roode, *cross, crucifix.*
Route, p. 113, *go about, travel.*
Rudd, *red, ruddy.*
Ruth, *pity.*
Ruthfull, *rueful, woful.*

S.

Sa, sac, s. *so.*
Saft, s. *soft.*
Saim, s. *same.*
Sair, s. *sore.*
Sall, s. *shall.*
Sarke, s. *shirt.*
Saut, s. *salt.*
Say, essay, *attempt.*
Scant, *scarce;* item, p. 242, *scantiness.*
Sed, *said.*
Seely, *silly.*
Seething, *boiling.*
Sel, sell, s. *self.*
Sen, s. *since.*
Seneschall, *steward.*
Sey, s. p. 89, *say, a kind of woollen stuff.*
Seyd, a *saw.*
Shee's, s. *she shall.*
Sheeld-bone, p. 117, *the blade-bone:* a common phrase in the north.
Sheene, *shining.*
Shent, *shamed, disgraced, abused.*

Shepenes, shipens, *cow-houses, sheep-pens,* p. 204. A.S. Scypen.
Shimmered, s. *glittered.*
Sho, scho, s. *she.*
Sholde, *should.*
Shoone, *shoes.*
Shope, *shaped.*
Shread, *cut into small pieces.*
Shreeven, shriven, *confessed her sins.*
Shullen, *shall.*
Sic, sich, *such.*
Sick-like, s. *such-like.*
Sighan, sighand, s. *sighing.*
Siller, s. *silver.*
Sith, *since.*
Skinkled, s. *glittered.*
Slaited, s. *whetted;* or, perhaps *wiped.*
Sleath, *slayeth.*
Slee, *slay.*
Sna', snaw, s. *snow.*
Sooth, *truth, true.*
Soth, sothe, *ditto.*
Sould, s. *should.*
Souldan, soldan, sowdan, *sultan.*
Spack, s. *spake.*
Sped, *speeded, succeeded.*
Speik, s. *speak.*
Speir, s. spere, speare, speere, spire, *ask, inquire[6].*
Speir, s. *spear.*
Spill, *spoil, destroy, kill.*
Spillan, spilland, s. *spilling.*
Spurging, *froth that purges out.*
Squelsh, *a blow,* or *bang.*
Stean, s. *stone.*
Sterte, *started.*
Steven, *voice, sound.*
Stint, *stop.*
Stound, stonde, (Introd.) *space, moment, hour, time.*
Stower, stowre, *stir, disturbance, fight.*
Stowre, *strong, robust, fierce.*
Stude, stuid, s. *stood.*
Summere, p. 113, *a sumpter horse.*
Surcease, *cease.*
Sune, s. *soon.*
Sweere, swire, *neck.*
Syne, *then, afterwards.*

[6] So CHAUCER, in his Rhyme of Sir Thopas:
——"He soughte north and south,
And oft he SPIRED with his mouth,"
i. e. 'inquired.' Not SPIED, as in the Canterbury Tales, vol. ii. p. 234.

T.

Teene, *sorrow, grief.*
Thair, s. *there.*
Than, s. *then.*
Thewes, *manners.* In p. 42 it signifies *limbs.*
Thir, s. *this, these.*
Tho, *then.*
Thocht, *thought.*
Thrall, *captive.*
Thrall, *captivity.*
Thralldome, *captivity.*
Thrang, *close.*
Thrilled, *twirled, turned round.*
Thropes, *villages.*
Tift, s. *puff of wind.*
Tirled, *twirled, turned round.*
Tone, t'one, *the one.*
Tor, *a tower;* also, *a high-pointed rock or hill.*
Trenchant, f. *cutting.*
Tres-hardie, f. *thrice-hardy.*
Triest furth, s. *draw forth to an assignation.*
Trisulcate, *three-forked, three-pointed.*
Trow, *believe, trust;* also, *verily.*
Troth, *truth, faith, fidelity.*
Tush, *an interjection of contempt or impatience.*
Twa, s. *two.*
Twayne, *two.*

U.

Venu, (Introd.) *approach, coming.*
Unbethought, p. 71, for bethought. So unloose for loose.
Unctuous, *fat, clammy, oily.*
Undermeles, *afternoons.*
Unkempt, *uncombed.*
Ure, *use.*

W.

Wad, s. walde, *would.*
Wadded, p. 36, perhaps from woad; i. e. *of a light blue colour[7].*
Wae, waefo', s. *woe, woful.*
Walker, *a fuller of cloth.*
Waltered, weltered, *rolled along;* also, *wallowed.*

Waly, *an interjection of grief.*
Wame, wem, s. *belly.*
Warde, s. *advise, forewarn.*
Wassel, *drinking, good cheer.*
Wat, s. *wet;* also, *knew.*
Wate, s. *blamed;* præt. of wyte, *to blame.*
Wax, *to grow, become.*
Wayward, *perverse.*
Weale, *welfare.*
Weare-in, s. *drive in gently.*
Weede, *clothing, dress.*
Weel, *well;* also, *we'll.*
Weïrd, *wizard, witch;* properly, *fate, destiny.*
Welkin, *the sky.*
Well-away, *exclamation of pity.*
Wem, (Introd.) *hurt.*
Wend, *to go.*
Wende, weened, *thought.*
Werryed, *worried.*
Wha, s. *who.*
Whair, s. *where.*
Whan, s. *when.*
Whilk, s. *which.*
Whit, *jot.*
Whittles, *knives.*
Wi', s. *with.*
Wight, *human creature, man or woman.*
Wild-worm, *serpent.*
Windar, p. 292, perhaps the contraction of Windhover, *a kind of hawk.*
Wis, *know.*
Wit, weet, *know, understand.*
Wode, wod, *wood;* also, *mad.*
Woe, *woful, sorrowful.*
Woe-man, *a sorrowful man.*
Woe-worth, *woe be to [you].* A. S. worthan, *(fieri) to be, to become.*
Wolde, *would.*
Wonde, (Introd.) *wound, winded.*
Wood, wode, *mad, furious.*
Wood-wroth, s. *furiously enraged.*
Wot, *know, think.*
Wow, s. *an exclamation of wonder.*
Wracke, *ruin, destruction.*
Wynne, win, *joy.*
Wyt, wit, weet, *know.*
Wyte, *blame.*

[7] Taylor, in his History of Gavel-kind, p. 41, says, *"Bright,* from the British word *Brith,* which signifies their *wadde-colour;* this was a light blue." —Minshew's Dictionary.

Y.

Yaned, *yawned.*
Yate, *gate.*
Y-built, *built.*
Ychulle, (Introd.) *I shall.*
Yese, s. *ye shall.*
Ylke, ilk, *same.* That ylk, *that same.*
Ylythe, (Introd.) *listen.*
Yode, *went.*
Yf, *if.*
Yn, *in.*
Ys, *is.*
Ystonge, ˌtrod.) *stung.*

Y-wrought, *wrought.*
Y-wys, *truly, verily.*

Z.

Ze, s. *ye;* zee're, s. *ye are.*
Zees, s. *ye shall.*
Zellow, s. *yellow.*
Zet, s. *yet.*
Zong, s. *young.*
Zou, s. *you;* zour, s. *your.*
Zour-lane, your-lane, s. *alone, by yourself.*
Zouth, s. *youth*

THE END.

PRINTING OFFICE OF THE PUBLISHER.

Printed in Great Britain
by Amazon